HOW TO BUY A HOUSE
WITH NO (OR LITTLE)
MONEY DOWN

The how-to guide with everything you need to know to get the most house with the least money down:

- creative financing sources
- planning tips
- tax angles
- instructions
- checklists

These and other valuable cash-saving techniques to help you buy your home with the smallest downpayment!

- seller financing
- special mortgages
- buying at the best price
- purchase-option leases
- family gifts
- nontraditional loans
- equity sharing

HOW TO BUY A HOUSE WITH NO (OR LITTLE) MONEY DOWN

MARTIN M. SHENKMAN, ESQ.

New York, New York

WARREN BOROSON

Senior Financial Editor
Sylvia Porter's Personal Finance Magazine
New York, New York

WILEY

JOHN WILEY & SONS

New York · Chichester · Brisbane · Toronto · Singapore

**To my wife Shelly
and my sons Yoni and Dov**

M. S.

**To my wife Rebecca
and my sons Bram and Matthew**

W. B.

Library of Congress Cataloging in Publication Data

Shenkman, Martin M.
   How to buy a house with no (or little) money down
Martin M. Shenkman and Warren Boroson.
     p. cm.
    Bibliography: p.
    Includes index.
    ISBN 0-471-50819-5.   ISBN 0-471-50818-7 (pbk.)
    1. House buying. 2. Real property. 3. Mortgages.   I. Boroson,
Warren. II. Title.

HD1379.S473 1989
333.33′8   dc19

89-30195
CIP

Printed in the United States of America

10 9 8 7 6 5 4

FOREWORD

Home Ownership—it's one of the most sought-after goals in our society today. It's a goal that reaches across social and geographic lines, across ethnic and racial differences. Whether we want a tax shelter, a place to raise a family, an investment, or just a shelter from the pressures of the outside world, owning a home has become an essential element in the modern-day American Dream.

Unfortunately, in many parts of our country the scarcity of land, the high cost of labor and building materials, and the competition for affordable housing have made realizing that dream more and more difficult.

No one understands that better than you, a prospective buyer. You've seen that the price of housing often increases faster than you can save for a downpayment. You have learned that the longer you wait and try to save, the farther and farther you fall behind. It's especially frustrating to know your income will support a mortgage, but your rent is so high you can't save for a downpayment.

At Schlott Realtors we've seen countless buyers in this kind of dilemma. They don't think they can afford to buy a new home . . . and yet, practically speaking, they can't afford not to.

Naturally, as a leading real estate broker we've tried to address the needs of these buyers, but for every person we can help to buy a home, there are tens of thousands of prospective buyers who need help and encouragement in dealing with the affordability crisis. And that's what this book offers you. Nationally known real estate attorney Martin Shenkman and distinguished financial writer Warren Boroson have drawn on years of practical experience to develop a wealth of creative ideas that might make it possible for you to buy a home.

Here, in clear and understandable English, they explain the ins and outs of buying a home with limited resources and offer a world of practical advice on how to do it.

Even the most popular method of getting a downpayment—borrowing from Mom and Dad—isn't as simple as it might seem. Is the money a gift, or is it a loan? If a loan, how will you pay it back? How will that loan affect your ability to get a mortgage? The authors explain ways to arrange your loans with relatives so that everyone is legally protected, and family harmony is preserved.

Equity sharing is another route for first-time buyers to obtain a new home, but it's a method that is rarely suggested by real estate agents and mortgage lenders because they often don't understand how it works. The authors have a section on equity sharing that explores ways to make equity sharing work and tells you how to avoid the pitfalls of buying real estate with another person.

Even if you don't think you will ever be a property owner (everyone feels that way at one time or another) read every chapter here. You'll be amazed at the financing possibilities you might never have considered.

It's worth your while to stand up to the affordability crisis. Buying a home is the most important financial move you'll ever make. It's the keystone to building your wealth and creating financial security for you and your family. It will give you the very best tax shelter available to most people, as well as a terrific hedge against inflation. That's a lesson people on the east and west coasts have learned very well. In the New York metropolitan area, for example, a typical house purchased in 1978 has trebled in value; many have increased even more. Where else would you find that kind of return on a conservative investment that shelters your income and offers long-term tax advantages?

Buying a home with limited resources is possible, as you'll see. It's a challenge and will require some hard work on your part. It's also exciting, and there's a tremendous sense of accomplishment when you finally move into your first home. Don't be beaten by the affordability crisis. Let Shenkman and Boroson help you buy your first home.

DICK SCHLOTT
President
Schlott Realtors

INTRODUCTION

Owning your own home is one of the goals and dreams almost every American aspires to. The reasons are endless, but the following are often heard:

- Having the pride and security of knowing it's yours.
- Reaping tax benefits (deducting mortgage interest and property taxes instead of collecting useless rent receipts).
- Building up equity (real estate historically has proven to be one of the best investments).

When trying to break into today's expensive housing market by purchasing your first home, or stepping up to a larger or more luxurious house, you must face one very critical question. Can you come up with enough of a downpayment to convince the seller to sell and the bank to lend you the balance of the money (your mortgage)? It's not easy. The affordability crisis is real. As a result, homeownership, particularly among younger households, has declined.

If you can't come up with the downpayment, you won't get the house you want. It's that simple. Almost. If you don't have the cash handy, what can you do? This major question—the answer to which will determine the biggest investment decision you may ever make— is what this book is all about. Every possible method for cutting corners, striking a deal, or maneuvering around barriers to get the downpayment for the home you want, is described in detail. This book will give you the real answers, along with a discussion of the real legal, tax, and financial issues involved. Everything you need to know to get the most "house for the buck" follows in the pages to come.

Before you plunge in, one caution must be noted. Since buying a home is unquestionably one of the most important financial decisions of your life, do it right. Hire a good attorney and accountant. The amounts of money involved in buying your home are likely to be very large. It will never pay to save the few hundred dollars (or perhaps a bit more) it will cost for a competent attorney and a qualified accountant if you risk losing your home or facing problems with the IRS. Use the ideas this book gives you to get the home you thought you could only dream about—and hire the right professionals to make sure that dream becomes a reality.

Good luck in your new home.

ACKNOWLEDGMENTS

A number of people at John Wiley & Sons, Inc. deserve recognition for their assistance and support in this project. Most important, Michael Hamilton, who helped conceive the idea of this manual, was a valuable help and inspiration throughout the process. Marilyn Dibbs, who keeps track of Michael, among her many other tasks, was a great help. Stephen Kippur and Ken Gesser made appreciated accommodations to this project.

Thanks to Stuart M. Saft, Esq., a partner in the New York City law firm of Wolf, Haldenstein, Adler, Freeman, and Herz, for his comments on selected portions of the manuscript.

Thanks to Dick Schlott, president of Schlott Realtors, for numerous helpful insights, examples, and ideas reflected in this book.

Thanks to Stan Perla, a partner in the New York city office of the international accounting firm of Ernst & Whinney for providing sample tax returns.

Most important, the greatest appreciation to my family—my wife Shelly, and my two dear sons Yoni and Dov—who are the source of my energy and joy.

MARTIN M. SHENKMAN

New York, New York
December 1988

Thanks to my wife Rebecca, and to Bram and Matthew, our two sons, for their help and tolerance.

WARREN BOROSON

Glen Rock, New Jersey
December 1988

CONTENTS

1 WHY BUY A HOUSE WITH LITTLE OR NO MONEY DOWN?

THE CASE AGAINST A LOW/NO DOWNPAYMENT

One powerful argument against buying a house with little or no downpayment is that, if you cannot afford the mortgage payments, you may end up losing the house. That could happen if you leave your job, become disabled, get divorced, or have large medical bills. Foreclosures do occur—right now, more than at any other time since World War II. Recently, over 300,000 homeowners were more than 90 days late on their mortgage payments, an increase of 100 percent from the rate for 1980.

Of course, if you lose the house, you're out money even if you had made no downpayment. You've probably paid moving expenses and closing costs. Your credit record will suffer. And you're personally liable on the mortgage and note. So it would be a true tragedy.

Another strong argument against a low/no downpayment: the less you put down, the higher your monthly mortgage payments will be and the longer it will take you to own the house free and clear. (See Chapter 2.) Besides, if you could make a 20-percent to 25-percent downpayment, you might get better terms—like a slightly lower interest rate.

These are, we grant, compelling reasons to hesitate before buying a house with little or no savings. And they point up a theme we'll repeat throughout this book: to succeed in buying a house with little savings, you should, above all, have a secure source of income—a steady job.

But primarily we'll look at the reasons why you should spring for it. Essentially, the argument is that in our society the difference between being prosperous and not being prosperous, to a large extent depends upon your being a homeowner. As the Joint Center for Housing Studies of Harvard University (Joint Center) has noted, "For decades, moving to better housing has been an important ingredient in the upward mobility of American households." But today many households, "rather than continuing to move up the ladder of housing progress, have stalled along the way." The reason is that fewer young people can afford to buy homes. And a formidable obstacle they face is the downpayment.

"Without doubt," states the National Association of Realtors in its book, *Homeownership—Key to the American Dream*, "the downpayment is a real barrier to the homeownership dreams of Americans who continue to rent."

THE DOWNPAYMENT BARRIER

Some renters, unquestionably, like renting. They want to pick up and move at will. They don't want to bother with mowing lawns, shoveling snow, raking leaves, and dealing with plumbers, electricians, carpenters, and so forth. But 55 percent of renters in a poll conducted for the National Association of Realtors, said they would very much like to own their own homes, and 92 percent had positive feelings about homeownership.

Why don't all these renters buy homes, then? Often because they can't afford them.

"Rental housing is increasingly the home of the nation's lower-income households," states the Joint Center, "while higher-income households increasingly choose to own a home."

Specifically, what renters cannot afford—first and foremost—is the required downpayment. Here are the results of a poll conducted by the National Association of Realtors on the top five reasons why renters rent and don't buy homes:

Reasons for Renting and Not Buying

	Under 35	35–54	55 and Over	All
No money for downpayment	82%	75%	42%	71%
Prices of homes too high	47	51	42	47
Found affordable rental housing	38	47	56	43
No money for maintenance/ mortgage	38	34	24	34
Interest rates too high	34	38	27	34

Source: NATIONAL ASSOCIATION OF REALTORS © Homeownership: Key to the American Dream, 1988, p. 35.

Clearly, lack of a downpayment is the major impediment for younger people—those under 35. For those 34 to 54, the downpayment is still the chief obstacle to obtaining a home of their own. More than twice as many young people are intimidated by the downpayment as are fazed by the prospect of monthly mortgage payments and the cost of maintenance.

RENTS KEEP INCREASING

Making life just a bit worse for tenants, rents have been increasing. More and more renters are now paying 30 percent, 40 percent, and even 50 percent of their incomes to their landlords.

Even though there are plenty of vacant apartments in some parts of the country, rents generally haven't declined. "Contract" rents—rental fees, not including utilities—have risen steadily since 1981, reports the Joint Center, "and now stand at their highest levels in more than two decades."

In 1987, contract rent for a modest average unit was $312—whereas in 1981, it had been $269. And because building rental housing has been getting more expensive, the Joint Center expects "continued high rent levels in the years ahead."

YOUNG PEOPLE ARE POORER

Compared with 1974, today's young households, on average, have lower incomes. The income of households with breadwinners less than 25 years old has fallen from $18,248 to $13,011. The income of households with breadwinners 25 to 34 has fallen from $27,366 to $24,230.

From 1980–1986, renters typically spent 94 percent to 95 percent of their incomes on everyday consumer expenses and living expenses. (Source: Bureau of Labor Statistics consumer expenditure survey.) Around 30 percent of their income went for housing (rent, utilities, etc.). Only 4 percent to 6 percent was left to save for a downpayment.

The typical renting household was able to comfortably put aside only $525 toward the goal of homeownership in 1980, and around $986 in 1985.

At the same time, a 20-percent downpayment for the typical single-family home in 1980 was $12,440; in 1985, it was $15,140. A year's savings in 1985 thus would have enabled typical renters to make a downpayment of $988 toward a $75,700 house—a little over 1.3 percent. They would have had to save 15 times as much to succeed in making the required downpayment.

What Renters Spent Money On (1985)*

Housing	29.9%
Transportation	18.5
Food	15.4
Insurance/pensions	7.1
Health care	3.8
Clothing	5.3
Other	14.1
	94.1%
Left over for savings	5.9%
	100.0%

Source: NATIONAL ASSOCIATION OF REALTORS © *Home-ownership: Key to the American Dream*, 1988, p. 36.
* Based on average income of $16,712.

HOUSE PRICES HAVE CLIMBED

It's bad enough that many young people cannot afford the down-payment to buy a house, and that rentals meanwhile are going up. But there is still another problem: while house prices have cooled off lately in many parts of the country, they are still very high compared with years gone by.

In 1977, the price of a typical first home was $44,000. In 1987, it was $95,000—up 116 percent. See Table 1 for a comparison of home prices in various parts of the country in 1977 and 1987. As the Joint

TABLE 1.   The Difference That Ten Years Made in
Typical Home Prices in Various Parts of the Country

Area	1977	1987	% Change
USA–Average	$44,000	$ 95,000	+116
San Francisco	72,000	169,347	+135
Los Angeles	65,000	142,900	+120
NY–NJ Metro	48,500	142,400	+194
Washington, DC	68,000	137,500	+102
Minneapolis	47,250	114,000	+141
Chicago	50,900	110,000	+116
Baltimore	47,000	106,500	+127
Philadelphia	45,000	99,000	+120
Columbus	42,000	88,000	+110
St. Louis	37,000	84,600	+129
Miami	48,500	78,900	+63
Milwaukee	42,900	76,400	+78
Houston	46,900	73,000	+56
Portland	35,500	72,950	+105
Pittsburgh	37,800	71,500	+89

Source: U.S. League of Savings Institutions.

Center notes, "Rising prices are a double-edged sword: while they make homeownership a good investment for those who already own, they also force young first-time buyers to make larger downpayments and/or larger monthly mortgage payments."

THE COST OF OWNING A HOUSE

Meanwhile, the cost of owning and running a modest single-family home during the first year of ownership has come down a little. The Joint Center reports that, "After rising steadily for 15 years, the after-tax cash cost of homeownership reached a peak of $9,599 in 1982." But in 1987 the cost was down to $7,449. In short, owning a home is still expensive—but not quite so expensive as it had been from 1982 through 1986.

It's no surprise, based on the above statistics, that young people are having a tough time trying to buy homes. They cannot raise the downpayments. Their incomes are shrinking. Their rents are increasing. The cost of houses has skyrocketed.

Some more depressing statistics are that for households aged 25 to 29, the homeownership rate fell from 43.3 percent in 1980 to 35.9

percent in 1987. Households aged 30 to 39 endured similar sharp declines.

FINANCIAL BENEFITS OF HOMEOWNING

Not owning a home doesn't just mean that a person isn't sharing the American dream. It may also suggest that the person is facing a less prosperous life—a life of high rents, of no appreciation on his or her housing, of no special tax benefits.

Many homeowners can deduct their mortgage interest and their property taxes in full from their taxable incomes. And because of their mortgage interest and property taxes, homeowners are more likely to be able to itemize their deductions (list all their deductions on Schedule A) instead of taking the standard deduction and perhaps save even more money on taxes.

If homeowners sell their primary houses, they can generally defer paying capital gains taxes on the appreciation if they buy and live in another primary home, at least as expensive, within two years of selling their former houses.

When they are over 55, they can just wipe out $125,000 of their capital gains on the sale of their main house (if they've lived there for three of the past five years and meet certain other requirements).

Besides that, homeowners are forced to save. Every monthly payment they make boosts ownership in their houses. After 15 years of paying a 30-year conventional mortgage at 10-percent interest, 22 cents of every dollar they fork over goes toward reducing their mortgage principal. After 20 years, 37 cents of every dollar reduces principal.

Then, too, if the homeowner has bought a good house in a good community, and maintained it, his or her house probably will grow in value. In 1968, the typical resale price of an existing home was $20,100; in 1987; the resale price had zoomed to $84,900—an increase of 322 percent. Of course, the inflation of the '70s and '80s had much to do with the rise in housing prices; it's very doubtful that houses will soar as much in value in the next few years. But over the long term, housing has handily bettered the inflation rate. Houses have appreciated as much as stocks have, and usually without the volatility of stocks.

True, unlike renters, homeowners must pay property taxes, must pay for maintenance, must pay for mortgages. But landlords work to make a profit. When you buy a home, you eliminate the landlord.

Renters become their own landlords and pay themselves (and the banks) what they used to pay the landlord.

Perhaps it's only because homeowners are richer to begin with, but they do save more of their incomes than renters. And they are twice as likely as renters to be saving for retirement—even renters who are the same age as the homeowners. (Renters of the same age are more likely to be saving to pay off bills.)

Perhaps homeowners are simply better able to control their spending. That may be why they succeeded in becoming homeowners in the first place. Or perhaps it's because of the tax breaks they enjoy once they become homeowners. Or maybe it's because they have eliminated the landlord's cut.

Homeowners themselves seem to think that owning a home gives them financial benefits. The National Association of Realtors reports that, asked why they bought homes, homeowners gave these reasons:

Reasons for Owning

Didn't want to pay rent	89%
Didn't want to depend on landlord	48
Wanted more privacy	46
Wanted to settle down, have roots	44
Found attractive residence	38
Found affordable mortgage plan	37
Investment purposes	34
Tax reasons	32
To build wealth for retirement	17

Source: NATIONAL ASSOCIATION OF REALTORS © *Homeownership: Key to the American Dream,* 1988, p. 40.

THE OTHER BENEFITS OF HOMEOWNING

As a group, homeowners are not just older and wealthier than renters. They are probably also happier. When a cross section of Americans were asked about the components of the "good life" in a poll conducted for the National Association of Realtors, this is how frequently the following were mentioned:

Components of the Good Life

A home you own	87%
A car	84
A happy marriage	80
A job that is interesting	78
A yard and a lawn	77
A high-paying job	66
A color TV	66
College for children	65
A lot of money	62
Really nice clothes	60

Source: NATIONAL ASSOCIATION OF REALTORS © *Home-ownership: Key to the American Dream*, 1988, p. 10.

One reason homeowners are happier is that they're more likely to be satisfied with their residences—with the privacy, the cost, the financial security, the desirability as a place to raise children. Here are the findings from another poll commissioned by the National Association of Realtors:

"Very Satisfied" with Residence

	Homeowners	Renters
As a place to live	89%	63%
Amount of privacy	84	63
Cost to live here	80	66
Amount of yard space	84	48
Quality of unit	81	53
Condition of unit	80	52
Amount of interior space	76	53
As a place to raise children	82	41
Safety from burglars	64	53

Source: NATIONAL ASSOCIATION OF REALTORS © *Homeown-ership: Key to the American Dream*, 1988, p. 14.

Homeowners are also more satisfied with their neighborhoods, with reasons ranging from the public school system to their safety from crime, as this National Association of Realtors poll shows:

Satisfaction with Neighborhoods

	Homeowners	Renters
As a place to live	88%	68%
Police/fire protection	76	68
Upkeep of other property	78	60
Friendliness of neighbors	78	59
As a place to raise children	81	48
Attractiveness of neighborhood	77	56
Public schools	72	56
Safety from crime	72	54

Source: NATIONAL ASSOCIATION OF REALTORS © *Homeownership: Key to the American Dream*, 1988, p. 14.

THE CASE FOR A LOW/NO DOWNPAYMENT

Granted, that most renters want to buy; that the downpayment is their single most formidable obstacle; that homeowners enjoy all sorts of financial benefits; that homeowners probably become wealthier; and that homeowners are happier.

The question remains: if a renter can't afford to save enough for a downpayment, how can the renter afford to pay off a mortgage, pay for property taxes, pay for maintenance, and so forth?

One answer is that the money renters have been giving to their landlords they can now use for their own houses. And, as we've seen in recent years, while rents have been climbing, the cost of owning a house has not always climbed as rapidly. In addition, as mentioned, homeowners get a cornucopia of tax benefits—which should go a long way toward balancing their budgets. (See Chapter 15.) And being a homeowner seems psychologically to help people save.

Certainly, the costs of homeownership are formidable. But not as formidable as the downpayment. Does anyone doubt that many of the renters who would love to own their own houses, but who cannot afford the downpayments, would be able to pay for their own houses—if they had less of a deposit to make?

Uncle Sam thinks so.

That's why Uncle Sam helps renters buy houses with small down-payments—as small as 0.51 percent of a house price. That's right, less than 1 percent. True, that percentage is for inexpensive houses, those under $50,000. But even if a renter buys a house as costly as $100,000, Uncle Sam will help him or her obtain a downpayment that's less than 5 percent. (See Chapters 9 and 10.)

Yet, with all the elaborate, costly studies that have been done about housing—like the ones mentioned in this chapter—nobody seems to have checked what percentage of renters are familiar with FHA-insured mortgages, let alone all the other techniques people can use to buy homes with little or no downpayments.

CHAPTER SUMMARY

Young people, as well as many others, are finding it harder and harder to buy houses, mainly because of high downpayments. Yet becoming a homeowner carries with it all sorts of financial benefits. People who don't buy homes, as a group, probably will never be as prosperous as those who do. After all, what other Americans, besides homeowners, don't have to pay taxes on $125,000 of their profits from an asset?

Granted, the transition from renter to homeowner can be difficult and stressful. But the rewards, as we've seen, may be well worth the risks. Especially if you take steps to lower those risks—by buying a good house in a good community, and making sure you have a steady job that provides you the income you need to succeed.

2 HOW MUCH HOUSE CAN YOU AFFORD?

TWO KEY QUESTIONS

Now that you've made the decision that you want to own your own home (the term home includes condominium, cooperative, townhouse, and so forth), the next, and most important, question is—what can you afford?

How much home you can afford is really a two-part question:

(1) How much downpayment can you make?

(2) How much can you pay monthly for mortgage interest and principal payments, as well as for property taxes and insurance?

Until you can answer these questions you can't really begin to look seriously for a home. The first question—how much downpayment can you come up with—is the tougher of the two, particularly for first-time home buyers. Coming up with the necessary downpayment, or using a planning technique to minimize the requested downpayment, is the focus of this book. But to understand the techniques involved, you must understand what the downpayment is and why it's so important to sellers of homes, and to banks and others who lend you money to buy your home.

After reviewing the basic information you need to know about downpayments, the second question—determining how much you can afford in monthly payments—will be addressed. Putting the answers to these two questions together will show you how much house you can afford. Throughout the rest of this book realistic techniques (not silly gimmicks) will be explained, which you can use to get the most house with the downpayment and monthly payments you can afford. You will learn how imaginative financing and a careful purchase can help you get much more house than you thought possible.

DOWNPAYMENTS—THREE REASONS WHY THEY ARE SO IMPORTANT TO SELLERS AND LENDERS

If you could know the cards in the hand of the person across the table from you it would be a lot easier to make the right bet. Well, it's no different in any type of negotiation. The more you as a buyer and borrower know about what the potential seller and lender want, the better you will be able to structure a deal they'll go for. The seller and lender may want a downpayment from you for any of a number of different reasons including:

(1) The seller may need cash for the downpayment on the next home he or she is buying.

EXAMPLE: Suzy Seller is selling her New York City condominium to Bill Buyer for $76,000. Suzy is insisting on a $16,000 downpayment (about 22 percent of the purchase price). Suzy is moving to Indiana and estimates that she needs $7,000 to cover her moving expenses and another $9,000 for her downpayment on a comparable condominium she will buy there.

---

(2) When the seller takes back a purchase money mortgage from you (acts as the bank for part of the purchase price), generally the seller wants as large a downpayment as possible to protect himself or herself in case the value of the house declines. This is because if you ever stop making the payments on your mortgage (default), the lender (or seller who holds your purchase money mortgage) will take back the house and sell it. If the house is worth less than what he or she lent you because the market is soft, the lender/seller will lose money.

EXAMPLE: Sammy Seller sold his house to Bob and Betty Buyer for $124,000. Sammy was eager to move because of a job transfer and agreed to take back a mortgage from Bob and Betty for $120,000 of the sale price. (See Chapter 5.) Shortly after Thanksgiving, Bob and Betty moved out, leaving Sammy holding the house and a worthless $120,000 purchase money mortgage (unless, of course, Sammy can find and sue them). The holiday season is always slow for house sales, and according to a broker

Sammy can get only about $118,000 after brokerage commissions if he tries to sell now. This will result in a loss to Sammy of $2,000 [$120,000 − $118,000]. His loss will be even greater if he considers the other costs he'll have to incur to get the house back from the Buyers and then sell it.

Sammy's other alternative is to hold the house until March, when the broker says the market should pick up and Sammy should be able to net $122,000 from its sale. If Sammy waits, however, he will have to pay insurance, gas and electric bills for three months, which will cost him about $575. Also, Sammy will have $120,000 of his money (the amount of the unpaid mortgage) tied up in the house and not earning interest. Assuming Sammy could get 10 percent on his money in a money market fund, he'll be losing another $3,000 [$120,000 mortgage × 10-percent interest rate × 3/12 months]. This second option is really not that much better than selling the house now for a lower price. Although Sammy should get $4,000 more [$122,000 sales price in March − $118,000 sales price now], he will have incurred $3,575 in additional costs [$575 expenses + $3,000 lost interest]. This additional $425 [$4,000 extra sales price − $3,575 extra expense] is not worth waiting for. Any additional repair or damage (up to the deductible on the insurance) may wipe out this modest additional profit.

Sammy asked the broker about renting the house while he waited to sell it. The broker advised him that the rental market was soft and that Sammy wouldn't get enough to cover his expenses.

After analyzing his alternatives Sammy regrets having sold his house with only a little over a 3-percent downpayment [$4,000 out of $124,000]. If he had insisted even on a minimum 5 percent down, he would have had $6,200 [$124,000 sales price × 5-percent downpayment] to protect himself against the risks and problems he is now facing. This extra $2,200 downpayment [$6,200 − $4,000] would have covered the losses he now faces.

---

(3) As you can see from the above example, lenders must always consider the possibility that they will have to take the property back from the buyers if they don't pay their mortgage. In the above example, Bob and Betty Buyer skipped town, but at least they didn't damage the house. Unfortunately, all buyers aren't so considerate.

This risk is another reason lenders want to have a minimum downpayment—to know that you, the buyer, have something invested in the property, so that you will treat it as your own.

NOTE: Roger Pickett, Vice President of the Express Financial Corp., a mortgage brokerage firm in Boca Raton, Florida, notes that most lenders insist that if the downpayment comes from a gift (say a parent gives his or her child a portion of the downpayment) at least 5 percent of the downpayment must come from the donee's (person who received the gift's) own funds. They count as the buyer's own funds only amounts that were in the buyer's bank account for at least three months. The reason, according to Pickett, is "We want the child to feel that he has an interest in the property too."

By understanding the needs, risks and concerns that sellers and lenders face, you can begin to address their needs in attempting to persuade them to accept a lower downpayment. The later chapters in this book will give you many specific suggestions on how to accomplish this.

HOW THE DOWNPAYMENT AFFECTS HOW MUCH HOME YOU CAN AFFORD

There are two important ways a downpayment can affect how much home you can afford to buy. The first and more obvious is that if a certain percentage is required, the amount of downpayment you can come up with will determine exactly how expensive a home you can buy. The following chart illustrates this:

EXAMPLE: Assume that the required downpayment is 5 percent of the purchase price:

Cash You Have to Put Down	Home You Can Afford
$ 2,000	$ 40,000*
5,000	100,000
10,000	200,000
15,000	300,000
20,000	400,000

Assume that the required downpayment is 10 percent of the purchase price:

Cash You Have to Put Down	Home You Can Afford
$ 2,000	$ 20,000*
5,000	50,000*
10,000	100,000
15,000	150,000
20,000	200,000

Assume that the required downpayment is 20 percent of the purchase price:

Cash You Have to Put Down	Home You Can Afford
$ 2,000	$ 10,000*
5,000	25,000*
10,000	50,000*
15,000	75,000*
20,000	100,000
30,000	150,000
40,000	200,000

* The asterisks indicate houses selling for less than the median single-family-home price (according to the National Association of Realtors' index for the third quarter of 1988).

If you lived in the New York area, where the median home price was $192,600 recently, it would take a downpayment of $38,520 to get a conventional bank mortgage, which requires 20 percent down. Fortunately, there are alternatives that later chapters will show you.

There is another way the downpayment determines the price of the home you can afford to buy. All home buyers have a limit to how much of their monthly take-home pay they can afford to spend on their basic home payments (mortgage payments of principal and interest, property tax escrow and insurance escrow). Once you know your limit, the other major variable in determining how much home you can afford is how much of a downpayment you can come up with.

EXAMPLE: Assume for each of the calculations below that you qualify for a conventional mortgage payable over 30 years at a 12-percent interest rate. If you have $500 a month to spend on a mortgage, and the downpayment listed, you can buy a home worth the amount shown:

Downpayment	Home You Can Afford
$ 5,000	$ 53,600
10,000	58,600
15,000	63,600
20,000	68,600

If you have $750 a month to spend on a mortgage, and the downpayment listed, you can buy a home worth the amount shown:

Downpayment	Home You Can Afford
$ 5,000	$ 78,000
10,000	83,000
15,000	88,000
20,000	93,000

If you have $1,000 a month to spend on a mortgage, and the downpayment listed, you can buy a home worth the amount shown:

Downpayment	Home You Can Afford
$ 5,000	$102,200
10,000	107,200
15,000	112,200
20,000	117,200

If you have $1,500 a month to spend on a mortgage, and the downpayment listed, you can buy a home worth the amount shown:

Downpayment	Home You Can Afford
$ 5,000	$150,800
10,000	155,800
15,000	160,800
20,000	165,800

HOW MUCH CAN YOU AFFORD TO SPEND EACH MONTH FOR YOUR HOME?

The charts in above examples demonstrate why it is so important to determine how much you can afford to spend each month on your mortgage and other house payments. Although the focus of this book is to tell you how to come up with the downpayment, the home-buying decision is just as tied to the amount you can afford to pay each month. The difference between these two considerations is that the amount you can pay monthly is pretty much fixed. Unless you get a raise, start a side business, or tighten your financial belt a bit more, there isn't much flexibility in the number you will be able to come up with each month. The cash you have for the down-payment may also be a pretty fixed number—but the later chapters will show you techniques to get more mileage out of what down-payment money you have, and in some cases how to even get more downpayment money.

How do you determine what you can spend each month? Many use a rule of thumb. The rule of thumb used to be that you should not spend more than about 28 percent of your take-home pay on your home (mortgage principal and interest, insurance and property taxes). Recently, as people began spending more of their money on homes, and as the growth of two-earner households permitted a larger percentage of take-home pay to go to housing expenses, this rule of thumb increased to about 33 percent. Some lenders may go even higher.

EXAMPLE: One-third of your monthly take-home pay supports the following amount of monthly house expenses. Assume that 15 percent of the monthly payment goes to property taxes and insurance and the 85-percent balance toward your mortgage interest and principal payments. Assume you have a conventional 30-year mortgage at a 12-percent interest rate. Finally, assume that you have cash for a downpayment equal to 15 percent of the home's purchase price.

Take-Home	⅓ Take-Home	Mortgage	House
$1,000	$ 333	$ 27,500	$ 32,350
1,500	500	41,300	48,600
2,000	667	64,850	72,300
2,500	833	81,000	95,300
3,000	1,000	97,200	114,350
3,500	1,167	113,450	133,500
4,000	1,333	129,600	152,500
4,500	1,500	145,800	171,500
5,000	1,667	162,000	190,600

Based on the figures in the above chart, a lot of homeowners would still be renters. Similarly, some homeowners would have their homes in foreclosure. The reason is that although rules of thumb may provide a good general indication for the average person, the average person is a lot like the average family with 2.3 children and so forth—he or she doesn't exist.

CAUTION: Rules of thumb are only as good as the thumb you use—and it better be your own.

The proper solution is to make an actual calculation of the money you reasonably will have available to meet your monthly payments of mortgage interest and principal, insurance and property taxes. This is important because it will prevent you from overextending yourself if you have unusual expenses (a handicapped child, alimony payments, etc.), which would not be considered in the general rules of thumb. It may also show that you can afford more house than either you or your banker thought because you are more frugal than many others.

CAUTION: In many cases banks and other lenders will sell your mortgage along with other mortgages they have. In these cases strict requirements (underwriting criteria) will have to be followed and your frugality won't change the lender's mind.

CAUTION: Notice that in the form on page 24 the amount of interest you expect to earn each month from savings accounts, money market funds, dividends on stock mutual funds, and so forth should all be included in income. If you are going to use this money (or sell those bonds or stocks) to come up with the downpayment, don't include the income these items are presently earning in your revenues. For example, if you have $15,000 in a money market fund earning 10 percent, which you will use for your downpayment, don't include the $125 monthly income in the above calculations—you won't have it.

The use of savings to pay for a downpayment reduces the income you have for monthly payments. This is another important relationship between the downpayment you make and the cash you'll have for monthly payments. The close connection between these two factors is why both have been discussed in this chapter.

The "Cushion for Emergencies" is a very important number. Never cut resources down to the last penny. Never, in spite of what the many faddish "no-money-down" books tell you, put every bit of savings into a house or any real estate. You should always save money for that inevitable rainy-day emergency. This is particularly true when you've highly leveraged yourself with a no- or low-money-down purchase.

The "Cash Available" number is the amount that you can reasonably afford to spend each month for your housing costs. When you combine this number with the cash you have available for a downpayment, you can use the above charts to determine the maximum price you can afford to spend for a home. But before feeling disappointed, read the rest of this book; you'll see exactly how to go about getting a more expensive home without changing your monthly income or cash savings.

WHY TRADITIONAL BANK FINANCING ISN'T ALWAYS ENOUGH

Traditional bank financing, if there is such a thing in these days of SAMs, ARMs, GEMs, GPMs, and other types of mortgages (see Chapters 8, 9, and 10), isn't always sufficient. This is particularly true for the first-time home buyer who is tight on funds for a downpayment.

The "traditional" mortgage is where the buyer qualifies by meeting certain income and employment tests. The longer and more stable your employment history, the better. The banker may also apply the one-third-of-take-home-pay rule of thumb discussed above, and certain other tests to see if you qualify. Finally, a substantial downpayment of 20 percent of the purchase price may also be required. Needless to say, not everyone can qualify for this type of mortgage. Even if you can qualify, this may not be sufficient for you to get the dream house your heart is really set on. For you and all these people, this book will provide guidance on what to do and how to do it, to help you get that dream house.

YOU'LL NEED CASH FOR MORE THAN THE DOWNPAYMENT

In the above discussions it was assumed that all the money you had available was used for the downpayment on your house. This down-payment then helped determine how much your monthly payments would be. This simplified approach, however, overlooks a very important point—there are other expenses: closing costs, moving expenses, and the cost of repairs, painting and other improvements. There are often substantial costs that a buyer has to pay in order to get financing, purchase a home, and then move in. These can include:

- Moving expenses. These include cost of movers, packing, shipping, and so forth.
- Points. Each point equals one percent of the mortgage that you get from a bank or other lender. Points can range anywhere from none to five, and occasionally even more.

EXAMPLE: Mary Mortgage gets a mortgage from the Bigcity Bank. Bigcity Bank charges her three points. She takes out a mortgage for $55,000. The points will cost Mary $1,650 [$55,000 × .03].

- Title search. There is a fee to have the ownership of the property you are buying investigated to make sure the seller really owns the property.
- Title insurance. This is an insurance policy that protects you in case someone ever claims to own the house and land you are buying.

- Casualty insurance. You will have to pay the first premium on the fire and casualty insurance on the home you are buying.

- Fuel adjustment. If the house has oil heat, for example, you will have to pay the seller the estimated value of the heating oil in the house at the date of sale.

- Legal fees. You will have to pay a fee to the attorney who represents you in the house purchase and who reviews all the documents. Expect a fee anywhere from $500 to $2,000, depending on the part of the country and the complexity of the transaction. Be certain to discuss the fee in advance. Some of the techniques described in this book for purchasing a house with little or no money down will require extra legal work to implement. This, incidentally, is something so many of the books promoting no-money-down purchases fail to mention. To help keep some of these additional legal fees down, this book contains illustrative legal documents.

CAUTION: Never try to use any of the sample legal documents on your own. They are for illustration only and do not necessarily contain all the terms you need. It is most important to note that the laws differ from state to state so that you always need a local attorney to assist with a real estate closing.

- Recording and filing fees. These fees vary from state to state and even from county to county. Have your attorney give you an estimate.

- Painting, cleaning, gardening and other costs may have to be incurred when moving to any new home. Few sellers leave a house in "move-in" condition.

Closing costs are an important component of the money you must have available to purchase a house. Review them with the broker and your attorney. For some tips on how to control closing costs, see Chapter 4.

CHAPTER SUMMARY

The first step in understanding how to buy a house with no (or almost no) money down is to understand the importance of the downpayment. This chapter has explained what the downpayment is, why it is important to buyers, sellers and lenders, and how it helps determine the most house you can afford to buy. Finally, the second critical component in the home-buying decision, the amount you can afford to spend each month on housing costs, which is integrally related to the downpayment, was also reviewed.

ADMINISTRATIVE OFFICES
1550 Route 23 North
Wayne, New Jersey 07470-0979
(201) 633-5000

FOR YOUR NOTEBOOK

The following form is used by Schlott Realtors to help determine how much house a prospective buyer can afford.

PREQUALIFYING WORKSHEET

CUSTOMER: _____ DATE: _____

1. Gross Monthly Income (GMI) .... $ _____
2. Recurring Monthly Payments
   Car _____   Other _____
   Credit Card _____   Other _____
   Credit Card _____   Other _____
   Loan _____   Other _____

Total Monthly Liabilities .... $ _____

3. 1st Qualifying Ratio

$$\underline{} \times 28\% = \underline{} \text{ (A)}$$
$$\text{(GMI)} \qquad\qquad \text{(PITI)}$$

4. 2nd Qualifying Ratio

$$\underline{} \times 36\% = \underline{} = \underline{} \text{ (B)}$$
$$\text{(GMI)} \qquad \text{Liabilities} \qquad \text{(PITI)}$$

The qualifying Monthly Payment (PITI) allowed will be the lower of (A) or (B).

22

PITI; Maximum allowed lower of
  (A) or (B)   _____ per mo

Homeowners Insurance ($3 to $4
  per $1000)   − _____ per mo

Real Estate Taxes   − _____ per mo

Private Mortgage Insurance (PMI)   − _____ per mo

Maintenance Fee (Condos,
  associations)   − _____ per mo

Principal and Interest   = _____ per mo

DIVIDE PRINCIPAL AND INTEREST BY THE INTEREST RATE FACTOR.
THIS WILL DETERMINE MAXIMUM MORTGAGE AMOUNT.

FACTOR	TYPE OF MORTGAGE	RATE	TERM	MORTGAGE $ AMOUNT	DOWN PAYMENT DOLLAR AMOUNT	MAXIMUM PRICE OF HOME
	FIXED 30 YR					
	A.R.M.					
	G.P.M.					
	FIXED 15 YR					
	OTHER					

Offices in New Jersey, New York, Connecticut, Pennsylvania and Florida.

FORM: *HOW TO ESTIMATE WHAT YOU CAN AFFORD IN MONTHLY PAYMENTS*

Revenues:
  Take-Home Pay—1st $ _____
              —2nd   _____
  Alimony/Child Support   _____
  Interest*   _____
  Other Income*   _____
    subtotal—income $ _____ (A)
Expenses:
  Utilities** $ _____
  Telephone   _____
  Car Payments   _____
  Food   _____
  Clothing   _____
  Life Insurance   _____
  Laundry   _____
  Entertainment   _____
  Charity   _____
  Education   _____
  Savings   _____
  Repairs**   _____
  Lawn Care**   _____
  Alimony/Child Support   _____
  Other   _____
    subtotal—expenses $ _____ (B)
Cash Available:
  Revenues [from (A)] $ _____
  Less 5%–15% Cushion for Emergencies   _____
  Less Expenses [from (B)]   _____
    Equals—Cash Available $ _____

* Reduced by estimate of taxes that will be due.
** Estimated for new home.

3 THE SMARTER YOU BUY— THE LOWER THE DOWNPAYMENT

INTRODUCTION

To lower the downpayment, to lower closing costs, and to lower your first year's expenses—the three main obstacles to your becoming a homeowner—try to buy any residence for less. Buy a good but less expensive house than you had planned to, or buy any decent house for less than it's worth. It's really not that hard to do. And make sure the house is really as good as you think: you don't want large, unexpected repair costs.

CAUTION: Never buy any house without having a professional house inspector check it over first. For names of inspectors, contact the American Society of Home Inspectors, 3299 K Street, N.W., Washington, DC 20007; (202) 842-3096. You will also receive a useful free brochure, "The Home Inspection and You."

Only about 40 percent of home buyers use house inspectors, but they can protect you against all sorts of grief as well as enormous unexpected expenses. Yet an inspection itself costs only $150 and up, depending on the size of the house and the area of the country.

Inspectors will check the soundness of the house structure (the roof, the floors) and its operating systems (furnace, water supply, electricity). Some check for termites, others don't. While inspectors won't tell you whether to buy a house or not, they will tell you about defects a house has—and the estimated cost to repair or replace them.

Look for an inspector who is an engineer. Don't rely on your uncle who once was a plumber, or a friend who runs a hardware store. Determining how long a furnace has before it expires, or whether a watermark in a basement means it floods in rainy weather or the washing machine once overflowed, calls for true expertise. Your uncle, the former plumber, probably hasn't the foggiest idea whether a horizontal crack in a wall is better or worse than a vertical crack. (A vertical crack may mean that the house is just settling; a horizontal crack may mean that the house is falling down.)

Forty percent of all houses for sale have at least one serious defect, reports HouseMaster of America, based in Bound Brook, New Jersey, the largest inspection service. A serious defect is defined as one costing at least $500 to repair or replace. The most serious defects are:

- Roofing. New asphalt shingling can cost $1,800 to $2,500. New wood shingling can cost even more.

- Structural flaws. If a wall needs more support, it can cost $3,000 to $4,000.

- Heating and cooling. A new warm-air furnace may cost $1,500 to $2,000; a boiler, $2,000 to $2,500; an air-conditioning compressor, $750 to $1,000.

- Plumbing. Replacing the entire plumbing system can cost several thousand dollars. Replacing the shower pan (the basin under the tiling) can run $900 to $1,600.

- Re-siding. Depending on the material, it can cost $8,000 to $20,000.

- Electricity. Boosting the supply can cost $600 to $1,200. Rewiring an entire house can cost many thousands.

Have an inspection performed on any house you're on the verge of buying. If you're signing a contract before an inspection, be certain that your attorney includes in the contract that the sale is contingent upon a house inspector's report indicating that no repair or replacement above $500 is needed. The $500 is typical, but you can modify it upward or downward. Many contracts provide that the seller must make repairs up to a specified amount. If the seller won't make repairs above the amount specified, the buyer can. If neither the seller nor buyer wants to make repairs above the specified amount, either can cancel the contract.

Insist that any repairs be done to your satisfaction. You don't want a roof patched when it should be replaced. Your house inspector can guide you.

SHOP IN THE OFF-SEASON

Spring is high season. Many homeowners want to sell in spring or early summer, so their children can start a new school in the fall. Fewer houses are available during the off-season, true. You won't have the variety of choices you would have, say, in the spring. But houses for sale in the depth of winter tend to be cheaper.

When is the off-season? It depends on the area of the country, but generally it's November and December (because of the holidays and the cold weather), and July and August (when people are vacationing). Your single best month for bargain hunting may be December. You'll have few competitors, and the sellers may be especially eager to come to terms. They may have just bought a house in a warmer part of the country. They may have been transferred to a new job and are under time pressure.

You can be pretty sure, too, that real estate agents will be unusually helpful during an off-season. They're not likely to be that busy.

Another drawback of shopping during the off-season, besides the limited number of houses available, is that you may not be able to inspect the grounds. You won't really be able to tell whether the lawn and the shrubbery are in good shape. On the other hand, there's no better time to check out the heating system and the tightness of the seals on the doors and windows than on a cold, windy day.

SHOP FAR OUT

The farther you are from your job, the more it will cost in travel expenses, whether you drive or use public transportation. But the closer you are to your job, usually the higher the cost of real estate. Housing near metropolitan areas may cost half again as much as housing elsewhere. So it's a trade-off.

But for first-time home buyers, it's often better to buy cheap and commute more—simply because of the cash-flow problems. If you work in New York City, you'll find that housing in nearby Tenafly, New Jersey is astronomical compared with housing in Succasunna, New Jersey, a good distance away. Besides that, the cost of everything else you buy in Succasunna—groceries, clothing, and so forth—may be lower, simply because commercial property is also less expensive and merchants can sell for less.

Once you've lived in your house in the boondocks for a while, consider taking advantage of the appreciation in your home and selling—then moving closer in. You'll deserve it. Then again, you may find that you prefer the quiet, wholesome, unpretentious life in Succasunna.

THINK SMALL

A Cape Cod should cost less than a colonial, which should cost less than a ranch. Here's a guide to house styles:

Colonial: Two stories. Good for young families, not necessarily for the elderly. Lots of stair climbing. Second floor is dangerous in case of a fire. But bedrooms and entertainment areas are far apart. Heating and cooling cost less than with a one-story. Less expensive to build—you don't need a large foundation or roof.

Split-Entry: The entrance is a foyer, and you climb up or down stairs. Lots of stair climbing. Lower level may be hard to heat evenly. But the basement is fairly high, so it may get more light.

Split-Level: Living area is on entry level; you walk down to the social area, up to the sleeping area. Lots of stair climbing. Bedrooms may be too warm. But it's a good design for a slanted lot.

Ranch: One story. Requires a large lot, large foundation, large roof, long walls. Costly to construct, and to heat and cool. But hardly any stair climbing. Easy to repair outside, easy to clean inside. Adaptable to outdoors life.

Tudor: Two or two and a half stories. Stucco or stone walls have half timbers. Roof more likely to develop leaks because of angles; house hard to heat evenly; second-floor rooms may be dark. But the slate roof tiles last a long time, and the house's appearance may entrance you.

Cape Cod: One and a half stories. If the attic is turned into bedrooms or finished, the house may be hot in summer, cold in winter. The rooms upstairs may be small, with small windows. But heating costs, and the price of the house itself, should be low.

INSPECTING A HOUSE YOURSELF

You don't want to pay a house inspector to report on every place you're interested in, so you should learn the basics, just to screen out inappropriate houses. It's also helpful to keep your house inspector on his or her toes. All inspectors aren't as careful as you would like them to be. Take a course. Read some books.

Exterior:

- A wide lot looks better than a long lot; a regularly shaped lot will be easier to sell. A tree to the south or southeast will cut down on summer heat.
- The area around the house should be graded, so water won't seep into the basement. The slant should be about six inches for the first six feet.
- A concrete driveway is better than asphalt, which is better than pebbles, gravel, or dirt. The driveway should slant away from the house, to keep water away.
- An attached garage will let you go directly into the house in cold weather, and keep your car a bit warmer in winter. But it may allow gasoline odors to invade the house. Two-car garages are desirable, even if you have one car, because of the extra storage space.
- The best foundation is poured concrete, with concrete block second best. If there's a crawl space under the house, it should be at least two feet high, and the soil covered by a layer of concrete or at least a plastic vapor barrier.
- No wood should touch the ground lest you get termites. A sign of termites: narrow mud tunnels leading to the ground.
- An outside wall of masonry is best. But check the mortar between the bricks or stones. Wood siding may need repainting. Check for peeling and blistering. If aluminum siding isn't vinyl clad and is chalky, it may need painting. Check that it has a solid backing and won't dent easily.
- Slate- or clay-tile roofs are best. Next in order come concrete tiles and metal panels, asbestos-cement shingles, and—most common—asphalt shingles, which should last 20 years. Check asphalt tiles for any that are broken, warped, or missing. If the

granules covering the tiles are almost gone, it may be time to replace them. And if there are two layers of tiles already, replacement can be very expensive. Check for tar patches, a sign of past leakage. A good roof has a wide overhang to protect the walls from water. If there's no snow on the house in winter, when other houses have snow, heat may be escaping from the house. A roof should have a 30-degree pitch.

Interior:

- An entrance foyer is desirable, to conserve heat in winter, coolness in summer. A large closet near the doorway is convenient.
- The kitchen should be near the dining room, the living room, and the garage. Look for lots of storage space and an area for a dining nook. The counter length should be at least two feet. An exhaust fan should be above the stove. The stove, refrigerator, and sink should be near one another.
- A bathroom should be on the same floor as the kitchen, and there should be one and a half bathrooms for every two bedrooms. Ideally, a bathroom will be off the main bedroom.
- Flush all toilets to test them, and lift the cover off the tank to inspect whether the workings inside are corroded. Visit the highest bathroom in the house, turn on all the faucets, and flush the toilet, to see if the water flows much more slowly. Interior baths are better than those that have an outside wall, but they should have exhaust fans. Check the ceilings below bathrooms for water stains.
- The fireplace should have an ash box, for ease of cleaning. Fireplace flooring should extend 18 inches in front, and one foot beyond each side of the fireplace. Check that the damper is working.
- The garage should slant down toward the outside, and it should have a window, along with a door besides the main door. An electrical outlet should be available.
- Check the walls of the basement for cracks; any crack one-third of an inch wide is worrisome. A horizontal crack is worse than a vertical crack; it may indicate that the wall is buckling.
- Look at the nails in the floorboards of the basement to see if they're rusty—a possible sign of flooding. And see whether the floor tiles have white stains at the joints, another sign of water

damage. Poke wood with a screwdriver; if it's soft, there may be termite damage.

- You should not have to walk through one bedroom to get to another. Any bedroom should have windows on two different walls for cross ventilation. Closets should have four feet of rod space per family member.

- In the attic, look for water marks on the ceiling. A window or louvers should give ventilation. Six inches of insulation are desirable in the attic—in the floor if it's unfinished, in the ceiling if it's finished.

Floors, windows, walls:

- Jump on the floor to see if it's too springy. Usually the better the carpet, the thicker the pile. If the carpet is glued over plywood or concrete, walk on it and listen for a snapping sound, which indicates poor adhesion.

- Casement windows can be troublesome; look for top-line models. Open and shut all windows. Look for small openings ("weep holes") at the bottoms of storms (to let rain escape).

- Plaster walls mute sounds better but crack more readily than drywall. A drywall should be half an inch thick, not just three-eighths. Quarter-inch panels are better than one-eighth inch. There should be at least three inches of insulation in the walls; remove the cover of a light switch plate to check.

Electricity:

- You should have 150 amperes and 110/220 volts coming into the house. Circuit breakers are better than fuses. Aluminum wiring installed before the 1970s may be a fire hazard; such wiring has AL stamped on it.

- Outlets should be 12 feet apart or closer. Every room (except bathrooms) should have at least four outlets. They are best placed at the corners of walls, so they're not blocked by furniture. Grounded (three-prong) outlets are also best. Electrical switches in a bathroom should not be reachable from showers or tubs, and should certainly be grounded. A light switch should be near the house entrance, and there should be lights outside in front and back. Weatherproof electrical sockets should also be in both the front and back.

Heating:

- Electrical heat is clean and can be regulated for each room, but it's the most expensive. If you have a warm-air system, the registers supplying heat should be on the outside walls; grills (returning air) should be on the inside. Both should be near the floor. There should be one heat source for each outside wall in each room. The thermostat should be located where it is not exposed to unusual variations in temperature—not next to a register, for example. Even in summer turn on the heat, just to see how quickly it comes on and how noisy the furnace may be. Carefully check for adequate heat in added-on rooms, rooms over a garage, and rooms on the house corners.

- The water heater should have a capacity of 40 gallons for a family of four, 50 gallons for five. A heater lasts around 10 years; check when this one was installed. Also check how quickly the water in the house gets hot.

Plumbing:

- Copper or brass pipes are better than galvanized iron, but the line leading to the main sewer should be iron. (Use a magnet to tell: iron is magnetic.) Some engineers hate plastic piping: it may break when you run a snake through to unclog it. Check the pipes for rust, wetness, discoloration, and mineral deposits. Examine the area around pipes for wet spots. A bad sign: the pipes are made of copper in one area, galvanized iron in another: this means the owner has been replacing them. The best pipe systems tend to have the fewest sharp angles.

- All toilets, sinks, and other fixtures should have shut-off valves underneath.

- A septic-tank system is nowhere near as desirable as a public sewage system.

QUESTIONS TO ASK

Among the questions you should ask the seller, in front of a real estate agent or other witnesses, to make sure your lawyer gets the seller's representations in the contract are:

- Has the house been checked for radon contamination, and what was the result? Consider having the house tested yourself.
- Have there ever been toxic-waste dumps nearby?
- Is the area in a flood plain?
- Is there anything about the house that would lower its value that I should know about?
- Is the roof leaking, and has it ever leaked? What damage resulted?
- What are the heating and cooling costs? Could I see a few years of past bills?
- Does the house need more insulation?
- Is the basement dry? If it has ever flooded, what damage resulted?
- Do fuses blow frequently, or circuit breakers open?
- Has the heating system ever not been able to keep the house warm?
- Has the air-conditioning ever not been able to keep the house cool?
- Has the house ever been treated for termites? What damage had the termites caused?
- Does anyone else have the right to use the property? A neighbor might have the right (an easement) to use your property to cross over to his or hers.
- Do you legally own the property beyond dispute? Does a former spouse exist, for example, who might claim part ownership? Make sure there are no defects in title. Have a title company do a search of the title records on the house and have your attorney review the report.
- Have any public assessments for sewers or pavements been announced? Are houses being reassessed for higher taxes?

CAUTION: If something the sellers say is important, ask your lawyer to put it into the contract; otherwise, you won't be protected.

LOW-COST HOUSING

Obviously, a smaller house will cost less to buy and less to maintain. This is also true for a house that shares walls with other houses— a townhouse; a residence that shares not just walls but a roof—a condominium or cooperative; and a residence that might be your very first choice: a two-family house, or duplex.

But face up to the fact that a low-cost house will probably appreciate less than other houses, if it appreciates at all. The most expensive antiques, dealers report, were expensive to begin with: Tiffany lamps always cost an arm and a leg. And if you buy a used mobile home for a song, expect to sell it for a song—or maybe just a few bars.

TWO-FAMILY HOUSES

Your single best bet in low-cost housing may be a two-family house. Two-family houses cost about a third less than two single-family detached houses. After all, duplexes share grounds, walls, a roof, heating and cooling systems. You're buying the large, economy size.

A two-family would be fine for relatives—parents and adult child. More and more young couples who are friends buy a two-family together.

But don't count on buying a two-family and renting out one floor to meet a hefty chunk of your expenses. You may have trouble obtaining a positive cash flow—more money coming in than goes out. And you may have trouble finding good tenants. Renters with cash to spare tend to buy houses. The remainder tend to be cash poor, and may have difficulty paying rents. Dispossessing a tenant can be difficult and expensive. Having one vacancy in your two-family house can be disastrous.

Certainly, renting out part of a two-family house can be profitable. But it doesn't always happen. Investigate before you try it. Check with your accountant, talk to local real estate agents, talk with other local landlords. And determine that you won't hate being a land-lord—listening to your tenants' gripes, warning them against late-night parties, dealing with midnight emergencies in two residences.

MANUFACTURED HOUSES

Since 1976, new manufactured homes have had to meet safety and construction standards set by the U.S. Department of Housing and Urban Development. You can get financing on them just as you would on any other homes—through banks, the Federal Housing Administration, and the Veterans Administration (though the mort-gages all may have 15-year terms). On the other hand, unless you buy a large ("double-wide") top-of-the-line manufactured home, and have it placed on an attractive, well-maintained site, you can't count on its appreciating much. In fact, the bottom-of-the-line models—mobile homes—may depreciate, just like cars.

One reason that most manufactured houses are inexpensive is that they can be made all year long, as opposed to site-built (or "stick-built") homes, where construction may be hampered by cold and wet weather. Typically, they cost half of what a site-built house goes for.

But not all manufactured homes are inexpensive. At the top of the class are panelized or prefabricated houses. In a posh area, they can go for as much as $250,000, but typically they run $100,000 to $120,000. The factory ships the roof panels, floors and walls, sometimes complete with wallpaper. Putting the house together can take two weeks to two months. On site, it may be indistinguishable from traditional housing. You have a wide choice of options and can create, in effect, a custom-made home—for significantly less money.

A step down from panelized houses are modular homes, and they would be a fine choice for cash-poor, first-time home buyers. They're typically smaller than panelized houses, and your choice of options is usually limited. Still, for the price ($45,000-$50,000), you get a modest but fine home, sometimes with all appliances, triple-pane glass, and eight inches of insulation in the walls.

TIP: Arthur H. Watkins, author of *The Complete Book of Factory-Built Homes*, singles out Cardinal Industries in Toledo as a manufacturer of top-notch modular homes.

Modular homes are also built in a factory, but in more sections. They are trucked to a site, then assembled. They can take as little as a week to put together because they're so standardized.

Mobile homes are made in a factory, in one or more sections, then placed on wheels to be carted to your building site—either a lot you own or one in a mobile-home park. While they are inexpensive, and some are very appealing, they have a poor reputation. Whenever there's a hurricane, you read about the damage done to mobile homes. Still, they deserve better—you can even buy fancy varieties with cathedral ceilings and bay windows. For what they cost—in some cases only $20,000–$25,000, excluding land, they can be excellent. About 50 percent of mobile-home owners rent space in a park.

Precut houses are for do-it-yourselfers, and are especially popular in the Northwest. Logs or two-by-fours are cut and marked in a factory, then shipped to the site. You can assemble everything yourself, using the packaged instructions. Usually these kits include only logs for the walls, not material for the foundation, doors, windows, and roof. Putting a kit house together can take three months to a year.

TIPS: Check a dealer's reputation, and make sure the price includes delivery and set-up expenses. Talk with people who have bought a particular model. Have any home checked out by an inspector. Look for a warranty for over a year. If you plan to rent a lot at a mobile-home park, make sure that your lease runs at least a year and that there's no rule against your selling your home at its park location.

BUILDING YOUR OWN

If you plan to build your own single-family house, you would be best advised to enroll in a school that teaches people how. And you should have a lot of free time and patience. Estimates are: If you act as the general contractor, supervising the plumbers, carpenters, and other workers, you'll save 20 percent of the cost of a new house. If you have the foundation and shell constructed by others but do the remainder yourself, you'll save 40 percent. Do everything yourself, and you'll save 60 percent.

CONDOMINIUMS AND COOPERATIVES

For people who hate housework, condominiums and cooperatives are a dream: you needn't mow lawns, shovel snow, or repair leaky faucets. In turn, you'll have to pay a monthly maintenance fee. Most coops are high-rise apartment houses in big cities. With a coop, you own stock in the corporation that owns the building. You have a lease on your apartment, and you share the blanket mortgage on the building. With a condo, you own your residence outright—be it an apartment, townhouse, garden apartment, whatever. You share ownership of the common grounds: the elevator, the pool, the hallways, the parking area.

By and large, a condo is better. In a coop, if a resident defaults, everyone may have to contribute to make up the deficit. One tenant's mechanic's lien can be attached against the entire coop. In a condo, the residents are protected because they have individual mortgages and individual deeds.

You may have an easier time getting a mortgage on a condo, too. (Actually, you don't get a mortgage on a coop—in some states it's considered personal property, not real estate; you just get a loan.) And the interest rate on a condo mortgage may be lower.

With a condo, you may have more freedom to decorate your own unit—to paint the walls, enlarge the kitchen. With a coop, there is a board that may object to your redecorating plans, if the coop rules give the board authority to review plans.

Condos also tend to appreciate more—partly because of the ease in getting mortgages, partly because in some coops shareholders can only sell their shares back to the coop or are otherwise restricted on resale. Still, because of overbuilding in some parts of the country, in recent years condo sales haven't exactly been brisk everywhere.

Coops have a few advantages. If there's an old mortgage, you may have a small downpayment, low interest, and small monthly payments to make. And the board can more easily get rid of someone whose behavior leaves something to be desired.

TIPS: If you're buying in a new development, check that the units are selling fast—and not just the units with good views, or the cheaper ones.

With any condo or coop, make sure you won't be charged extra for using the pool or for parking space. Be sure that you own the land too—it isn't being leased from the developer. Investigate the developer's reputation, at least to the extent of calling your state's department of consumer affairs.

For a true bargain, look for an apartment being converted into a condo. Prices at the outset may be unusually low, and if you're already a tenant, you may get a special (insider) price. Check that the management can be replaced by a reasonable percentage vote of the membership, and that any professional manager has only a short-term contract—so he or she can be dispensed with in a reasonable amount of time if necessary.

Make sure that a balloon mortgage on a coop isn't coming due soon, lest your mortgage payments soar. Also check whether major repairs are slated soon, like a new furnace, and whether there's a limit on the amount that the assessments can be raised in a single year. See how much money is in reserve to cover emergency expenses—10 percent to 20 percent of the total annual assessment should do. Find out what the maintenance fee is now, whether it was recently increased, and whether it's slated to rise soon. Find out whether the place has adequate fire and liability insurance, and make sure there aren't any big lawsuits outstanding.

Expect that the higher floors in tall buildings (those with elevators) will cost more: they will be quieter and have better views. (But in three-story walkups, the units on the third floor will be cheaper.)

Before buying any condo or coop, talk to tenants. Are repairs made promptly? Has there been a large turnover? Are units appreciating? Are many units rented out? (If so, it's a bad sign: renters don't take as good care of a place as owners.) Find out whether pets are allowed, and whether the residents are mostly your age.

As for individual units, check the soundproofing. Have someone talk next door, or put on a radio, so you can hear how the sound carries. Check the view. See whether the unit is near a noisy elevator or a trash disposal.

If you're looking at a condo conversion, study the engineering report on the entire building. The same goes for a coop.

If you're buying a used condo, make sure the seller has paid all of his or her assessments, so you won't be liable for them. And make sure that you can eventually sell your unit without the approval of the owners' association, or even giving the association the right to buy the condo first (a right of first refusal).

BUY FROM A FIZZBO

Fizzbos are sellers who aren't using brokers. (The name comes from "For Sale By Owner"—FSBO.) Usually fizzbos just want to save the 6-percent to 7-percent brokers' commission. If that's so, they can afford to sell you a house for a bargain price. Alas, all too many fizzbos ask too much for their houses, not granting buyers any of the commission they expect to save. But you may be more successful in bargaining with them, because they have more leeway in the price.

Other fizzbos weren't successful in selling through brokers, so they have undertaken the job themselves. Perhaps they were asking too much, or their house has problems, or the market has been slow. In any case, the longer a house has been on the market, the more eager the owners may be to unload the place.

You can find fizzbos by looking for classified ads that say, "For Sale By Owner," or that simply list a private phone number rather than a brokerage firm number. Or you can just drive around town and look for "For Sale By Owner" signs.

ASSUME A MORTGAGE

By taking over a seller's existing mortgage, you might get a low interest rate and reduce your closing costs. And lowering closing costs is equivalent to lowering the downpayment. In many states, fixed-rate mortgages now have due-on-sale clauses—which means buyers cannot assume them. But your state may be an exception. Besides, you can assume FHA-insured or VA-guaranteed mortgages. (See Chapters 9 and 10.) If those mortgages were obtained in the past two years, though, you will have to obtain approval.

You probably won't have any problem taking over an adjustable-rate mortgage. (See Chapter 14.) By doing so, you'll save some closing costs, of course. And if the mortgage's interest rate has already been boosted several times, so that it's at or near its permissible lifetime limit ("cap") on increases, that mortgage would be very appealing.

If the sellers' house has appreciated a great deal, assuming their mortgage won't be enough, you'll have to come up with the difference between their mortgage balance and the selling price of the house. The same may be true if they've had the mortgage for many years: the balance may be on the low side. Ideally, you'll buy where the sellers have lived in their house only a few years, and their house has not appreciated much.

OTHER INEXPENSIVE HOUSING

To learn about bargain houses, you must be energetic. Get acquainted with a variety of real estate agents. Talk with lenders. Telephone various government housing offices. Scrutinize the classified ads in newspapers. That way, when a bargain house becomes available, someone will phone you first.

The ideal inexpensive house is one that is simply underpriced. Typically, the owners have lived there for 20, 30, or more years and just can't comprehend that the house they bought for $10,000 is now worth $90,000. They offer the house for sale, at $70,000, on a Saturday morning, and by Saturday afternoon there are a half-dozen offers, all at the full asking price. If you arrived at 9:15 in the morning, yours could have been the first offer. Other sources of bargain houses:

- Foreclosed houses. Check with lenders and brokers in the area. Lenders call foreclosed houses "real estate owned" (REOs), and they sell such houses through brokers or at sheriff's auctions. If you're interested in a foreclosed house, you might be able to arrange favorable financing, including minimal downpayments. Also check with your local Department of Housing and Urban Development, Veterans Administration, Federal National Mortgage Association, and Farmers Home Administration, which sometimes also sell foreclosed houses.

One danger presented by foreclosed houses is that there may be liens you don't know about. Use some of the money you save on the price and downpayment to hire an experienced lawyer. To learn whether any foreclosed houses are being sold at auction in your area, call the Auction Information Center in Gilbert, Arizona at (602) 926-0149. Also call the FHA—1-800-553-4636. At an auction, you will need earnest money to bid—$2,000 in cash, certified check, or cashier's check for a one-family house, and $5,000 for a group of units. Lenders will usually be available to help you with a mortgage if your bid is accepted.

- Tax-delinquency sales. You can learn about them from a county clerk's office. Tax-delinquency auctions are similar to auctions of foreclosed houses, but here you bid to pay the outstanding taxes. Properties are sold "as is," and you may not even have a chance to inspect them. Worse yet, the current owner may have two years to redeem the property by paying the back taxes—and all you'll receive is a return of your payment plus interest. Even if you succeed in buying such a house, there may be liens you don't know about.

- Housing for first-time home buyers. Around 48 states have programs for first-time home buyers that allow them to obtain mortgages with as little as 5 percent down (but with private mortgage insurance—see Chapter 10). These programs also give a break on the interest rate—perhaps two to two and one-half percentage points. To find out if your state has such a program, look for "Housing Finance Authority" under the state government listings in your phone book.

In New York, the Affordable Housing Program is part of the State of New York Mortgage Agency (SONYMA); call 1-800-342-HOME. The program sells tax-exempt bonds to raise money to buy mortgages from lenders. The mortgages must be fixed rate and have 20-, 25-, or 30-year terms. There are income limits and purchase-price limits, but they vary tremendously from area to area. A one-family house can be new, but a two-, three-, or four-family home must be five years old or older. SONYMA has bought 23,000 loans in the past five years.

Not all mortgages purchased come from first-time homeowners. A small percentage—4 percent—comes from homeowners who are buying in special target areas, and the income limits and purchase prices are higher. You can call SONYMA to learn which lenders in your area are in the program, and what the income and purchase-price limits are in the community where you intend to buy a house.

TIP: A first-time home buyer is someone who hasn't had an interest in a principal home during the past three years. If you have only a vacation home, or you sold your principal home over three years ago, state housing finance agencies will consider you a first-time home buyer.

- Fixer-uppers. A house that's shabby on the outside may be even worse on the inside. If the lawn and siding have been neglected, the same might be true of the furnace and the roof. Fixer-uppers and handyman's specials are best left for pros, not for first-time home buyers. If you do want to try your luck, be sure to have any dilapidated house thoroughly checked out by a house inspector first. Bear in mind that your best bet may be a dilapidated house in a good community, even if it costs far more than the same house in a deteriorating community.

"Gentrified" neighborhoods—areas of cities that are being spruced up—tend to be high priced. Your best course may be to look for a house in an area near an already restored section, especially if the houses are impressive—brownstones and Victorians. But check with local real estate agents to make sure that the area seems poised to rise again. A basic rule of thumb: Don't spend more buying and fixing up a house than two-thirds of what the house would have cost new. If you buy a house for $20,000 and plan to spend $20,000, the house should be equivalent to a $60,000 new house.

Sometimes you can even buy a deteriorated house in an inner-city neighborhood for as little as $1, providing that you promise to fix it up within a year or two and live there for three years. Check your city housing agency to see if it has an urban homesteading program. Many cities offer low-interest mortgages if you agree to restore a house in a historic district. You might also try the National Park Service, which can provide money to help restore historic areas. Write to the National Park Service, Office of Architectural and Historic Preservation, Department of the Interior, Washington, DC 20040.

A GUIDE TO BARGAINING

Whether you are interested in a handyman's special or a two-family house, you may succeed in knocking thousands off the purchase price if you know the rudiments of negotiation. That, in turn, will lower your downpayment, your closing costs, and your mortgage payments. In fact, if you bargain skillfully, you may also be able to persuade a seller to give you a mortgage—with a low or no downpayment. (See Chapter 5.)

Be Courteous: Above all, when a real estate agent takes you house shopping, or when you meet homeowners who are trying to sell their houses on their own, don't be aggressive. Remember that you want a favor from the sellers: a low price. Keep in mind that sellers are proud of their homes. They are more apt to sell for less to someone they like than to someone who riles them. And it's easy to like a young person buying a first home, especially if that young person is courteous—if, for example, you ask permission before opening any doors or testing the faucets.

When you're dealing with large amounts of money—like $90,000—a few thousand may not seem so important, at least to the person receiving the $90,000. So don't ruin everything by criticizing the seller's taste. You might mention that the wallpaper in the house needs replacing, that the appliances are old, that the plaster ceilings are cracked, that the carpeting is worn, that the furnace is old, that the faucets leak, that the roof is 25 years old. But do it courteously, not harshly. Mention good things about the house as well as the imperfections. Certainly, never criticize the design of the wallpaper, the color of the carpet, the landscaping, or anything else that reflects on the seller. In fact, keep reminding the sellers that you like their house. The furniture is beautiful; the decorations are tasteful.

Never be overbearing. Don't say, "I can't understand how you can expect anyone to pay $65,000 for a house with a defective furnace." Instead, say, "This is a wonderful house, just perfect for us, but I wonder if we can carry it if we have to pay $65,000—and then, a few months from now, have to pay for a new furnace and new wallpaper." Your goal is to seem fair, not come across like a money-mad yuppie out to steal a fine house for a mere pittance.

Plead Poverty: You have a perfect excuse why you're offering so little for a house. You can't afford to pay any more than you're offering. If the seller says, "Look, we're just $5,000 apart. How about we split the difference? Just throw $2,500 more into the pot and we've got a done deal." Your answer: "I'd like to, I really would. But I just can't afford it."

Do Your Homework: Before bargaining with any seller, do some research. Check out at least a half-dozen houses in any area to get an idea of what houses are selling for. Try to find out how lively or how slow the housing market is. Try to learn why any particular homeowner wants to sell. Has the homeowner bought another house, and is he or she paying taxes on it and having to maintain it? Has the seller been transferred elsewhere? Is the seller retiring to a warmer place? Have the sellers been divorced?

Definitely find out how long the house has been on the market. If it's been for sale longer than normal for the area and that time of year, you may have a bargaining edge. But also learn whether the seller has reduced his or her price during that time. A recent price cut isn't auspicious.

Also try to learn whether the seller owns the house free and clear, or whether he or she has a large mortgage balance. (Sellers with small or no mortgages may be more willing to help you with financing.) Inquire whether the seller needs cash to buy another house. Check whether the seller's mortgage is assumable—and decide whether you want to assume it.

The more eager a seller is to unload a house, the more successful your bargaining efforts will be. And time is an ingredient in bargaining. Don't waste much time bargaining with a homeowner who isn't especially eager to sell, whose house has just recently been put on the market, who has a large mortgage and needs cash to buy another house. A friendly real estate agent can provide you with valuable guidance.

CAUTION: Never tell a real estate agent your bargaining strategy. An agent is, legally and ethically, on the side of the seller. The agent must try to obtain the highest possible price for the seller, and the very best terms. So don't tell an agent that you'll offer, say, $60,000, but are willing to pay $70,000. An agent would be obliged to tell the seller, "The buyer is willing to pay $70,000, so hold out for at least that much."

SET GOALS

With most house shopping, you simply want a low price. But if cash is tight, you have other goals:

- A low downpayment.
- A first or second mortgage from the seller (especially if the house is free and clear). (See Chapter 5.)

You might even be willing to pay the full asking price for a house if you can dispense with the downpayment and get a mortgage from the sellers. Determine what your goals are. If you can afford 10 percent down, you might bargain hard over the selling price. If you're planning to get an FHA-insured mortgage for less than 5 percent down, or a VA-guaranteed loan for nothing down, again your aim should be a low sales price. (See Chapters 9 and 10.) But if you absolutely need the lowest possible downpayment, that— and not a low selling price—should be your foremost goal.

To persuade sellers not to require a downpayment, you must negotiate with someone who owns a house without a mortgage, who doesn't need cash, and who will grant you a mortgage. Otherwise, with a downpayment less than 5 percent, you may never get a mortgage from a traditional lender. Even putting less than 20 percent down, you would probably be required to buy private mortgage insurance.

Explain to the sellers that you have a good job with rising earnings. Would the seller be willing to wait six months for a downpayment? To accept installments toward a downpayment? In that case, you can afford a higher purchase price. If the sellers trust you, why shouldn't they accept a higher selling price than they had expected? The interest on any mortgage they grant will probably be more than they could get by investing their money elsewhere.

On the other hand, all you want may be the lowest selling price. Assume that the asking price is $100,000. Sellers tend to have added 5 percent to 10 percent to that price, so they may expect $90,000 to $95,000. Based on your own assessment, you think the house is worth $90,000. (Your assessment comes from what similar houses have recently sold for, how well the house has been maintained, and the area—as well as your view of how eager the sellers are to sell and the briskness or slowness of the market.)

Now you can determine the following:

(1) The highest offering price you can afford, assuming that it's equal to or less than the house's value. The first price might be $90,000—if you can get by with little or no downpayment.

(2) An offering price that strikes you as fair. The second price would also be $90,000.

(3) A price that would be a bargain. This might be $87,500.

(4) An offering price that would make the house a steal, but still be considered reasonable: $85,000.

(5) A price so low that the sellers would have to be anxious to unload the place were they to accept. The fifth price might be $80,000.

START LOW AND MAKE SMALLER CONCESSIONS

One theory states that you want to dampen the sellers' expectations, so you should open the bidding with price (5)—the lowest offer that any sellers might accept. This is a risky tactic. The sellers might not only reject the offer, but angrily refuse to negotiate with you any further. If you want to negotiate for a low downpayment and a seller's mortgage, you might be a better off starting with price (4).

If you offer $80,000, don't say, "That's what your house is really worth in this stagnant market." Say, "Well, $80,000 is all we can afford—and that's with no downpayment and your giving us a mortgage." In the bidding that follows, make progressively smaller concessions, again to dampen the sellers' expectations that you'll come up much more. If the sellers tell you that their rock-bottom price is $95,000, you might go toward price (4)—$85,000. Your subsequent concessions, if you decide to make them, might be progressively smaller—$1,000 and $500, say. So your next two prices are $86,000 and $86,500. You'll still be $1,000 away from price (3), which you think would make the house a bargain, and $3,500 away from prices (1) and (2), which would just be fair prices. Your own concessions might match the amount of the sellers' concessions.

Your concessions should head toward a nice, round number. In the negotiation above, $86,500 is heading toward $87,500—which is price (3), a house at a terrific bargain.

How much time you take between concessions depends on how badly you want the house and how interested you think the sellers are. As the saying goes, "He who wants it most pays the most." Negotiating experiments have shown that the bargainer who makes more concessions, and makes them more quickly, typically winds up paying too much or getting too little.

If the sellers tell you, "Take it or leave it, $95,000 is my final price," or the equivalent, just ignore it. Continue bargaining.

OFFER SOMETHING BESIDES MONEY

If you reach an impasse in the negotiations, remember that you're not just bargaining about the house price. You can negotiate about terms, too, and about cash equivalents.

- Offer to arrange the sale and move-in date to please the sellers. Do they want to be out of their house quickly? You'll oblige them. Do they want to remain for six months and postpone the closing? You'll be amenable—or you might suggest, instead, that you close quickly, and they pay you rent until they move out (a good way for you to amass cash).

- Agree to raise your offering price if the sellers will pay some of your closing costs, such as points on any mortgage you are getting (but you'll lose your tax deduction and the sellers can't deduct points they pay on your mortgage), or the cost of a termite inspection. Try to make your price concessions lower than the closing costs you want the sellers to pay. This will give the sellers a way of saving face, while indirectly granting you price concessions.

- Suggest that you do some work for the sellers in return for price concessions. Do they need help moving? You and a few friends will rent a truck and do it for them. Be careful—barter transactions are taxable.

- Propose that they skip any fixing up they were planning to do—replacing broken window panes, removing an old carpet, finishing painting the interior or exterior. You'll do those chores yourself.

- Mention that, in order to persuade them to lower their price, you will let them take certain items they might not have been planning to—lawn furniture, lawn mower, appliances, chandeliers, built-in bookcases.

These concessions will help persuade the sellers that you're dead serious about not having enough money. And they will help assuage any feelings the sellers may have that they are "losing" the bargaining contest.

CHAPTER SUMMARY

To lower your downpayment, reduce your closing costs, and keep mortgage payments low, all at the same time, buy a cheap house, or buy an expensive house cheaply. Whether you buy a traditional house or a mobile home, don't try to save money by skipping a house inspector's report. But do shop off-season—when bad weather is keeping other buyers away. Look at houses far away from a metropolitan area. Check into two-family houses that you can buy with other people. Investigate modular houses, mobile homes, precut homes, and—if you can afford it—panelized houses. Condominiums and cooperatives are other types of residences you should consider. Be on the lookout for houses being sold without agents, and houses with mortgages that are assumable. For further savings, check into foreclosed houses, houses delinquent on their taxes, housing for low-income people, and fixer-uppers in communities making a comeback. Finally, be prepared to bargain over the price.

FOR YOUR NOTEBOOK

FORM: *COMPARING HOUSES**

	1	2	3
Address	_____	_____	_____
Asking price	_____	_____	_____
Take-back mortgage	_____	_____	_____
Mortgage amount	_____	_____	_____
Downpayment	_____	_____	_____
Size of lot	_____	_____	_____
Size of house	_____	_____	_____
House style	_____	_____	_____
Property taxes	_____	_____	_____
Heating bill	_____	_____	_____
Age of house	_____	_____	_____
Stories	_____	_____	_____
Exterior	_____	_____	_____
Storm windows	_____	_____	_____
Garage	_____	_____	_____
Water bill	_____	_____	_____
Type of heating	_____	_____	_____
Electric bill	_____	_____	_____
Age of furnace	_____	_____	_____
Central air/age	_____	_____	_____

* Courtesy U.S. Department of Housing and Urban Development.

	1	2	3
Bedrooms/size	___	___	___
Living room/size	___	___	___
Dining room/size	___	___	___
Bathrooms/size	___	___	___
Closets/size	___	___	___
Refrigerator/size	___	___	___
Disposal/dishwasher	___	___	___
Stove/age	___	___	___
Washer-dryer/age	___	___	___
Laundry space	___	___	___
Water heater/age	___	___	___
Basement area/size	___	___	___
Finished basement	___	___	___
Finished attic	___	___	___
Attic area/size	___	___	___
Fireplaces	___	___	___
Carpeting	___	___	___
Drapes	___	___	___
Public sewer	___	___	___
Backyard patio	___	___	___
Fencing	___	___	___
Landscaping	___	___	___
Other	___	___	___

FORM: COMPARING NEIGHBORHOODS*

Neighborhood quality	Yes	No
1. Are the homes well taken care of?	___	___
2. Are there good public services (police, fire)?	___	___
3. Are there paved roads?	___	___
4. Are there sidewalks?	___	___

	Yes	No
5. Is there adequate street lighting?		
6. Is there a city sewer system?		
7. Is there a safe public water supply?		
8. Are the public schools good?		

Neighborhood convenience
1. Will you be near your work?		
2. Are there schools nearby?		
3. Are there shopping centers nearby?		
4. Is public transportation available?		
5. Are child-care services nearby?		
6. Are hospitals, clinics, doctors nearby?		
7. Are parks and playgrounds nearby?		

Neighbors
1. Will you be near friends or relatives?		
2. Are children of your kids' ages nearby?		
3. Will you feel comfortable with the neighbors?		
4. Is there an active community group?		

Does the neighborhood have any problems?
1. Increasing real estate taxes?		
2. Decreasing price of homes?		
3. Many families moving away?		
4. Heavy traffic or noise?		
5. Litter or pollution?		
6. Factories or heavy industry?		
7. Businesses closing down?		
8. Vacant houses or buildings?		
9. Increasing crime or vandalism?		

What is your overall rating of the neighborhood?

Good __ Fair __ Poor __

* Courtesy U.S. Department of Housing and Urban Development.

4 CUTTING CLOSING COSTS

THE IMPORTANCE OF CLOSING COSTS

To buy a house when you have very little cash, you have three hurdles to jump over: (1) the downpayment, (2) closing costs, and (3) first-year expenses. The downpayment is the highest hurdle, but don't neglect the other two.

Closing costs are not usually considered part of the downpayment, yet you can't become a homeowner without paying them. And the more you can lower your closing costs, the less likely you are to endure a cash-flow crisis after you buy a house.

NOTE: A study by the National Association of Realtors found that new homeowners spent over $2,000 more than regular homeowners on their homes within 12 months after buying them—for furniture, appliances, clothing, linens, curtains, and so forth.

The "closing" is generally when the title (ownership) to a property changes hands. In many areas, buyer, seller, attorneys for each, the real estate broker and lender meet. The buyer hands over the downpayment, presents the seller with a check (from the mortgage lender) for the rest, and pays various other expenses. In the western part of the country, the closing may be handled by an escrow agent, and lawyers are rarely employed. The buyer and seller may not even meet at the closing.

If you play your cards right, you can probably lower your closing costs by several hundred dollars, or more. What you must do is shop around. Don't leave it to your lawyers, your real estate agent, your lender, or to providence to reduce your closing costs. You must go out there and work at it.

Your mortgage lender is supposed to give you a "good faith" estimate of closing costs within three days after you apply for a mortgage, along with a copy of *A HUD Guide to Home Buyers*, published by the U.S. Department of Housing and Urban Development. Under the Real Estate Settlement Procedures Law (called RESPA), the lender is also required to give you a list of actual closing costs one day before closing.

Obviously, you won't have enough time then to comparison shop, so you must start early.

WHAT YOU MUST PAY FOR

Real estate practices vary around the country. Even two counties next to each other may have different traditions. So it is with closing costs. In some places, the buyer pays for a termite inspection. In others, the seller pays. In still others, no one worries about termites. In some cases, purchasing title insurance is deemed essential; in other cases, it may not be as important (check with an attorney).

But in most cases, the buyer pays. And pays and pays. You've heard of interest-rate shock—when the cost of an adjustable-rate mortgage suddenly becomes far higher? Welcome to closing-cost shock. One man, scrutinizing all the expenses he was presented with at a closing, turned ashen, excused himself from the lawyers, bankers, sellers, and everyone else in the room—and was never seen again. Here's approximately what you can expect to pay at the closing:

- Mortgage application fee: $100–$300.
- Mortgage points: each one is 1 percent of the mortgage. These enable the lender to hold down the interest rate. Buyers with VA-guaranteed mortgages must pay one point, and usually no more. Three points may be par for everyone else, but there can be a lot of variation, so investigate carefully.

TIP: If you can spare the money, pay for points at the closing so you can deduct them for tax purposes in the current year. Pay by separate check, so you can prove to the IRS that the money went only for those points. Don't let the lender simply reduce the money lent to you by the points the lender will earn. The IRS may claim they're not deductible. If you pay off the cost of the points monthly along with the mortgage, you can deduct only a portion of the cost every year as you pay them—until you sell the house.

- Mortgage insurance: The FHA charges 3.8 percent of the mortgage; the VA, 1 percent; private mortgage insurers, about 1.25 percent. You won't normally have to buy this insurance if your downpayment is 20 percent of the house price, though some lenders insist on mortgage insurance unless the downpayment is 25 percent.
- Appraisal: $125–$200.
- Credit report: $30.
- Loan origination fee: $100–$200.
- Inspection reports: $25–$100 for termites; $150–$300 and up for engineer's inspection.
- Title search plus title insurance: $300–$1,500. This is to protect you and the lender in case the seller doesn't really own clear title to the property. Perhaps his former spouse owns half, and the seller doesn't have the right to sell it without the ex-spouse's permission. You probably won't be required to obtain title insurance for a cooperative, but you probably will pay for a title search. (For further discussion, see below.)

TIP: Ask the seller which company provided his or her title insurance coverage. Buy a policy from the seller's title insurance company, and if the old policy was issued recently you may get a discount.

- Homeowners insurance: Several hundred to a thousand dollars or more, depending on the value of your house and the location. (For further discussion, see below.)
- Prepaid property taxes: A few hundred to thousands, depending on the tax assessment, the tax year, and so forth.
- Recording fee and tax stamps: About ½ percent of the mortgage amount.
- Lawyers' fees: The lender's lawyer usually receives $500–$1,000; yours, up to 1 percent of the price of the house. Some charge more and some less depending on what is involved. (For a further discussion see below.)
- Survey: $100–$300.

TIP: If a survey was made within the past five years, maybe you can persuade the lender to skip it. If you're not successful, try to hire the previous surveyor, at a discount.

- Adjustments: What you owe the seller for taxes he or she has paid past the date of closing, for remaining oil in the tank, for furnishings or appliances you've bought, and a prorated portion of the gas and electric bill (unless you can have the utility company change billing over at the date you close).

It's hard to say what closing costs typically will amount to, but a ballpark estimate is 2 percent to 3 percent of your purchase price, plus whatever points you must pay.

HOMEOWNERS INSURANCE

Don't wait until the day of the closing to arrange for homeowners insurance. Start comparison shopping several weeks before. By shopping around, you can probably slice a few hundred dollars off the bill—and wind up with a better policy.

Homeowners, or hazard, insurance comes in "packages"—one for renters, another for condominium owners, another for owners of single-family detached homes, and so forth. The packages are identified by HO (HomeOwners) numbers 1 to 8. In the past, HO 3 was recommended for homeowners. But a new homeowners contract, Special HO 3, is even better. HO 3, unlike HO 1 and HO 2, provides coverage for water damage, glass breakage, burned kitchen counters, and so forth.

Each package protects your home, its contents, and any detached buildings (like a garage). You also get personal liability protection—in case someone slips in front of your house and sues you.

You can save up to 20 percent of your premium if you insure a house for only 80 percent of the cost of replacing it. Yet you will receive complete coverage for any damage less than 80 percent of the value of the house. The reason for considering this: A house is seldom totally destroyed. Even in a fire, the ground under your house (typically constituting 20 percent to 25 percent of its value) will emerge intact, and so will a good deal of the foundation. Policies vary though, so be careful to read the fine print and ask your insurance agent. Watch out for co-insurance rules when cutting back.

The contents of your house—the furniture, clothing, appliances—are usually insured for half of your total coverage automatically. If your home is insured for $100,000, your personal possessions will be insured for up to $50,000. Detached buildings get 10-percent coverage. If you can't live in your house because of a disaster such as a fire, you get 20-percent coverage for living costs—the amount for temporary living quarters plus the difference between the cost of your meals out and meals at home.

But any really expensive articles you have—computers, silverware, jewelry, antiques, collectibles—won't be properly covered. An insurance company will rarely pay more than $1,000–$2,500 for these items, and that's why you might consider paying for special "floaters," in case your losses exceed your coverage.

Be sure to buy a "replacement cost" rider. If your old TV set is stolen in a burglary, you don't want to receive only the cost of an old TV set. You want what a new TV will cost.

Ask your real estate agent or insurance agent whether your area qualifies for flood insurance. Your property must be in a community that has agreed to plan and carry out measures to reduce future flooding. (Around 20,000 communities are in such areas, and 18,000 have qualified.) The Federal Insurance Administration of the U.S. Department of Housing and Urban Development, as well as many private companies, provide this insurance in flood-prone areas, often for very reasonable fees. States where the most policies are sold are Florida, Louisiana, Texas, New Jersey, and California.

For general coverage, get quotations from at least three different companies, because prices probably will be very far apart. You may lower your premiums by 10 percent if you deal with companies that are "direct writers" (don't employ agents).

In Florida, the state department of insurance compared the amounts charged by different companies for insuring a $70,000 masonry home with a $250 deductible, $100,000 liability coverage, and 80-percent replacement cost. In Orlando, one insurance company charged $132 a year, while another charged $254. Difference: $122, or 92 percent.

In New Jersey, the state insurance department reports that the annual premium for $110,000 coverage on a wood house in Asbury Park, insured under an HO 3 policy, costs $229.83 with one company. An equivalent policy costs $858.34 with another insurance company. Difference: $628.51, or 273 percent!

If there's no difference in the premiums or the coverages, which is unlikely, throw in with the company that also insures your life and your car. You should have more clout there in case of a dispute.

TIPS: Consider a high deductible—the amount you yourself must pay before the insurance company starts paying. A $250, $500, or especially a $1,000 deductible will reduce your premium considerably. If you raise a $250 deductible to $500, you may be able to cut your premiums by 5 percent.

Ask about discounts for burglar alarms, smoke and heat alarms, automatic sprinklers, and dead-bolt locks. While you may get only $20 off for a smoke alarm, you might get 10 percent off with an automatic sprinkler system, 20 percent with a sophisticated home-security system.

Check into policies that will cover both your house and your car. One major insurance company offers a 10-percent discount on auto insurance and a 5-percent discount for homeowners insurance, if you get both. Even if you don't get a discount, you may be hit with only one deductible. Say, for example, your car is destroyed by a fire in your garage. With a combined deductible, you would pay only one deductible for the damage to both your car (auto insurance) and the garage (house insurance).

If you're buying a condominium, check out the building's coverage, so you don't pay for duplicate protection.

Rather than pay extra to insure valuable objects you own, consider keeping them in a bank's safe-deposit box. Examples are stamp collections, jewelry, silverware, small antiques, coin collections.

If yours is a new home—built within the past two years—you may be eligible for a 20-percent discount. The discount sinks by three percentage points every two years. A 10-year-old home might qualify for an 8-percent discount. [8 years/2 years = 4 × 3 percentage points = 12%; 20% − 12%=8%]

Perils covered by a special HO 3 homeowners policy can include:

- Fire or lightning
- Windstorm or hail
- Explosion
- Riot or civil commotion
- Aircraft
- Vehicles
- Smoke
- Vandalism or malicious mischief
- Theft
- Damage by glass or safety-glazing material that is part of the building
- Volcanic eruption
- Falling objects
- Weight of ice, snow, or sleet

- Accidental discharge or overflow of water or steam from within a plumbing, heating, air-conditioning, or automatic fire-protective sprinkler system, or from within a household appliance
- Sudden and accidental tearing apart, cracking, burning, or bulging of a steam or hot-water heating system, an automatic fire-protective sprinkler system, or of an appliance for heating water
- Freezing of a plumbing, heating, air-conditioning, or automatic fire-protective sprinkler system, or of a household appliance
- Sudden and accidental damage from artificially generated electrical current (does not include loss to a tube, transistor, or similar electronic component)

All perils except flood, earthquake, war, nuclear accident, and others specified in your policy are typically covered.

LEGAL FEES

You should shop for a lawyer, too. A real estate agent or your lender can give you names of those who specialize in house closings. Run the names by your friends and see whose name keeps popping up the most. Make sure any lawyer you use has local experience, and therefore is familiar with local real estate practices.

When you call a lawyer, ask what he or she will charge, how the charges are computed, how many closings he or she has actually handled in the past year, who will be doing the work, and any other questions you may have.

Mention to the lawyer the names of the people who referred you. Indicate whether you may be sending more business his or her way: you need a will, your uncle needs estate-planning help, your cousin is starting a business. If the lawyer and his or her practice, policies, expertise, and price seem satisfactory, make sure you get a written contract (a retainer agreement) specifying how much the lawyer will charge, and the services that will be rendered, so there is no disagreement afterward.

TITLE INSURANCE

To be sure you are really the owner of a new home, you must make sure that the former owners were really the former owners. That's why you pay for (1) a title search—having a lawyer or title insurance company check into the past ownership of your new home to make sure there's no doubt it belongs to the seller and that there are no delinquent taxes or liens on the property or other defects in the title to the property; and (2) title insurance—protection against defects in the title not turned up by the title search.

To protect yourself thoroughly, also be certain that you purchase a homeowners title policy in addition to any policy the mortgage lender requires. Defects in the title to a property are rare. Lately, insurance companies have been paying out less than 9 percent of their title insurance premiums; in earlier years, they paid out only 4 percent or 5 percent.

Yet title insurance is expensive. To some extent, the problem is that there hasn't been much competition among title insurance companies. In fact, some states actually allow title insurance companies to agree on what to charge.

Another problem is that some title insurance companies pay commissions to the lenders, real estate agents, or lawyers who refer their clients. These lenders, real estate agents, or lawyers are "controlled business agents," and can collect 60 percent of your premiums just by referring you.

What you must do is—yes—shop around. Don't let your real estate agent, lender, or lawyer obtain title insurance for you. Look in the Yellow Pages for title insurance companies, and find out what they will charge you for a search, for title insurance, and for homeowners title insurance.

The price differences may be sizable. In California, some title companies give you a discount if you're buying a house those companies insured within the past five years; others will give you a discount only if you're buying a house those companies insured within the past two years.

In Chicago, here's what one company was recently charging, compared with the competition:

Comparison of Title Insurance Premiums

Property Value	Average Chicago-Area Price	One Company
$ 75,000	$ 507	$452
100,000	592	500
250,000	973	500
500,000	1,607	500
1,000,000	2,802	500

CHAPTER SUMMARY

Closing costs can amount to 2 percent, 3 percent, or more of the price of your buying a house. To prevent a cash crunch after the closing, do your utmost to lower the expenses. You can succeed if, before the closing, you go shopping—for a reasonably priced home-owners insurance policy, for a capable, efficient lawyer who will charge a reasonable fee, and for reasonably priced title insurance coverage.

FOR YOUR NOTEBOOK

The following is a sample form used to advise borrowers of closing costs.

INTERSTATE MORTGAGE SERVICE INC.
LICENSED MORTGAGE BANKER
292 MAIN STREET
SUITE 23
HACKENSACK, NEW JERSEY 07601

(201) 488-2662

GOOD FAITH ESTIMATE OF CHARGES FOR SETTLEMENT SERVICES

APPLICANT(S): _____

_____

MAILING ADDRESS: _____

_____

PROPERTY ADDRESS: _____

_____

SALES PRICE $ _____ MORTGAGE LOAN REQUESTED $ _____

DATED _____ TYPE OF MORTGAGE _____

IN CONNECTION WITH YOUR APPLICATION FOR A LOAN SECURED BY A MORTGAGE COVERING THE ABOVE CAPTIONED PREMISES, LENDER IS FURNISHING YOU WITH THE FOLLOWING GOOD FAITH ESTIMATE OF CHARGES FOR SETTLEMENT SERVICES YOU ARE LIKELY TO INCUR. THIS IS REQUIRED BY HUD PURSUANT TO THE REAL ESTATE SETTLEMENT PROCEDURES ACT AND DOES NOT MEAN THAT THE LOAN HAS BEEN APPROVED.

801) LOAN ORIGINATION FEE: .... $ _____

802) LOAN DISCOUNT: .... $ _____

803) APPRAISAL FEE: .... $ _____

804) CREDIT REPORT: .... $ _____

805) LENDER'S INSPECTION FEE: .... $ _____

806) MORTGAGE INSURANCE APPLICATION FEE: .. $ _____

901) INTEREST PREPAID (MAXIMUM, 1 MONTH): . . . $ _____

902) MORTGAGE INSURANCE PREMIUM: . . . . $ _____

1107) DOCUMENT PREPARATION & REVIEW FEE: . . . $ _____

1108) TITLE INSURANCE-LENDER'S COVERAGE: . . . . $ _____

OWNER'S COVERAGE (OPTIONAL): . . . . $ _____

1201) RECORDING FEES: DEED AND MORTGAGE: . . . $ _____

1203) MISCELLANEOUS: . . . . $ _____

1301) SURVEY (IF REQUIRED): . . . . $ _____

1302) PEST INSPECTION: . . . . $ _____

1303) TAX SERVICE FEE: . . . . $ _____

1304) UCC1 FEE: . . . . $ _____

1305) FNMA CO-OP FEE: . . . . $ _____

1306) MISCELLANEOUS: . . . . $ _____

808) LOAN APPLICATION FEE (NON-REFUNDABLE):

$ _____

TOTAL: $ _____

THIS FORM DOES NOT COVER ALL ITEMS YOU WILL BE REQUIRED TO PAY IN CASH AT SETTLEMENT. FOR EXAMPLE, DEPOSIT IN ESCROW FOR REAL ESTATE TAXES AND INSURANCE. YOU MAY WISH TO INQUIRE AS TO THE AMOUNTS OF SUCH OTHER ITEMS. YOU MAY BE REQUIRED TO PAY OTHER ADDITIONAL AMOUNTS AT SETTLE-MENT.

ITEM No. 1107, DOCUMENT PREPARATION & REVIEW FEE, IS DESIGNATED AS THE LENDER'S FEE FOR REVIEW OF THE FILE, PREPARATION OF THE BOND, MORTGAGE AND ALL OTHER LEGAL DOCUMENTS NECESSARY TO OBTAIN A VALID FIRST MORT-GAGE LIEN, ASSEMBLY OF AND TRANSMITTAL OF THE COMPLETED LOAN PACKAGE. I HAVE RECEIVED THIS FORM, AND THE TRUTH IN LENDING DISCLOSURES, AND THE BOOKLET "A HUD GUIDE FOR HOMEBUYERS—SETTLEMENT COSTS."

_____

SIGNATURE   DATE

_____

SIGNATURE   DATE

5 LET THE SELLER BE THE BANKER TOO

WHAT IS SELLER FINANCING?

Seller financing is where the sellers of the house you are buying help you finance the purchase. They do this by letting you owe them money instead of paying the full price of the house at the closing.

In the traditional house-purchase transaction the buyer uses savings to pay for about 20 percent of the purchase price. The remaining 80 percent is usually obtained from a bank as a loan. This loan is secured by a mortgage on the house the buyer is buying. In this traditional type of purchase the seller receives cash for the house at the closing—part from the buyer and the rest from the bank.

In some instances, the buyer may want to use the seller as a bank, instead of, or in addition to, the regular bank. Many times the seller will agree. From a legal perspective there are two basic ways that a seller can loan the buyer money, or give the buyer credit. The first, and more common, approach is for the seller to take back a mortgage from the buyer.

When a seller (mortgagee) accepts a mortgage from the buyer (mortgagor) it is called a purchase money mortgage (PMM). This is the equivalent of the seller loaning the buyer an amount of money equal to the mortgage, since the seller will not receive that money at the closing. In other words, the seller accepts the buyer's "paper" (the mortgage), signed by the buyer at the closing, instead of cash. The seller may provide all of the financing or only some, and the borrower will get the rest of the financing from a bank or other lender.

In the second approach to the seller loaning money to the buyer, the seller conveys the property to the buyer on the installment method (also known as a land contract). Under the installment method the buyer typically gives the seller a downpayment and makes payments for the balance over a number of years. This has some legal distinctions from the seller accepting the buyer's mortgage. Unlike a mortgage, where the buyer receives the title to (ownership of) the property at the closing, in an installment-sale contract the buyer usually doesn't receive title to the property until all of the required payments are made. Since the buyer doesn't have legal title (ownership) of the property until it is fully paid for, this approach is generally only usable where the seller provides all of the financing, because it may be difficult for the buyer to obtain additional funds from another lender.

Some of the technical legal distinctions between a purchase money mortgage and the installment method will be discussed later in this chapter.

NOTE: Dick Schlott, president of Schlott Realtors, observes that "Many sellers have immense amounts of equity in their homes, particularly in the Northeast and California. They can benefit by being the lender if they don't need all of the equity to purchase another home. They shouldn't be embarrassed to ask their Realtor to help arrange for financing.

"A common situation is where an older couple is selling and moving to Florida or another southern area where homes can be obtained for less money. The $125,000 exclusion older couples can qualify for often isn't enough to avoid tax on a large gain that isn't being reinvested in another house. Also, some people take early retirement and don't qualify for this tax benefit. Using seller financing can get the sellers a great return on their money and can defer the tax they have to pay on the gain of the sale of their old home.

"For the buyers, seller financing may be the only way they can qualify for the house they really want. Seller financing can be a great result for both parties."

WHY BUYERS SHOULD BE INTERESTED IN SELLER FINANCING

As a buyer, you receive a number of advantages from seller financing, particularly if you are trying to buy with little or no money down:

- Speed. Seller financing can be arranged as quickly as the buyer and seller can agree on the basic terms of the transaction and the lawyers can draft the loan documents and have them ready for signature. This can be far more rapid than bank financing, which typically (although not always) has long and formal review procedures from the initial loan application to the final disbursement of funds. If either the buyer or seller is in a big hurry, seller financing may be the way to go. This can happen when, for example, either the buyer or seller is about to be relocated to a new city, is leaving on a lengthy trip, or has a personal matter that must be attended to.

On the seller's side, if a seller will not be buying another house, the seller won't qualify for the tax-free treatment available when a homeowner sells one home and replaces it within two years with a more expensive home. If the seller will face a tax on the gain from selling the home, it may be very advantageous for him or her to have that gain taxed in a specific year. The flexibility and speed of consummating a purchase money mortgage may enable the seller to choose which tax year to take the gain.

- Easier qualification. Seller financing may be much easier for a buyer to qualify for. The seller may be willing to accept back a mortgage from the buyer for part of the purchase price without subjecting the buyer to the stringent qualifying criteria a bank or other traditional lender may impose. If you can't meet the strict requirements of a major lender, perhaps seller financing will be the answer. Perhaps you had a personal bankruptcy a few years ago, or had a prior house foreclosed upon. Traditional lenders may not be willing to extend a loan to you. However, a seller, particularly if you hit it off, might extend you the credit. If your bankruptcy was caused by a business failure that was not avoidable, a seller may be willing to consider the circumstances.

TIP: In some cases, according to Dick Schlott, if the seller will accept 25 percent of the price as seller financing with no interest for five years, the buyer can automatically qualify with certain commercial lenders for an immediate loan for the remaining 75 percent of the price. This easy qualification for primary financing can be a great advantage to a seller in a hurry to sell, or who has been held up in the past by buyers who cancelled the purchase because they couldn't get a mortgage.

- Downpayment. If you can't meet the downpayment required by traditional lenders, a seller who is willing to accept a lesser downpayment may be your sole route to buying the type of home you want.

EXAMPLE: Paul and Pauline Purchaser wish to buy a house from Heidi Homeowner. Heidi wants $89,000 for the house. The Purchasers called the local banks and savings and loan associations and found that the financing they want requires no less than 20 perrcent down. Unfortunately, they can't afford to pay the $17,800 downpayment, the estimated $1,500 for moving expenses, and the $4,350 their lawyer says they'll need for closing costs. They really want the house, so they work out an arrangement with Heidi. Heidi will take back a $15,000 second mortgage. Since Heidi will be getting cash equal to the amount of the mortgage the Purchasers get from another lender, she is willing to delay her receipt of this additional amount in order to earn a good interest rate on it. This will give the Purchasers enough breathing room to make a 20 percent downpayment on a $75,000 loan from a local savings and loan association, while leaving them with enough money to to move, close, and have a bit of a cushion for a rainy day. Without the seller financing from Heidi, they never could have made the deal.

- Amount of loan. Many traditional lenders will extend a loan to a house buyer only up to a specified percentage of the appraised value of the house. Seller financing can fill this gap.

EXAMPLE: Bob and Betty Buyer are buying a home from Suzy Seller for $125,000. The Buyers have saved carefully for a number of years and now have $18,750 that they can use as a respectable 15 percent downpayment. They believe they've obtained a reasonable price, and, most important, the house meets their special needs. Betty is a free-lance writer and needs an extra room that could be converted to an office. Bob is an artist and needs a scenic place to paint. The backyard of the house abuts a small river, which Bob will use for much of his work.

   The local bank recently changed its loan policy and will now finance a house purchase up to only 80 percent of appraised value. The appraiser hired by the bank values the home at only $112,000; apparently he doesn't have the artistic appreciation of Bob and Betty. Based on this value the bank will lend the Buyers only $89,600. The Buyers are thus coming up short of the purchase price for their dream house. Enter seller financing.

   Ready to close on the deal with Suzy Seller, the buyers suddenly find themselves short on the downpayment—a big disappointment after they had saved and planned so carefully. They need an additional $16,650 [$125,000 purchase price − ($18,750 downpayment + $89,600 bank financing)]. If Suzy can be persuaded to take a $16,650 second mortgage, they can close the deal. A second mortgage means the bank's mortgage, which is a first mortgage, gets paid off first if the Buyers default and the house is foreclosed upon.

CAUTION: The Buyers must have their lawyer carefully examine the loan documents with the bank to see if there are any restrictions on having a second mortgage on the house. Also, the Buyers should carefully revaluate their ability to meet their monthly payments on both the first mortgage to the bank and the second mortgage to Suzy. Any time more interest is paid to buy a property, the risks of missing payments, defaulting, and losing the house increase. Second mortgages often have higher rates.

- Interest rates. When bank and mortgage interest rates get very high, as they did in the early 1980s, seller financing can be a critically important component of the purchase price for a home.

WHY SELLERS SHOULD CONSIDER FINANCING THE SALE OF THEIR OWN HOUSE

Although some sellers may think that taking back a purchase money mortgage is a step of desperation to sell a house in a slow market, this is far from being the only benefit or use of seller financing. Buyers will benefit from understanding the benefits to the sellers, since this will give them the knowledge to negotiate the best deal from a seller—maybe even one who is not familiar or comfortable with seller financing:

- High return. The typical homeowner who is selling a house probably invests savings in such things as stocks, bonds, money market funds, certificates of deposit (CDs), and the like. Stocks and bonds may generate better returns over time when compared to money market funds and CDs, or they may not. This risk factor in the actual return is one of the drawbacks of investments in stocks and bonds. Money market funds and CDs, on the other hand, are more secure. Their principal investment may even be guaranteed or insured. The yields on these investments, however, are not always high.

Taking back a purchase money mortgage on the sale of a house may offer less risk and more reward than many of the alternative investments open to a seller. The interest rate on a purchase money mortgage is likely to be higher than what the seller could earn on money market funds or CDs. The risk, however, must be considered carefully.

- Lower risk. Well, maybe and maybe not. Some arguments can be made that taking back a purchase money mortgage from the buyer of their house is a lower risk investment than many of the other types of investments that typical house sellers have available. This is because the seller knows the house and thus knows the security for the loan. Also, the seller has met and had an opportunity to interview the borrower and thus is in a position to assess the risks. If the borrower defaults, the seller/lender gets back the same house he or she owned originally.

These arguments, however, must be tempered a bit by reality. First, depending on the size of the purchase money mortgage the sellers are taking back, they are placing a large portion of their net worth in a single asset—the purchase money mortgage. While, admittedly, the sellers had a major portion of their assets in their home before, this doesn't change the fact that a new investment decision is being made to concentrate assets in the purchase money mortgage. The sellers are unlikely to have any formal background as lending officers, so it is questionable whether they really know how to evaluate the buyer's qualities as a borrower. Perhaps one of the biggest risks is that the buyer of the house will not maintain it, or worse yet damage or destroy it. There is no assurance that if house prices fall, the buyer will not walk away. If the sellers move to another state and the buyer defaults, the sellers will be forced to handle the problems at a distance. Finally, foreclosing on a house on which they hold a purchase money mortgage is not always the best deal for the sellers/lenders.

As a result of these concerns, sellers may prefer buyers who have some reasonable net worth (say, a closely held business) that will give some assurance that the buyer's personal guarantee on the purchase money mortgage has value. Alternatively, the sellers could request that the buyer have a guarantor. If a parent, relative, or friend who is more established and secure financially than the buyer guarantees the loan, this will give an extra measure of protection to the sellers. The attorney preparing the necessary legal documents for the sellers can assist in these matters.

- A sale is made. If the housing market is soft, it very well may be that providing financing to the borrower is the best, or perhaps the only, way to consummate a sale on a house at a price that the sellers will accept. Sellers who wish to stick to their prices in a soft market may have to provide favorable financing in order to entice buyers to meet their prices.

- It's not forever. If the seller/lender needs cash and cannot wait for the purchase money mortgage to be paid off, it is often possible to sell the purchase money mortgage to a bank or a private investor and obtain cash immediately. This process is called "discounting" because the person buying the purchase money mortgage from the seller typically pays the seller less than the face value of the mortgage. This reduction, or discount, reflects the investor's concerns about risk as well as the legal and other expenses associated with the transaction.

EXAMPLE: Suzy Seller took a purchase money mortgage from Bob and Betty Buyer for $16,650, as in the above example. Suzy thought the interest rate on the mortgage would provide her with a good investment. Suzy, always on the lookout for a good real estate buy, found a great house for sale by an estate at a very low price. She needed cash to close the deal so she placed an advertisement in the real estate section of the local paper for the $16,650 purchase money mortgage. She sold it to an investor for $14,500, which she used as the downpayment on the estate property.

TIPS: Suzy should make sure that her attorney properly records (files) the mortgage she receives from the Buyers with the appropriate county's recording office (or other appropriate government agency) to ensure that her lien on the property is publicly known. This will help Suzy foreclose on the property if the Buyers don't pay, and collect the money due her before other creditors of the Buyers get paid (except for the bank holding a first mortgage, which will have priority over Suzy).

If Suzy thinks she may try to sell the mortgage to an investor, a bank, or other purchaser (into the secondary market), she should consult an attorney or banker before consummating the loan to make sure that she uses the appropriate forms and has the necessary terms to facilitate such a later sale.

HOW THE PURCHASE MONEY MORTGAGE BETWEEN THE BUYER AND THE SELLER CAN BE ARRANGED

The purchase money mortgage that the seller takes from the buyer can be arranged in almost any way the seller and buyer agree. If the seller is planning to sell the mortgage, he or she will strongly prefer to use standard mortgage documents and standard terms to make the mortgage readily saleable. If the seller is planning to hold the mortgage, the major restrictions are generally what the parties can agree to.

CAUTION: The interest rate that the seller charges can't exceed certain limits specified by state law. These rules are called usury laws. Since they differ from state to state it is important to check with your lawyer in the state where the house is located, to see how these rules may affect the transaction. Be particularly careful where additional interest (penalty) charges are assessed, because they could push the total interest charges over the allowable limits.

Other than these restrictions, the terms of the mortgage are generally open to negotiation. This is where the benefits of seller financing come in for the buyer. When you want to buy a house and are tight on cash, try to negotiate a deal where the seller will provide financing and accept a low, or even nominal, downpayment. Alternatively, if you qualify for bank or other financing, try to get the seller to lend you the additional money you need for part or all of the downpayment. Be careful to have your lawyer analyze the bank loan documents to determine whether there are any limitations on such additional financing. Many banks require borrowers to complete forms specifying where all the money being used to buy the house came from, a major reason being to find out whether there is seller or other financing. See the sample form, "Source of Funds Statement," at the end of this chapter. If there are restrictions, then you have to negotiate your deal with the seller within the parameters your lawyer advises that the primary lender will accept.

A few basic mortgage terms need to be explained so that some of the purchase-money-mortgage arrangements can be understood. "Amortization" is the process of paying off the principal amount of a debt. Amortization occurs when your payments are greater than the interest that you owe.

EXAMPLE: Bill Borrower owes Linda Lender $1,000. He agreed to pay Linda interest at a rate of 10%. He therefore owes Linda interest of $100 [$1,000 × 10%]. If Bill pays Linda anything more than $100 the excess portion will reduce (amortize) the principal due.

A traditional mortgage is amortized over a 25- or 30-year period—the "term." At the end of this period the mortgage "matures" (comes due) and the remaining principal and any interest due must be paid. Often mortgages are structured to mature before they are paid up. This is called a "balloon." For example, a mortgage could have a 30-year amortization period (i.e., if you made payments for 30 years you would repay all the principal and interest) but may balloon in five years. This means that most of the principal would still be due, since in the early years most of the payments go toward interest rather than principal reduction.

EXAMPLE: Barbara Buyer is purchasing a condominium from Howard Homeowner for $178,000. Barbara has just finished putting herself through law school at night while working during the day as a secretary. She has no substantial salary history and little money for a downpayment, as a result of high tuition fees. She can't qualify for a conventional loan to buy Howard's condominium. Howard is eager to move and thinks he has a good deal with Barbara. He is confident she will get a top-paying job and do well. Besides, he trusts her not to damage the condominium even if for some reason things don't work out. Howard can earn only about 8 percent on his money in a money market fund.

Barbara is willing to pay Howard 14 percent interest on a three-year purchase money mortgage if she can have the condominium for only $2,500 down. Barbara is confident that after three years she will be able to refinance the condominium and repay Howard.

Barbara's monthly payments will be substantial. Assuming Howard and she agree to a 30-year amortization schedule and a three-year balloon, her payments will be approximately $2,055 per month. After the three years, when the mortgage matures, Barbara will owe Howard about $175,000.

HOW SELLER FINANCING IS DONE—THE PAPERWORK AND THE PROCEDURES INVOLVED

The most common type of seller financing, as noted in the introduction to this chapter, is for the seller to take back paper—a purchase money mortgage—from the buyer. The mechanics and legal documentation for this transaction are set out below. There are two basic legal documents involved in the loan portion of the house purchase:

(1) *A Note:* Where the seller provides financing, the seller is lending money to the buyer. This loan is written in the form of a legal document called a "note," which comes from the buyer to the seller. A note states the terms (interest rate, maturity date, late payment charges, and so forth) on which the loan was made, including the terms according to which the buyer/borrower will repay the seller/lender. The note is the buyer/borrower's personal promise to repay the money borrowed. This is why the note is sometimes called a "promissory note." This note gives the seller the right to collect any of the borrowed money from the buyer/borrower personally, if the seller isn't paid and the property can't be sold for enough money to pay back the loan. The note provides the basis for a deficiency judgment against the borrower.

(2) *A Mortgage:* The seller, in order to secure the repayment by the buyer of the note, will take back a mortgage on the house. Thus, the mortgage gives the seller/lender a claim against the house for the repayment of the loan. Since this claim is a lien against real estate, it can be recorded in the public records so that anyone seeking to purchase the property, or investigating the possibility of making another loan against the property, will see the seller/lender's mortgage. This is critically important for the seller/lender's protection, because any mortgages or other liens recorded in the public records at a later date will generally be paid after the seller's mortgage if there is a foreclosure. The seller/lender's mortgage is said to have "priority" over the liens recorded later.

These are two general types of legal documents used to safeguard the seller/lender's interest in collecting on the note, depending on the laws of the state where the house is being sold subject to a purchase money mortgage. In most states the mortgage involves only the buyer/borrower and the seller/lender. However, in some states a legal document called a "deed of trust" is used (primarily in the South and the West), an approach that involves a third person. This third person (called the trustee) holds the security interest in the house for the seller/lender (called the beneficiary). The technical legal difference between the two approaches is that where a mortgage is used, the seller must go through a process called foreclosure in order to get the property back from a buyer/borrower who fails to make payments (see below). Where the deed of trust approach is used, the process for a seller/lender to get the house back historically has been somewhat simpler. However, in most cases a legal process which is similar to foreclosure must be used where a lender seeks to take property held under a deed of trust or a mortgage. A practical difference will be that you use a mortgage agreement in mortgage states and a deed of trust agreement in states that use the deed of trust approach. Your lawyer will help you with any distinctions that you must know.

The seller/lenders should understand what the foreclosure process requires. The buyer/borrowers should also understand the consequences of the transaction they are undertaking. If the buyers don't repay the loan as required (they default), the sellers can foreclose on the house. This process sets a limit on the borrowers' right to pay the amounts due on the mortgage and keep the house. The court can cut off these rights and have the property sold at an auction to repay the seller/lenders their loan, with any remaining money going to the buyer/borrowers. The process is generally carried out by a sheriff, who sells the property at public auction.

WRAPAROUND MORTGAGES AND OTHER SELLER FINANCING TECHNIQUES

Although more complicated arrangements, such as wraparound mortgages, are common in larger commercial real estate transactions, they are not frequently used in residential real estate transactions. A wraparound mortgage is most readily understood from a simple example.

EXAMPLE: Sam Seller sells his house to Betty Buyer for $90,000. Sam has an existing mortgage with a balance of $60,000 with interest at 8 percent. Betty puts $5,000 down and gives Sam a mortgage for the remaining $85,000 at the prevailing interest rate of, say, 11 percent. Sam receives monthly payments from Betty and then uses a portion of the money to make the monthly payments on his underlying $60,000 mortgage. In addition to making 11 percent interest on the $25,000 Sam is effectively lending to Betty to buy his house, Sam is also making the interest spread (11 percent to 8 percent) on the underlying mortgage of $60,000. The new $85,000 mortgage to Betty is said to "wrap around" the old mortgage— hence the name "wraparound mortgage." This interest spread is the reason most residential mortgages can't be assumed—the banks and savings and loans want to earn the additional interest by requiring a new loan.

CAUTION: Sellers should be certain to have their lawyers carefully review the provisions of their existing mortgages before attempting this type of arrangement. The bank (or other lender) will probably forbid this procedure, or at minimum, have some requirements sellers will have to meet.

Sometimes, in the case of VA- and FHA-backed mortgages, which can be assumed by the buyer, some type of wraparound financing may be used. (See Chapters 9 and 10.) Most conventional mortgages aren't assumable, so these techniques won't be practically applicable very often. Occasionally, however, an older mortgage at a low interest rate may be available for assumption. If so, it is likely that the principal balance on the mortgage won't be very substantial. The legal and other costs of these techniques should also be considered.

TAX CONSEQUENCES OF SELLER FINANCING

There are important tax considerations that both the buyer/borrowers and the seller/lenders should consider about seller financing.

For the buyer/borrowers the most important tax benefit is to be able to deduct the interest paid on a home mortgage. Interest paid on a mortgage incurred to acquire a house used as a primary (or a qualified second or vacation) residence can be deducted if certain additional requirements are met. The loan on which the interest is paid must be secured by an instrument that makes the buyers' ownership in the house specific security for the payment of the loan. A mortgage will qualify if it is also recorded (filed with the appropriate government agency). Be certain that all the proper formalities are observed so that the interest will be deductible.

For the sellers the primary benefit of taking back a purchase money mortgage, or selling on an installment contract, is the ability to use the installment method of reporting gain for tax purposes. So long as the sellers aren't dealers in real estate (in the trade or business of buying and selling houses), this method should be available. The installment method permits the sellers to defer paying tax on the gain realized on the sale until the sellers actually receive the cash payments from the buyer/borrowers. This is an important negotiating point for buyers to use to encourage sellers to cooperate.

If the sellers were to sell their real estate for cash—all to be paid in the year of sale—they would have to recognize any gain (the proceeds less their investment or tax basis) in that year. There is an alternative to this. A very common approach is for the buyers to pay some amount as a downpayment and the rest over a period of time (with interest on the unpaid balance). In this situation it would seem unfair to tax the sellers on the entire proceeds in the year of sale. Not only would they not have received all the money due, but the tax they would owe could be more than the downpayment received.

The installment sales rules address this problem. If you buy a house and make payments over time the sellers generally will have to report income only as they receive payments from you over a number of years. For most real estate sales this installment treatment is automatic any time at least one payment is made after the end of the year in which the sale occurs.

EXAMPLE: Howard Homeowner purchased a house in 1980 for $100,000. He sold it at the end of 1988 for $450,000. The buyer negotiated a deal where Howard provided all of the financing and got only about an 11 percent downpayment, or $50,000, in cash at the closing. The balance is to be paid at the rate of $100,000 at the end of each year for four years with interest at prime plus 2 percent.

CAUTION: "Prime" is generally the interest rate that banks charge their best customers. There is a lot of confusion concerning the status of the prime rate; therefore, whenever borrowing or lending money at a rate pegged to the prime rate, specify which bank's prime and perhaps even that bank's definition of prime. Alternatively, use a rate regularly set by the IRS.

The sale in the above example is automatically treated as an installment sale since at least one payment (actually four) was made after the end of the tax year in which the sale occurred (i.e., after 1988). The installment sales treatment will apply to any similar sale unless the seller specifically elects not to have the installment sales rules apply.

When the seller receives installment payments under a purchase money mortgage or an installment contract, only a portion of each payment is taxable. The basic rule is that the portion of each payment is taxable that is equal to the same proportion that the seller's gross profit on the entire sale bears to the total contract price the buyer is to pay. This concept is much more easily understood with an example.

EXAMPLE: In the example used above, Howard Homeowner sold his house for $450,000, and he had paid $100,000 for it. Thus, his taxable gain is $350,000 [$450,000 amount realized − $100,000 investment or tax basis]. The contract price is $450,000, and this is the amount that Howard is to receive. What portion of each installment payment does he report as income?

$$\frac{\text{Gross Profit}}{\text{Contract Price}} = \frac{\$350,000}{\$450,000} = 77.78\%$$

Howard will recognize the following amounts of income on each of the scheduled payments:

Year	Payment	Profit %	Profit Recognized
1988	$50,000	77.78%	$38,889
1989	100,000	77.78%	77,778
1990	100,000	77.78%	77,778
1991	100,000	77.78%	77,778
1992	100,000	77.78%	77,777
	$450,000		$350,000

The tax laws require that a certain minimum interest rate be charged in many transactions subject to the installment sales rules. If the interest rate charged is too low interest may have to be imputed at a rate set by the tax rules.

EXAMPLE: Assume that a fair-market interest rate at the time of the above transaction is 9 percent. Howard, however, only charged the purchaser interest at a 5-percent rate. Why would Howard charge less than the going market rate? A below-market rate probably means one thing—the principal amount of the transaction (the $400,000 purchase price) is overstated. No seller would charge less than the going rate unless he got something for it—and that something is, according to the assumptions made by the tax laws, an excessive purchase price (principal amount).

The seller and the buyer will have to impute interest at a minimum rate required by law, say the 9 percent in the example. What will happen is that Howard will report a lower gain on the sale and a higher annual interest income on the purchase money mortgage (or on the unpaid installment obligations if an installment contract was used) than what the buyer is actually paying. Similarly, the buyer will show a lower purchase price for the real estate than the $450,000 actually paid, and he will report interest deductions greater than the amount he actually pays.

End Year	Payment Balance*	Actual Rate	Interest Paid	Total** Payment	Present Value at 9% Imputed
1988	$450,000	5%	—	$ 50,000	$ 50,000
1989	400,000	5%	$20,000	120,000	110,088
1990	300,000	5%	15,000	115,000	96,796
1991	200,000	5%	10,000	110,000	84,942
1992	100,000	5%	5,000	105,000	74,382
			$50,000	$500,000	$416,208

* Payment Balance is the amount of the installment notes outstanding for the year and thus the amount on which interest must be computed. Since the sale occurred on December 31, 1988, no interest is due in 1988. The payment balance is calculated by subtracting from the contract price the principal payments required by the contract—$50,000 at closing and $100,000 at the end of each of the next four years.

** Total Payment is the sum to the principal payments required under the contract plus the interest payments at the 5 percent contract rate on the outstanding balance. The example assumes 5 percent simple interest with all payments made at the end of each year.

The payment schedule which must be used when the true 9-percent market interest rate is charged on the true imputed principal amount (sales price) is as follows:

End Year	Principal Balance*	Imputed Rate	Interest Payment	Principal Payment	Total Payment
1988	$416,208	9%	—	$50,000	$50,000
1989	366,208	9%	$32,959	87,041	120,000
1990	279,167	9%	25,125	89,875	115,000
1991	189,292	9%	17,036	92,964	110,000
1992	96,328	9%	8,672	96,328	105,000
			$83,792	$416,208	$500,000

Assume in the above examples that adequate interest was charged. The seller sold real estate for $50,000 down and took a purchase money mortgage from the buyer for $400,000. The seller may have been willing to sell the real estate subject to a large purchase money mortgage because he had no urgent need for the cash and was content to receive payments over four years with interest. On the other hand, he may have been willing to take back the purchaser's notes because it was the only way to make the deal. Suppose the seller has a strong need for cash shortly after the sale.

It may be possible to sell the installment notes, but if he does, he will be forced to report all the remaining gain for tax purposes. If Howard Homeowner sold his $400,000 of installment notes right after the sale for $400,000, he would have had to recognize the remaining $311,111 of unreported profits. The total profit on the sale transaction was $350,000. The seller had to report $38,889 in profit on the receipt of the $50,000 downpayment (see the chart above showing the gross profit to be reported on each scheduled payment). The remaining profit would have to be reported on his sale of the installment note for its face value of $400,000. If a seller pledges purchase-money-mortgage notes as collateral for loans, he will be denied the special benefits of the installment method and will have to pay tax on the portion of the notes pledged.

SAMPLE FORMS

The forms at the end of this chapter are illustrative of the types of legal documents that you may encounter when negotiating for seller financing in order to make a purchase with a small (or no) downpayment. These forms merely illustrate some of the possibilities. Don't attempt to make a sophisticated real estate transaction without first getting qualified legal help. Remember that the real estate laws are different in every state so you must get professional advice as to how these transactions should be done in your state.

- Source of Funds Statement. This is illustrative of the type of disclosure statement which a bank may use to determine whether you are using seller (or other) financing as well as theirs.
- Purchase Money Mortgage. This is illustrative of the type of mortgage agreement that you may sign with a seller who takes back paper.
- Promissory Note. This is illustrative of the type of note that may be used in conjunction with the mortgage when a seller provides financing using a purchase money mortgage.

CHAPTER SUMMARY

This chapter has illustrated how you may be able to arrange a purchase in which the seller of the house you want provides the financing in a way that permits you to buy with little or no money down. These techniques really can work. However, there are a number of important risks that you should address when attempting to use the approaches illustrated. First, consult a competent attorney who can not only draft and record the necessary legal documents, but who can articulately explain your rights and obligations under these documents, many of which are very important. Second, as with all low- or no-money-down purchase techniques, carefully evaluate with your accountant or financial adviser what this approach will mean to your future monthly payments. This is particularly critical when the seller's financing will use a balloon mortgage—where the mortgage must be paid off in its entirety at what may be a relatively near date.

FOR YOUR NOTEBOOK

This appendix contains a few samples illustrative of the documents mentioned in the chapter. A sample source-of-funds statement furnished by Dan Koenigsburg, president of Interstate Mortgage Service, Inc., is included. Also, an illustrative house sale contract calling for seller financing, and a secured promissory note for the amount of the seller financing, are shown. The mortgage for the transaction is not illustrated. Remember, these samples are for illustration only. They are not meant for actual use. Consult a qualified attorney to properly protect your legal interests.

INTERSTATE MORTGAGE SERVICE INC.

LICENSED MORTGAGE BANKER

292 MAIN STREET

SUITE 23

HACKENSACK, NEW JERSEY 07601

———

(201)488-2662

SOURCE OF FUNDS STATEMENT

RE: _____

_____

_____

I CERTIFY THAT THE $ _____ DEPOSIT GIVEN
FOR THE PROPERTY LOCATED AT _____
CAME FROM:

NAME OF INSTITUTION – ACCT NUMBER	AMOUNT	BALANCE IN ACCT
NAME OF INSTITUTION – ACCT NUMBER	AMOUNT	BALANCE IN ACCT
NAME OF INSTITUTION – ACCT NUMBER	AMOUNT	BALANCE IN ACCT

I FURTHER CERTIFY THAT THE ADDITIONAL MONIES NEEDED AT THE
CLOSING IN THE AMOUNT OF $ _____ WILL BE
OBTAINED FROM: _____
_____ AND HAVE NOT BEEN
BORROWED.

PURCHASER	DATE	CO-PURCHASER	DATE

80

HOUSE SALE CONTRACT—WITH SELLER FINANCING

CONTRACT of sale dated December 1, 1988 between Sam and Sue Seller, residing at 123 Main Street, Centerville, Onestate (the "Seller"), and Paul and Pat Purchaser residing at 456 Redwood, Apt. 12E, Ridgewood, Onestate (the "Purchaser").

1. *Sale.*
    The Seller agrees to sell, and the Purchaser agrees to buy the property, including all buildings and improvements thereon, erected, situated, lying, and being in the City of Centerville, County of Oakland, State of Onestate, more particularly described as follows:

ALL that tract or parcel of land and premises, situated, lying and being in the City of Centerville, in the County of Oakland, and State of Onestate. BEING known and designated as Lot No. 3 in Block No. 13 on a certain map entitled "Map of Elmora Manor, Centerville, Onestate, O.L.P. Jones, Surveyor, dated June 10, 1812" and filed in the Registrar's Office as Case #38-CH-4.

BEGINNING at a stake in the Northeasterly side of Main Street, at a point therein distant 50 feet Southeasterly from the intersection formed by the said Northeasterly side of Main Street and the Southeasterly side of Glenwood Road; thence running (1) North 36 degrees 01 minutes East, a distance of 100 feet to a stake for a corner; thence running (2) South 54 degrees 18 minutes East a distance of 48.02 feet to a point for another corner; thence running (3) South 35 degrees 42 minutes West a distance of 100 feet to a point in the aforesaid line of Main Street; thence running (4) North 54 degrees 18 minutes West a distance of 48.57 feet to the point or place of BEGINNING. BEING also known as 123 Main Street, Centerville, Onestate.

BEING known as Lot 3 in Block 13, Account No. 10-504B on the official tax map of the city of Centerville, Oakland County, Onestate (the "House").

2. *Street Rights.*
    This sale includes all the right, title, and interest, if any, of the Seller in and to any land lying in the bed of any street, in front of or adjoining the House, to the center line of such street.

3. *Condemnation.*
    This sale also includes any right of the Seller to any unpaid award by reason of any taking by condemnation any damage to the House.

The Seller shall deliver, at no additional cost to the Purchaser, at the closing, or after the closing, on demand, any document which the Purchaser may require to collect any such award.

4. *Personal Property.*
   (a) Included in this sale are all fixtures and articles of personal property attached to or used in connection with the House, unless specifically excluded. The Seller represents that the fixtures and personal property are paid for and owned by the Seller free and clear of any security interests or liens other than the existing mortgage. Fixtures and personal property included in this sale are the following: heating, air-conditioning, plumbing, electrical and lighting fixtures (except the breakfast-room ceiling fixture), bathroom and kitchen fixtures and cabinets, storm windows and doors, screens, shades, mail box, wall-to-wall carpets, sump pump, shrubbery, fences, range, refrigerator, freezer, washing machine, clothes dryer, dishwasher, and drapery in the dining room, including the hardware and rods.

   (b) Not included in this sale are the following: furniture, drapes (other than the dining room), curtains, microwave oven, fireplace equipment, breakfast-room ceiling fixture, and lawn ornaments.

5. *Purchase Price.*
   The purchase price is One Hundred Forty-Two Thousand Dollars ($142,000).

6. *Payment of Purchase Price.*
   (a) The Purchase Price shall be paid as follows:
   (i) By check on the signing of this Contract, to be held in escrow by Seller's attorney .... $ 10,200

   (ii) By allowance for the principal amount remaining unpaid on the Existing Mortgage .. $ 23,569

   (iii) By a Purchase Money Mortgage and Note from Purchaser to Seller $105,000

   (iv) Balance due and payable at closing .... $ 3,231

   Total $142,000

   (b) All money payable under this contract shall be paid, unless otherwise specified, as follows:

(i) Cash, but not over $1,000,

(ii) Certified check of the Purchaser, or an official check of any bank, savings bank, trust company or savings and loan association having a banking office in the State, payable to the order of the Seller,

(iii) Money other than the purchase price, payable to the Seller at closing, may be by check of the Purchaser up to the amount of $1,000, or

(iv) As the Seller or Seller's attorney may otherwise agree in writing.

(c) All monies held in escrow shall be held in interest-bearing accounts and Purchaser shall be entitled to all interest earned.

7. *Seller Financing—Purchase Money Mortgage.*
(a) The Purchaser shall give to the Seller, and Seller shall accept, a purchase money mortgage and a note (the "Purchase Money Mortgage and the Note"). The Purchase Money Mortgage and the Note shall be drawn by the attorney for the Seller at the expense of the Purchaser, and shall be substantially in the form of the Purchase Money Mortgage and the Note attached to this Contract. Purchaser shall pay the mortgage recording tax, recording fees, and the attorney's fee in the amount of $600 for the preparation of these documents.

(b) The Purchase Money Mortgage and Note shall each state that it is subject to the prior lien to the Big City Bank (the "Existing Mortgage"), and to any extension or modification of the Existing Mortgage made in good faith. If any required payments are made on an Existing Mortgage between now and Closing, which reduce the unpaid principal amount of an Existing Mortgage below the amount shown in this agreement, then the balance of the price payable at closing will be increased accordingly. The interest rate on the Purchase Money Mortgage shall be Thirteen percent (13%), and principal and interest shall be payable based on a Twenty-Five (25) year amortization schedule with any remaining principal and interest payments due Ten (10) years from the date which is the last day of the first full month following the Closing of this Contract.

8. *Existing Mortgage.*
(a) The House shall be conveyed subject to the lien of an Existing Mortgage to Big City Bank which at the date of this Contract has an

unpaid principal amount of approximately $23,569, and on which interest is paid at the rate of Ten percent (10%) per year. Payments are in monthly installments in advance, on the first day of each month. Such payments include principal, interest, hazard insurance, and real property taxes. Any balance of principal and interest shall be due and payable on December 1, 1997.

(b) Seller shall assign the mortgage escrow account that is held for the payment of taxes, insurance and other expenses to the Purchaser, if it can be assigned, and the Purchaser shall pay the amount of the escrow account to the Seller at the Closing.

(c) The Seller represents and warrants that: (i) The principal amount shown above for the Existing Mortgage is reasonably correct and that only the payments required pursuant to the Existing Mortgage shall be made; (ii) The Existing Mortgage does not contain any provision allowing the holder of the mortgage to require its immediate payment in full or to change the interest rate or any other term by reason of the transfer of title or closing; and (iii) The Existing Mortgage shall not be in default at the time of closing.

9. *Flood Area.*

If the House is located in a state or federal flood hazard area, Purchaser may cancel this Contract on written notice to Seller within Ten (10) days from the date of this Contract, in which case the provisions of Section 14 of this Contract shall apply.

10. *Assessments.*

If, at the time of closing, the House is subject to any assessment which is, or may become, payable in annual installments, and the first installment is then a lien, or has been paid, then for the purposes of this contract all the unpaid installments shall be deemed to be due and shall be paid by the Seller at closing.

11. *Mortgage Estoppel Certificate.*

Seller agrees to deliver to the Purchaser at the Closing a certificate dated not more than Thirty-One (31) days before closing signed by Big City Bank, the holder of the Existing Mortgage, in a form appropriate for recording, certifying the amount of the unpaid principal and interest, date of maturity, and rate of interest of the Existing Mortgage. The Seller shall pay the fees for recording this certificate.

12. *Violations.*

All notices of violations, any regulations, codes, laws, ordinances, orders, or other requirements by any governmental agency affecting the House at the date of this contract, shall be complied with by the Seller, at Seller's expense, and the House shall be conveyed free of any violations. This provision shall survive closing.

13. *Adjustments At Closing.*

(a) The following items are to be apportioned as of midnight of the day before closing: (i) interest on the Existing Mortgage; (ii) taxes; (iii) sewer rents, if any, on the basis of the fiscal year for which assessed; and (iv) fuel oil, if any.

(b) The adjustment on account of the mortgage escrow account on the Existing Mortgage shall be made as required in Section 8(b) of this Contract.

(c) If the Closing shall occur before a new tax rate is fixed, the apportionment of taxes shall be based upon the old tax rate for the prior period applied to the latest assessed valuation.

(d) If there is a water, electric, or other utility meter on the premises, the Seller shall furnish a reading to a date not more than Ten (10) days prior to the Closing, and the charges, if any, shall be apportioned on the basis of the last reading.

(e) The Seller may credit the Purchaser, as an adjustment to the purchase price, with the amount of any unpaid taxes, assessments, water charges and sewer rents, together with any interest and penalties, to a date not less than Ten (10) days after the Closing, provided that the official bills, computed to that date, are provided to the Purchaser at Closing.

14. *Default by Seller.*

If the Seller is unable to convey title in accordance with the terms of this Contract, the sole liability of the Seller will be to refund to the Purchaser the amounts paid on account of this Contract, plus all reasonable charges made for examination of title and any additional searches made under this Contract, including the survey, termite and structural inspection charges. Upon such refund and payment this Contract shall be considered cancelled, and neither the Seller nor the Purchaser shall have any further rights against the other by reason of this Contract.

15. Closing.

The closing of this transaction shall include the payment of the purchase price to the Seller and the delivery to the Purchaser the deed described in Section 16 below (the "Closing"). The Closing will take place at the Seller's attorney's office at 100 Legal Street, Centerville, Onestate, on or about 11:00 a.m., February 1, 1989.

16. Deed.

At the Closing the Seller shall deliver to the Purchaser a bargain and sale with covenants against grantor's acts deed in the proper statutory form for recording to transfer full ownership, fee simple title, to the Premises, free of all encumbrances except as stated in this Contract (the "Deed").

17. Quality of Title.

(a) The Seller shall give and the Purchaser shall accept such title as a reputable title company which regularly conducts business in this State will be willing to approve and insure at standard rates with their standard form of title insurance policy. This title insurance policy must transfer ownership of the property to the Purchaser free of any rights and claims except the following: (i) restrictive covenants of record which do not and will not impair the normal use of the property; (ii) utility and similar easements which do not impair the normal use of the property or inhibit the Purchaser from constructing any reasonable improvements or additions to the House; (iii) laws and government regulations that affect the use and maintenance of the House, provided that they are not violated by the existing House and improvements or by their current use; (iv) consents by the Seller or any former owner of the House for the erection of any structure or structures on, under, or above any street or streets on which the House may abut but which are not within the boundary lines of the House.

(b) Seller shall deliver to Purchaser an affidavit of title at Closing. If a title examination discloses judgments, bankruptcies, or other returns against other persons having names the same as or similar to that of the Seller, the Seller shall state in the affidavit showing that they are not against the Seller.

(c) If required pursuant to local law, Seller shall deliver to Purchaser, at Seller's sole expense, a certificate of occupancy. Seller shall make any repairs necessary to obtain the certificate of occupancy at Seller's sole expense up to a maximum of One Thousand Dollars ($1,000). If repairs in excess of such amount are required and Purchaser is unwilling to assume the cost, then either party hereto may cancel this contract, and the provisions of Section 14 of this Contract shall apply.

18. *Risk of Loss.*

The risk of loss or damage to the premises by fire or other casualty until the delivery of the deed is assumed by the Seller. If there is a fire or other casualty to the House prior to the Closing and the cost of repairing the damage exceeds Ten Thousand Dollars ($10,000), Purchaser may cancel this Contract and the provisions of Section 14 of this Contract shall apply.

19. *Transfer and Recording Taxes.*

The Seller shall deliver a check at the Closing payable to the order of the appropriate State, City or County officer in the amount of any applicable transfer tax, recording tax, or both, payable by reason of the delivery or recording of the Deed together with any required tax return. The Purchaser's attorney, at Purchaser's expense, shall complete any tax return and cause the check and the tax return to be delivered to the appropriate office promptly after Closing.

20. *Broker.*

The Purchaser and Seller state that neither has dealt with any broker in connection with this sale other than Joe's Real Estate Company, Inc., and the Seller agrees to pay the broker the commission earned pursuant to a separate agreement at the rate of Five Percent (5%). Each party agrees to hold the other party hereto harmless in the event of any misrepresentation as to the use of brokers.

21. *Condition of the House.*

The Purchaser agrees to purchase the House, buildings and personal property as is, which shall mean in their present condition subject to reasonable use, wear, tear and natural deterioration between the date of this Contract and Closing, except as specifically provided otherwise in Section 22. The House and personal property shall be delivered in broom-clean condition, and all personal property not included in this sale shall be removed. All systems and appliances shall be in good working order. The roof shall be free of leaks and the basement free of seepage. Purchaser shall have the right to inspect the House prior to the Closing to verify the condition of the House.

22. *Inspections.*

The Purchaser has Ten (10) days from the signing of this contract to obtain a termite inspection of the House, and a structural inspection by a qualified home inspection service, at the Purchaser's sole cost and expense if Purchaser so chooses. If the inspection reports indicate the presence of termite infestation or any structural problem, the Seller shall eliminate the infestation or correct the structural problem at Seller's expense, if the cost does not exceed One Thousand Dollars ($1,000). If the costs exceed such amount, and Purchaser is unwilling to bear the additional cost, this Contract will be cancelled and the provisions of Section 14 of this Contract shall apply. Notice of the Seller's intent to cancel this Contract must be given to the Purchaser's attorney within Ten (10) days after Seller's receipt of the termite or structural inspection report. If notice is not given to the Purchaser's attorney within this Ten (10) day period, it shall be the Seller's responsibility to eliminate the reported problem at the Seller's sole cost and expense. If the attorney for the Seller has not received the termite inspection report within Twenty (20) days from the signing of this contract, this paragraph shall be unenforceable and of no effect.

23. *Entire Agreement.*

All prior understandings and agreements between the Purchaser and the Seller are superseded by this Contract which contains their entire agreement. This Contract is entered into after full investigation by both parties and no reliance is made on any matter not set forth in this Contract.

24. *Modification.*

This Contract may not be changed or terminated except in a writing signed by both parties. However, each of the parties authorizes their respective attorneys to agree in writing to any change in dates and time periods provided for in this Contract.

25. *Binding Effect.*

This Contract shall apply to and bind the heirs, executors, administrators, successors, distributees, and assigns of the respective parties.

In witness whereof this contract has been executed by the parties:

_____	_____
Purchaser	Seller
_____	_____
Purchaser	Seller

STATE OF ONESTATE)

         : ss.:

COUNTY OF OAKLAND)

 On this _____ day of _____ , 19 ___ , before me personally came PAUL PURCHASER, to me known and known to me to be the individual described in and who executed the foregoing instrument, and he duly acknowledged to me that he executed the same.

            _____

               Notary Public

STATE OF ONESTATE)

         : ss.:

COUNTY OF OAKLAND)

 On this _____ day of _____ , 19 ___ , before me personally came PAT PURCHASER, to me known and known to me to be the individual described in and who executed the foregoing instrument, and she duly acknowledged to me that she executed the same.

            _____

               Notary Public

STATE OF ONESTATE)

         : ss.:

COUNTY OF OAKLAND)

 On this _____ day of _____ , 19 ___ , before me personally came SAM SELLER, to me known and known to me to be the individual described in and who executed the foregoing instrument, and he duly acknowledged to me that he executed the same.

            _____

               Notary Public

STATE OF ONESTATE   )
                                    : ss.:
COUNTY OF OAKLAND   )

    On this _____ day of _____ , 19 ___ ,
before me personally came SUE SELLER, to me known and known
to me to be the individual described in and who executed the
foregoing instrument, and she duly acknowledged to me that she
executed the same.

                        _____
                                            Notary Public

SECURED PROMISSORY NOTE

$105,000   Centerville, Onestate
                                                                     December 1, 1988

FOR VALUE RECEIVED, the undersigned jointly and severally promise to pay to the order of Sam Seller and Sue Seller or the holder hereof ("the Payee") at Centerville, Onestate, or at such other place as the Payee may, from time to time, designate in writing to the undersigned, without offset or defalcation or relief from appraisement or valuation laws, the principal sum of One Hundred Five Thousand Dollars ($105,000) in lawful money of the United States of America in equal monthly installments of Nine Hundred Seventy-One and 21/00s ($971.21) on January 1, 1989 and the first day of each month thereafter inclusive of interest at the rate of Thirteen percent (13%) per year. The remaining principal balance and any unpaid interest shall be due and payable on January 31, 1999, unless accelerated to an earlier date in accordance with the terms of this Secured Promissory Note ("Note").

Payments made under the Note shall first be applied against payments of interest and then toward the reduction of principal.

A default shall occur in the event of: (i) the nonpayment of any sums due under this Note after a Ten (10) day grace period; (ii) the breach of any other covenant, warranty or agreement in this Note or the Purchase Money Mortgage dated the same date as this Note ("Mortgage") after written notice and a Thirty (30) day grace period; or (iii) then at the option of the holder hereof immediately and without notice upon the appointment of a Receiver or Trustee in bankruptcy or the filing of a petition in bankruptcy ("Default"). Upon the occurrence of a Default the entire unpaid principal balance and interest due shall immediately become due and payable. Following any Default, interest shall accrue at the rate of Eighteen percent (18%) per year or the highest rate allowed by law.

The undersigned does hereby pledge, transfer and grant to Payee, security for the payment of his obligations under this Note his entire right, title and interest in ALL that tract or parcel of land and premises, situated, lying and being in the City of Centerville, in the County of Oakland, and State of Onestate. BEING known and designated as Lot No. 3 in Block No. 13 on a certain map entitled "Map of Elmora Manor, Centerville, Onestate, O.L.P. Jones, Surveyor, dated June 10, 1812" and filed in the Register's Office as Case #38-CH-4.

BEGINNING at a stake in the Northeasterly side of Main Street, at a point therein distant 50 feet Southeasterly from the intersection formed by the said Northeasterly side of Main Street and the Southeasterly side of Glenwood Road; thence running (1) North 36 degrees 01 minutes East, a distance of 100 feet to a stake for a corner; thence running (2) South 54 degrees 18 minutes East a distance of 48.02 feet to a point for another corner; thence running (3) South 35 degrees 42 minutes West a distance of 100 feet to a point in the aforesaid line of Main Street; thence running (4) North 54 degrees 18 minutes West a distance of 48.57 feet to the point or place of BEGINNING. BEING also known as 123 Main Street, Centerville, Onestate.

BEING known as Lot 3 in Block 13, Account No. 10-504B on the official tax map of the City of Centerville, Oakland County, Onestate (the "House").

Together with all the appurtenances attached thereto, all easements, rights of way, buildings, structures, improvements, and fixtures thereto described in the Mortgage.

All covenants, conditions, warranties and agreements made by the undersigned in the Mortgage are hereby made part of this Note, and undersigned shall keep same as if each one were set forth herein.

The undersigned may prepay any portion of the principal amount due under this Note without penalty.

Notwithstanding anything in this Note or the Mortgage to the contrary, the total interest payments and payments which could be characterized as interest, shall not exceed the amount allowed to be charged under the applicable usury laws. Any interest payments in excess of the amount permissible shall be refunded by first applying such excess against amounts due under this Note and refunding any excess remaining to the undersigned.

If the Payee shall institute any action to enforce collection of this Note, there shall become due and payable from the undersigned, in addition to the unpaid principal and interest, all costs and expenses of that action (including reasonable attorneys' fees) and the Payee shall be entitled to judgment for all such additional amounts.

The undersigned (and any guarantors, endorsers or surities) irrevocably consent to the sole and exclusive jurisdiction of the Courts of the State of Onestate and of any Federal court located in Onestate in connection with any action or proceeding arising out of, or related to, this Note. In any such proceeding, the undersigned waives personal service of any summons, complaint or other process and agrees that service thereof shall be deemed made when mailed by registered or certified mail, return receipt requested to the undersigned. Within Twenty (20) days after such service, the undersigned shall appear or answer the summons, complaint or other process. If the undersigned shall fail to appear or answer within that Twenty (20) day period, the undersigned shall be deemed in default and judgment may be entered by the Payee against the undersigned for the amount demanded in the summons, complaint or other process.

The undersigned (and any guarantors, endorsers or surities) waive presentment, demand for payment, notice of dishonor and all other notices or demands in connection with the delivery, acceptance, performance, default or indorsement of this Note.

The undersigned agree that they shall each be unconditionally liable on this Note without regard to the liability of any other party to this Note.

No delay or failure on the part of the Payee on this Note to exercise any power or right given hereunder shall operate as a waiver thereof, and no right or remedy of the Payee shall be deemed abridged or modified by any course of conduct. No waiver whatever shall be valid unless in a writing signed by the Payee.

This Note shall be governed by and construed in accordance with the State of Onestate applicable to agreements made and to be performed in Onestate.

This Note cannot be changed orally.

IN WITNESS WHEREOF, the undersigned jointly and severally intend to be legally bound by this Note and execute their signatures as of the date first above written.

Witness: _____   _____
                                   Paul Purchaser

Witness: _____   _____
                                   Pat Purchaser
                                   Address for Communication:
                                   123 Main Street
                                   Centerville, Onestate

6 MOM AND DAD GIVE THE DOWNPAYMENT

INTRODUCTION

With the cost of the average house in excess of $90,000, affordability is a crucial problem, particularly for the first-time home buyer. The word "average," however, can be very misleading. In certain parts of the country the price of an average home can be almost double the national average—$190,000 and more! However resourceful first-time home buyers can be, and however many of the techniques discussed in this book are used, more and more first-time home buyers have resorted to parental assistance to get a foot into the housing market. GI financing (Generous In-laws) is common. In some cases a relative other than a parent or in-law will render the assistance. However, to simplify the discussions following, it will be assumed that it is parents lending the hand. If another relative is assisting, the results will generally be the same.

CASE STUDY: Dick Schlott, president of Schlott Realtors, cites a recent example where a young couple bought their first home in West Milford, New Jersey for $111,000. The couple had saved a downpayment of $12,200. Their parents gave them a gift of $10,000 toward the downpayment. With this assistance they were able to qualify for a mortgage for the remaining $88,800.

EXAMPLE: Ned and Nancy Newlywed dream of buying a home with a backyard. They hate paying rent and having nothing but rent receipts to show for it at year end. The tax benefits of homeownership are also a strong enticement to them. The Newlyweds, however, while earning a combined income of $45,000, just haven't been working long enough to have saved up much of a downpayment. Their take-home pay is about $31,000 per year, or $2,580 per month. They figure that they can spend about 40 percent of that, or about $1,000, on mortgage payments. Homes in the area within a reasonable commute to where they both work run about $135,000. Even if they could find a way to buy a house with no money down, they couldn't afford the monthly mortgage payments. On a 25-year mortgage with an 11-percent interest rate their payments would be about $1,300 per month (before including property taxes and insurance).

Each set of parents has agreed to give them $20,000 as a wedding present to use as a downpayment on a home. If they use $35,000 of this as the downpayment (the remaining $5,000 to cover closing and moving costs), their monthly payments would be reduced substantially to about $970 per month. Although this will be a bit tight when property taxes and insurance are added in, it will be manageable. Without their parents' help they just couldn't do it because even a low- or no-money-down purchase would require monthly payments that they couldn't afford.

Parental assistance has become more common, but too few children and parents understand the many consequences that parental assistance can have. There are gift, estate and income tax implications. There are legal implications as to how the transaction is structured. There are important personal and emotional issues that must be dealt with. The effect on the financial position of both the parents and the children should be considered. Finally, the manner in which the parental assistance is structured can have implications for any bank financing the children may seek for the purchase. This chapter will review many of these implications and provide guidance as to how best to plan parental help so that everyone can benefit. Understanding the tax and other nuances of parental assistance will make it easier for a couple buying their first home to persuade their parents to help.

ARE THE PARENTS GIVING OR LENDING THE MONEY?

The first issue that must be addressed is whether the parents will give the children the money, or lend it to them. There are very important differences in the tax and legal consequences of a gift versus a loan. This chapter will review the implications of the parents giving the money to the children. Some parents may prefer to lend the money to their children rather than give it to them outright. For example, the parents may want the money back later for retirement, or perhaps they feel a loan will teach the children responsibility. Chapter 7 will review the consequences of the parents lending money to their children to help them buy their home.

ADVANTAGES OF PARENTS GIVING RATHER THAN LENDING THE MONEY TO THE CHILDREN/HOME BUYERS

The advantages to the children of receiving a gift of money rather than a loan are obvious:

- It will be easier for the children to obtain financing from a bank or other commercial lender if the parental assistance is a gift.
- The money will not have to be repaid, so it will increase the children's net worth and not increase future monthly payments as would a loan.

Surprisingly, there can also be important advantages to the parents in making a gift of the money to their children, rather than lending it:

- The outright transfer of money can remove it from the parents' estate and save them substantial estate tax costs (the estate tax is explained below).
- Giving money during their lifetime, rather than as an inheritance, can save on estate administration (legal and other) costs.
- Parents can use a gift of money, such as the downpayment for a home, to see how their children react to receiving large sums of money. For moderately well-off and well-to-do parents who may hope to leave money or other property to their children after their deaths, a gift while they are alive affords them an opportunity to see how the children use the money, and how it affects their lifestyle and attitude. The parents then can alter their estate plans and wills accordingly.
- Parents may wish to put the money beyond the reach of their creditors. A gift to their children to buy a home may be an ideal way to accomplish this.

EXAMPLE: An internationally known dentist was concerned that his fame and wealth created the risk of malpractice suits. He gave outright to his children a substantial sum of money to use as the downpayment on a beautiful vacation condominium in Florida. The children will own and benefit from the use of the apartment. Any appreciation in the value of the condominium won't be included in the dentist's already large estate, resulting in a potentially large savings in estate tax. Should he be the subject of burdensome malpractice suits he can be confident that this earlier gift to his children, made before any such suits were brought, will be beyond the reach of any judgment. When the dentist visits his children in Florida he will be able to enjoy the use of the vacation home with them.

In addition to the advantages of parents giving rather than lending money to their children for a downpayment, an obvious disadvantage must be carefully weighed by the parents before making any gift. Once the money is given, the parents can't expect or count on getting it back. If the parents aren't positive that they can continue to lead the lifestyle they want, and have the security and peace of mind that they have striven for, they shouldn't make a gift. If the parents are planning to retire in the near future, they must make certain they won't need the money for retirement. If the parents' income is subject to risks, for example a business that is experiencing financial difficulty, or that may in the future, they must carefully weigh all these factors. If an outright gift is inappropriate, then a loan may make more sense. (See Chapter 7.)

GENERAL TAX CONSEQUENCES OF GIVING CHILDREN MONEY FOR A DOWNPAYMENT

When parents give money to be used by their children to purchase a house, the parents will have no legal interest in the house and thus will not be entitled to claim any tax deductions for interest on any mortgage, property taxes paid, or casualty losses. If the parents are in a higher tax bracket than the children, and their accountant thinks there is merit in their trying to claim some portion of these deductions, then some form of equity-sharing arrangement, rather than an unrestricted gift, may be appropriate. (See Chapter 8.)

Before parents begin giving large sums of money, they must be aware of two taxes that could affect them: (1) the gift tax, and (2) the estate tax.

(1) The gift tax is a tax assessed when an individual transfers any asset for less than a full purchase price—a gift. If you give someone

$50,000, or property worth that much, you could owe a tax which can be assessed at rates as high as 55 percent of the value of the gift, or $27,500 on the $50,000 gift.

(2) The estate tax is assessed on the value of property you transfer at death. For example, when a taxpayer dies leaving a house, investments, and other assets, a federal tax is charged on the value of those assets. The tax rate can also reach up to 55 percent.

The following discussions will provide an overview of how the gift and estate taxes work and will highlight how these taxes affect parents who give their children money for a downpayment on a house. Since the gift and estate taxes are closely related (unified), some aspects of each will have to be discussed with the other. Finally, with this background some planning suggestions for parents considering such gifts can be made.

THE GIFT TAX

The gift tax may apply to any transfer of money or property by a party where no consideration (payment) is received in return. These rules apply no matter who makes a gift—a parent or anyone else; however, to keep the discussion simpler, the person making the gift will be referred to as the parent. The gift tax is applied in a very broad and all-encompassing manner so that a gift of any property, whether direct or indirect—whether it is money, personal property (furniture, a car, draperies, and so forth), or real estate—can trigger the tax.

The simplest way to conceptualize the gift tax is that when a parent makes a gift subject to tax, the gift tax rate is applied and the tax paid. Unfortunately, the calculation is a bit more complicated. The gift tax is based on all taxable gifts a parent makes during his or her lifetime. Thus, the gift tax calculation is different from the income tax in at least two important ways: (a) each parent has his or her own gift tax calculation even if the two file their income tax return together; and (b) this calculation is generally based on gifts over an entire lifetime and not on each year alone, as is the federal income tax. Thus, to calculate the gift tax due, the parent making the gift uses the following general approach:

(1) Add up all taxable gifts made in all prior years and the taxable gifts made during the current year (i.e., on cumulative lifetime transfers).

(2) Calculate the gift tax on the amount obtained in (1) using the gift tax rate schedule.

(3) Next, all gift taxes that were paid in prior years are subtracted. The net amount left is the gift tax that must be paid as a result of gifts made for the most recent year.

Fortunately, there are a number of important exceptions (exclusions) to the gift tax which can help parents avoid many of these complexities. One exclusion permits any parent to give a child up to $10,000 per year without incurring a gift tax. Although parents (or anyone else for that matter) can make a $10,000 tax-free gift to anyone, the following discussion will assume it's to a child. Thus, a parent can make gifts of up to $10,000 to any number of people he or she wants to during the year and avoid all gift taxes. If both parents join together to make the gift, the two of them can give up to $20,000 in any year to any child.

This raises a common question. What if the mother has the money in her bank account and the father is tight on cash? How can the couple give their child the maximum $20,000 annual tax-free gift amount? The answer is to use a technique called "gift splitting." With the consent of the nongiving spouse (the husband in the above example), the gift will be treated as if one-half had been given by each spouse. Thus, with gift splitting the mother can give her son $20,000 and the gift will be treated as if made one-half each by the husband and wife, and each of their annual $10,000-per-person gift tax exclusions will be available to eliminate any gift tax (or use of the unified credit).

CAUTION: If gift splitting is elected during any year, then all gifts made by the couple must be subject to gift splitting. For wealthier taxpayers who have made substantial gifts in the past this may not always be the best approach. This situation could occur if one spouse is in a higher marginal gift tax bracket than the other spouse. Be sure to consult your tax adviser if this applies to you.

To use gift splitting the couple must both be citizens or residents of the United States, they must be married at the time the gift is made and cannot remarry during the remainder of the year. They must also file a statement with the IRS within a certain time period (see below).

If the parents also want to give their child's spouse (their son-in-law or daughter-in-law) money for the downpayment, they can give each person $20,000, for a total of $40,000 per year. If they make the gifts near year end, they can give up to $80,000 in a short time—$40,000 in December and another $40,000 in January. If the spouse's parents are also willing and able to make comparable gifts, all of the above amounts can be doubled.

TIP: Careful use of the annual gift tax exclusion can enable parents to give their children money to be used for a downpayment on a house without incurring any gift tax cost, and without using up any of their unified credit (see below).

There is another important exception to the gift tax laws called the unified credit. This credit allows any taxpayer to give up to $600,000 of money or property away without paying any gift tax. Unfortunately, a parent (or other taxpayer) can only use this credit once in his or her lifetime. When it's used up—it's gone. This credit is called "unified" because the same credit is allowed to be used to reduce either the gift or estate tax, or any portion of each up to the single maximum $600,000 amount. This will be discussed further in the section below concerning the estate tax.

The first reaction many people have to the unified credit is, "Wow! Its such a large amount. How could I (or my parents) ever accumulate so much money?" It's true, the unified credit is a very large amount. Congress intentionally set it very high so that most taxpayers could avoid paying the tax. But many people are caught by the gift and estate taxes in spite of this large unified credit. And it's not only the wealthiest people.

CAUTION: Too often, it isn't the wealthiest people who get stuck paying Uncle Sam gift and estate taxes: it's people who consider themselves middle-class or upper middle-class and who don't plan properly. Inflationary increases in real estate values, large insurance policies, and pension and retirement accounts that accumulate over time can push unsuspecting taxpayers into what they consider to be a tax that is only for the rich.

EXAMPLE: Andy and Amy Average never considered themselves particularly wealthy. Andy and Amy both work and between them earn what they consider a nice living. Over the years, they have carefully salted away the maximum in pension plans, 401(k) plans, IRAs, and whatever was appropriate (the tax law changes and switches in employers determined which plans they used at different times). The balances in all their various pension and retirement accounts total about $220,000. Andy has always been very conservative regarding insurance. He maintains a sizable $250,000 policy on his life, wanting to make sure Amy is well provided for. The Averages bought a simple home in a suburb of New York many years ago for about $45,000. The dramatic inflation in house prices in the greater New York area over the years has pushed the value of their home to $385,000. Their furniture, two cars, and mutual fund investments are worth about $112,000. Because they never considered themselves wealthy, they kept all property in joint name. On Andy's death, all his property went to Amy. The estate is now worth a whopping $967,000, and on Amy's death her estate will have to pay an estate tax. Some simple estate planning at an earlier date, a credit trust or perhaps including gifts of cash to their children to purchase their first homes, may have eliminated the estate tax costs.

Now that it's clear that the large unified credit isn't necessarily the answer to all gift and estate taxes, it's important to see how this unified credit works. When a parent makes gifts subject to the gift tax (for example, a gift to a child in excess of the annual amount excluded as described above), a gift tax must be calculated. After the gift tax is calculated, it is reduced by the amount of the unified credit which that parent hasn't yet used.

NOTE: The unified credit is actually equal to $192,800. A credit of this amount eliminates the tax on a transfer of a taxpayer's first $600,000 of property. Only after a gift tax is incurred in excess of $192,800 (i.e., only after $600,000 of property is transferred) will any gift tax have to be paid. After this point the gift tax is assessed at a rate of 37 percent and can go up to 55 percent. It is still important to conserve the unified credit to the extent possible. This is because whatever amount of the unified credit is used during a parent's lifetime to avoid tax on gifts won't be available at the death of the parent to eliminate the estate tax.

EXAMPLE: Amy Average in the above example has an estate worth a whopping $967,000. Her will leaves everything equally to her four children. Assuming that Amy has not used up any of her unified credit, her estate will be able to claim the benefit of the full $600,000 amount. Thus, only $367,000 of the estate will be subject to the estate tax. If Amy had used up her credit during her lifetime by making taxable gifts, the entire estate of $967,000 would be subject to tax. This additional $600,000 of taxable estate will be taxable at rates from 18 percent to 37 percent. The actual calculation of the estate tax is quite complicated, and is explained in general terms later in this chapter.

Planning a proper gift program to take maximum advantage of the tax opportunities available, while being ever careful of the parents' financial position, is a cornerstone of estate tax planning. A properly planned gift program, taking maximum advantage of the annual exclusions and the unified credit, can completely eliminate what might otherwise be a costly estate tax. With proper planning parents can make sure that what's left of their hard-earned dollars goes to benefit their children and family, and not to Uncle Sam. What this means to a parent making a gift of money for a downpayment can be illustrated with a simple example.

EXAMPLE: Paul Parent's daughter Betty from a prior marriage needs some help to buy a condominium. Paul's present wife, Sally, doesn't want to give any of her own money. Betty's mom doesn't have the financial means to help. Betty needs $40,000 for a closing scheduled December 1. If Paul makes a gift to Betty of the full $40,000, he will use up $30,000 of his unified credit, or pay gift tax on $30,000 if his unified credit has already been used up [$40,000 gift−$10,000 annual exclusion]. If Paul uses some planning he can avoid using up his unified credit. Paul can give $20,000 of his money now and ask his present wife to elect to split the gift (treat it as if one-half of the gift were made by her). She may be willing to do this since Paul is making the gift from his separate money and there won't be any cost to her. Paul can then lend the remaining $20,000 to Betty. In January, Paul and Sally can give Betty another joint gift by way of canceling the loan. (See Chapter 7.) This type of planning will save $30,000 of unified credit, which may ultimately save Paul's estate $16,500 [$30,000 × 55% maximum estate tax rate].

There is one other important exclusion from the gift tax. Parents (or anyone) can give unlimited amounts for tuition and medical care without incurring any gift tax. In some instances these can be used as the means to help children indirectly with the purchase of a home, if the children have substantial medical or education expenses. For example, if one or both members of a couple are going to college full or part time, and they need more money for a downpayment than the annual exclusion will allow, the parents may consider paying the children's college tuition. This may free up additional savings the children have, to be used as the downpayment on the house.

EXAMPLE: Alice Ambitious works during the day as an accountant and attends law school in the evenings. Her tuition is about $9,400 per year. She decides to buy a condominium to live in and needs her parents' help with $30,000 for the downpayment. Her parents can use gift splitting to give her $20,000 tax free during the year. What about the remaining $10,000? In the above example, a loan was used. But for Alice, a more direct approach may be possible. Alice's parents can pay for her law school tuition for one year (and perhaps a few of her uninsured medical expenses) in addition to making the $20,000 tax-free gift. This enables them to give Alice the amount she needs in a single year without the complications, legal expenses, and tax risks of using a loan arrangement. Alice can then use the money she had set aside for tuition toward the downpayment on her new condominium.

THE ESTATE TAX

The estate tax is important to understand since it can provide a motivation for moderate to wealthy parents to consider giving children money for a downpayment. It is also important since ideally, any gifts of substantial amounts of money should be made in the context of an overall estate and gift tax plan, so as not to forgo important tax benefits, or excessively deplete the parents' financial resources.

Since the estate and gift taxes are closely related (by a single unified credit), it was difficult to explain the gift tax without also explaining the estate tax. The following discussion will thus complete many of the comments above and provide an overview of the estate-tax system.

The estate tax is a tax imposed on the value of all the property that a taxpayer leaves to others on his or her death—for example, all of the property a taxpayer's will gives to his or her children and other family members. The estate tax, however, is much broader than that and can apply to property not governed by a person's will (probate property). The estate tax is really an excise tax on the right of a deceased person to transfer property he or she owned.

The basic structure of the estate tax is as follows:

(1) Add up the value of the taxpayer's entire estate. This includes all of the property the taxpayer owned at death, such as cash, real

estate, stocks, and so forth; certain transfers of property made by the taxpayer within three years before his or her death and over which the taxpayer retained certain controls or powers; transfers of property made during the taxpayer's lifetime in which the taxpayer kept some rights to possess or enjoy the property. For example, if a parent gives a child the family home, but retains the right to live in that home until death, the value of the home will be included in the parent's estate. Also, a property that the taxpayer gave away during his or her lifetime, but over which he or she retained the right to revoke the gift, is included in the estate. Certain gifts to children under the Uniform Gifts to Minors Act, where the taxpayer serves as the custodian of the property, may be included as a result of this rule.

(2) Subtract from the value of all of the property in (1) above the following: (a) funeral expenses, (b) administrative expenses of the estate, (c) certain debts (for example, a mortgage on property included in the gross estate) and losses of the estate, (d) the marital deduction (a deduction for the property which the taxpayer's spouse gets), and (e) charitable contributions.

(3) The result of the above computation equals the taxable estate of the taxpayer.

Unfortunately, as with the gift tax discussed above, the calculation of the actual tax due is a bit more complicated than would be anticipated. The tax is not merely calculated on the amount of the taxable estate determined in (3) above. Rather, the remaining steps must be used:

(4) Add to the amount of the taxable estate in (3) the total amount of taxable gifts (don't include amounts given that weren't taxable as a result of the annual $10,000 per-person exclusion) the taxpayer made during his lifetime.

(5) Calculate the estate tax due on the total amount in (4).

(6) Reduce the tax due by the amount of unified credit and the gift taxes paid during the taxpayer's lifetime on gifts he or she made. Note how the portion of the unified credit used against gift taxes during the taxpayer's lifetime will not be available again to offset the estate tax due.

The reason for this somewhat confusing calculation is that the same progressive tax rate (the tax rate gets higher on larger transfers), with a single unified credit to offset it, is applied to transfers of property a taxpayer makes during his or her lifetime or at death (through a will, or without a will, through intestacy). The more property a taxpayer owns, whether that property is given away while he or she is alive, or following his or her death, the higher the rate of tax will be. Although combining the gift and estate taxes into a closely integrated system makes the calculations more difficult, it accomplishes the objective of taxing gifts made during one's lifetime the same as gifts made after one's death.

DOCUMENTS AND FORMS USED WHEN PARENTS MAKE A GIFT

One of the basic documents that may have to be used when parents make a gift to their children of a downpayment is a gift tax return. The gift tax return must be filed (and the gift tax, if any, paid) once each year. The tax return is due by April 15 of the next year. If the parents extend the due date for their income tax return (by filing a special form with the IRS), they will generally get an automatic extension of the due date for their gift tax return as well. A gift tax return will generally have to be filed for any gifts of property except where the gift is excluded under the annual $10,000-per-person exclusion, or the special exclusion for gifts of tuition and medical payments. This means that if the parents use the gift-splitting technique they must file a gift tax return. A sample gift tax return is included in the appendix to this chapter.

If a couple wish to use the gift-splitting technique described above, they must file a statement (election) with the IRS consenting to have the gift-splitting rules apply for that year. This election must be filed by April 15 of the next year.

Some parents may be concerned about giving large sums of money to a newly married couple. How can they protect their gift if the marriage falters? Additional legal documentation, such as an unrecorded mortgage, may be necessary.

OBSERVATION: When parents make a gift of money to help children buy a home, the amounts involved are generally large. Unless the parents of the daughter-in-law or son-in-law also make an equivalent gift, some parents become concerned about the consequences of a divorce. With such a large number of marriages ending in divorce, this concern is very real.

One approach is a prenuptial agreement which specifically addresses what happens with the home and the money given by the parents. In other situations, some parents have their lawyer prepare a mortgage which

> the parents hold, according to Richard Hofflich, an attorney with Hofflich and Rosenbloom in New York City. The parents don't record the mortgage, so it does not become a matter of public record. If the marriage falters and the children get divorced, the parents use this unrecorded mortgage to reacquire their gift. The potential problem with this approach is that an unrecorded mortgage won't always provide the hoped for protection.

Use of an unrecorded mortgage presents a number of problems. If the mortgage isn't recorded it may become unenforceable after a number of years, depending on the laws in the state where the property is located. For example, in some states, after six years the parents would not be able to enforce the mortgage. The hope by the parents, however, is that if the marriage lasts that long it should be a stable marriage.

Another problem is that if the parents insist on having an unrecorded mortgage, what will be said in the Gift Letter Certification the parents will probably have to sign if the children are seeking a bank loan for the balance of the purchase price? The parents can't state that the money was an outright gift to the children if they hold a mortgage. It's fraud. If they indicate the true nature of the transaction, the children may have difficulty in qualifying for a loan. The solution may be for the children to have a prenuptial or some other form of agreement concerning the funds. Another solution would be for the parents to give outright the amount of money the bank deems necessary for the children to qualify for the mortgage loan they need, and then to treat any additional money above that amount as a loan to the children. (See Chapter 7.)

The use of this type of mortgage also raises some complicated gift tax issues. If there is a mortgage on the children's property equal to the amount of cash purportedly given, for gift tax purposes the gift will not be considered to have been made (in technical terms, the gift will not be complete until there is an irrevocable transfer of the money). This will disqualify the "gift" for the annual $10,000-per-person exclusion. If the IRS considers the gift to be complete only when the mortgage lapses according to state laws (or is canceled by the parents), the entire amount of money given may be considered a gift for gift tax purposes in that year. This could wreak havoc with the parents' estate planning. These problems are complicated and should be addressed by an attorney specializing in estate planning.

TIP: If the soon-to-be-married couple is going to have a prenuptial agreement to address the concerns of the parents making the gift of money for a downpayment, be certain that both members of the couple have their own lawyers (never use one lawyer) review the agreement. Prenuptial agreements can have important legal (and emotional) ramifications and should not be taken lightly.

A final document that is commonly encountered when parents make a gift of money for children's use as part of the downpayment, will be a Gift Letter Certification the children's bank or mortgage company will want. If the bank is going to consider the cash that the children received from the parents for purposes of evaluating the children's loan application, they will often want a signed letter from the parents stating that the money was in fact a gift and not a loan. A sample Gift Letter Certification is included later in this chapter.

WHERE PARENTS CAN GET THE CASH TO MAKE THE GIFT OF THE DOWNPAYMENT TO THEIR CHILDREN

For some parents who wish to help their children break into the housing market, it isn't so easy to come up with the cash. Most parents just don't have the financial resources to worry about many of the gift and estate tax problems discussed in the earlier parts of this chapter. There are a number of possibilities that parents can pursue to obtain cash to help their children with a downpayment.

Parents may have a lot of equity in their own homes. They can tap that equity with a home-equity loan and provide their children with money to use toward the downpayment on their new home. If the total of the home-equity loans that the parents have outstanding doesn't exceed $100,000, they will often be able to deduct the interest expense they pay. They're allowed to tap up to $100,000 of home equity for any purpose and deduct the interest on it. If they've used up part or all of their $100,000 equity line, then they will be able to deduct only part of the interest.

NOTE: "Although the $100,000 limit sounds high, when parents are helping a number of kids through college, or have children from both a current and prior marriage, the $100,000 limit gets used up very quickly," says Dick Schlott, president of Schlott Realtors.

If the parents have a rental property, they may be able to refinance the property or take out a second mortgage and provide some or all of the proceeds to the children as a gift (or loan). If the parents own more then 10 percent of the rental property, are actively involved in its management (approve tenants, hire, or make repairs, etc.), and have income (modified adjusted gross income) of $100,000 or less, they can deduct up to $25,000 in tax losses on the rental property (the passive loss limitations won't apply to limit their deductions). Thus, if the parent refinances, the additional interest will be tax deductible.

If the parent has stocks or bonds that have appreciated in value, another approach is to give the children the stocks or bonds to use toward the downpayment. When the children sell the stocks or bonds they may be in a lower tax bracket than the parents, so that the tax cost of the sale will be lower.

CHAPTER SUMMARY

A more and more common source of financing the downpayment for many first-time home buyers is a helping hand from their parents. The inflation in the value of homes over the years has put the price of a house out of reach of many first-time home buyers without this assistance. This type of help, however, is not without its legal, tax, and emotional complications. To best utilize parents' generosity, review the many considerations discussed in this chapter. While it is always best to obtain the assistance of a qualified attorney, as the amounts given get larger, the tax complications become substantial, and obtaining competent professional advice becomes critical.

FOR YOUR NOTEBOOK

Two sample forms used for gifts given to home buyers, plus federal gift tax forms that may have to be filed by the parents giving money to their home-buying children, are shown below and on the following pages. The forms for actual filing can be obtained from the IRS. However, it's always best to consult an accountant and estate planner before filing any gift tax forms. The instructions for these forms contain additional details and information about gift taxes which were not discussed in the brief overview provided in the chapter.

FORMS: *GIFT LETTERS*

INTERSTATE MORTGAGE SERVICE
LICENSED MORTGAGE BANKERS
292 MAIN STREET
SUITE 23
HACKENSACK, NEW JERSEY 07601

(201) 488-2662

GIFT LETTER CERTIFICATION

RE:

This is to certify that I, _____ , am
giving a gift in the amount of $ _____ to _____
_____ who is purchasing property
at _____ .
My relationship to the applicants is _____ .
This is a gift and does not have to be repaid.

_____   _____
                                 DATE

_____   _____
                                 DATE

ADMINISTRATIVE OFFICES
1550 Route 23 North
Wayne, New Jersey 07470-0979
(201) 633-5000

GIFT LETTER

Below is text required for a Gift Letter.

We _____ do
hereby certify that we have given/will give a gift of $ _____
_____ to my (relationship) _____
on _____ to be applied toward the purchase of
the above property. Our address is _____
_____ . We certify that
this is a bona fide gift and that there is no obligation, expressed or
implied to repay this sum in cash or in other services of any kind.

We understand that this gift will require documentation, including
proof that we have the ability to give the gift and that the funds both
have been given by us and received by the applicants prior to
closing.

For confirmation of the availability of funds, please contact the
below mentioned institution.

Name of Depository _____
Address of Depository _____
_____

Account Number _____
Account Held under the name of: _____
_____

_____
Signature of Donor and Date

_____
Signature of Donor and Date

_____
(continued on p. 112)

Funds for closing utilizing gift monies must be verified in the following manner:

1. Gift letter completed and signed. Typically, gifts must come from a family member. Family member is defined as father, mother, sister, brother, grandparents.
2. Verification of deposit sent to savings institution to verify that the funds are available to give or a copy of the donor's bank statement is required.
3. When the funds are given to the applicant, a copy of the check or passbook showing withdrawal of gift and deposit slip showing funds being deposited in applicant's bank account.
4. If the gift funds are given directly to the escrow attorney, a copy of the check and letter from the attorney certifying receipt of the funds.
5. If the gift funds were given prior to application, the above items will still be required.

Offices in New Jersey, New York, Connecticut, Pennsylvania and Florida

---

FORMS: *GIFT TAX RETURNS*

EXAMPLE: Assume the following facts: Max and Laura Smith are a married couple. Max wishes to give his daughter and son-in-law, Judy and Mark Jones, $50,000 in cash.

An individual is allowed to make a cash gift of up to $10,000 to as many different individuals as he or she desires in one tax year, without incurring any gift or estate tax ramifications. If his or her spouse so chooses, he or she can elect to split such gift, thus increasing the annual exclusion to $20,000 per donee. A Federal gift tax return (Form 709) must be completed to make such an election. (See the sample gift tax return.*)

In this case, Laura consents to split the gift with Max. If the gift is made payable to only one of the children, then it is deemed paid to one donee. To further save taxes the gift could be paid equally ($25,000 each to Judy and Mark) or made out on a check jointly "to the order of Mr. and Mrs. Mark Jones." Then Mark and Judy are deemed to be two separate donees; thus $40,000 in total gifts can be made to the two of them without any gift or estate tax ramifications.

On gifts above these dollar levels, a unified tax is imposed. However, each individual is allowed to make $600,000 of either lifetime gifts, or transfers at death, free of gift or estate taxes. The gift tax return must be

---

* Tax forms and example were prepared by Ernst & Whinney, New York, NY.

filed to show the gifts made, and the reduction of this lifetime exemption. The $600,000 exemption is recorded on the return as a credit on the taxes that would be due on the gifts made above these annual exclusion limits. (The tax on $600,000 is $192,800, which is the maximum lifetime "unified credit.")

In the Smiths' case, the gift of $50,000 exceeds the $40,000 annual maximum. The gift tax returns that must be filed for both Max and Laura show the $5,000 of lifetime exclusion that each is using. The $900 of tax on these excess gifts is reflected as a credit against this $192,800 credit. They can each still make up to $595,000 of additional lifetime gifts or transfers at death tax free.

Form 709
(Rev. December 1988)
Department of the Treasury
Internal Revenue Service

United States Gift (and Generation-Skipping Transfer) Tax Return

(Section 6019 of the Internal Revenue Code) (For gifts made after December 31, 1986, and before January 1, 1990)

Calendar year 19 _88_

► For Privacy Act Notice, see the Instructions for Form 1040.

OMB No. 1545-0020
Expires 10-31-91

Part 1.—General Information

1 Donor's first name and middle initial **Max**	2 Donor's last name **Smith**	3 Social security number **123-45-6789**

4 Address (number and street) **Anytown Drive**	5 Domicile

6 City, state, and ZIP code **Gotham City, Metropolis 12345**	7 Citizenship **USA**

	Yes	No
8 If the donor died during the year, check here ► ☐ and enter date of death _____ , 19 ____		
9 If you received an extension of time to file this Form 709, check here ►☐ and attach the Form 4868, 2688, 2350, or extension letter.		
10 If you (the donor) filed a previous Form 709 (or 709-A), has your address changed since the last Form 709 (or 709-A) was filed?		X
11 Gifts by husband or wife to third parties.—Do you consent to have the gifts (including generation-skipping transfers) made by you and by your spouse to third parties during the calendar year considered as made one-half by each of you? (See instructions.) (If the answer is "Yes," the following information must be furnished and your spouse is to sign the consent shown below. If the answer is "No," skip lines 12–17 and go to Schedule A.)	X	

12 Name of consenting spouse **Laura Smith**	13 SSN **987-65-4321**

	Yes	No
14 Were you married to one another during the entire calendar year? (See instructions.)		X
15 If the answer to 14 is "No," check whether ☐ married ☐ divorced or ☐ widowed, and give date (see instructions) ►		
16 Will a gift tax return for this calendar year be filed by your spouse?		X

17 **Consent of Spouse**—I consent to have the gifts (and generation-skipping transfers) made by me and by my spouse to third parties during the calendar year considered as made one-half by each of us. We are both aware of the joint and several liability for tax created by the execution of this consent.

Consenting spouse's signature ►   Date ►

Part 2.—Tax Computation

1 Enter the amount from Schedule A, Part 3, line 15		1	5,000
2 Enter the amount from Schedule B, line 3		2	0
3 Total taxable gifts (add lines 1 and 2)		3	5,000
4 Tax computed on amount on line 3 (see Table for Computing Tax in separate instructions)		4	900
Note: *If you are reporting gifts made before January 1, 1988, see instructions.*			
5a Enter the lesser of line 3 or $21,040,000	**5a** 5,000		
b Subtract $10,000,000 from line 5a (do not enter less than zero)	**5b** 0		
c Enter 5% (.05) of line 5b		5c	0
6 Total tentative tax on the amount on line 3 (add lines 4 and 5c)		6	900
7 Tax computed on amount on line 2 (see Table for Computing Tax in separate instructions)		7	0
8a Enter the lesser of line 2 or $21,040,000	**8a** 0		
b Subtract $10,000,000 from line 8a (do not enter less than zero)	**8b** 0		
c Enter 5% (.05) of line 8b		8c	0
9 Total tentative tax on the amount on line 2 (add lines 7 and 8c)		9	0
10 Balance (subtract line 9 from line 6)		10	900
11 Maximum unified credit (nonresident aliens, see instructions)		11	192,800 00
12 Enter the unified credit against tax allowable for all prior periods (from Sch. B, line 1, col. C)		12	0
13 Balance (subtract line 12 from line 11)		13	192,800
14 Enter 20% (.20) of the amount allowed as a specific exemption for gifts made after September 8, 1976, and before January 1, 1977 (see instructions)		14	0
15 Balance (subtract line 14 from line 13)		15	192,800
16 Unified credit (enter the smaller of line 10 or line 15)		16	900
17 Credit for foreign gift taxes (see instructions)		17	0
18 Total credits (add lines 16 and 17)		18	900
19 Balance (subtract line 18 from line 10) (do not enter less than zero)		19	0
20 Generation-skipping transfer taxes (from Schedule C, Part 4, col. H, total)		20	0
21 Total tax (add lines 19 and 20)		21	0
22 Gift and generation-skipping transfer taxes prepaid with extension of time to file		22	0
23 If line 22 is less than line 21, enter BALANCE DUE (see instructions)		23	0
24 If line 22 is greater than line 21, enter AMOUNT TO BE REFUNDED		24	0

Under penalties of perjury, I declare that I have examined this return, including any accompanying schedules and statements, and to the best of my knowledge and belief it is true, correct, and complete. Declaration of preparer (other than donor) is based on all information of which preparer has any knowledge.

Donor's signature ►   Date ►

Preparer's signature
(other than donor) ►   Date ►

Preparer's address
(other than donor) ► Ernst & Whinney, 787 Seventh Avenue, New York, N.Y.   10019

For Paperwork Reduction Act Notice, see page 1 of the separate instructions to this form.

Form **709** (Rev. 12-88)

SCHEDULE A Computation of Taxable Gifts

Part 1.—Gifts Subject Only to Gift Tax. *Gifts less political organization, medical, and educational exclusions—see instructions*

A Item number	B Donee's name and address and description of gift. If the gift was made by means of a trust, enter trust's identifying number below and attach a copy of the trust instrument. If the gift was securities, enter the CUSIP number(s), if available.	C Donor's adjusted basis of gift	D Date of gift	E Value at date of gift
1	Mark Jones - Cash	25,000	7/1/88	25,000
2	Judy Jones - Cash	25,000	7/1/88	25,000

Part 2.—Gifts Subject to Both Gift Tax and Generation-Skipping Transfer Tax. You must list the gifts in chronological order.
Gifts less political organization, medical, and educational exclusions—see instructions

A Item number	B Donee's name and address and description of gift. If the gift was made by means of a trust, enter trust's identifying number below and attach a copy of the trust instrument. If the gift was securities, enter the CUSIP number(s), if available.	C Donor's adjusted basis of gift	D Date of gift	E Value at date of gift
1				

Part 3.—Gift Tax Reconciliation

1	Total value of gifts of donor (add column E of Parts 1 and 2)	1	50,000
2	One-half of items ____1-2____ attributable to spouse (see instructions)	2	25,000
3	Balance (subtract line 2 from line 1)	3	25,000
4	Gifts of spouse to be included (from Schedule A, Part 3, line 2 of spouse's return—see instructions) . If any of the gifts included on this line are also subject to the generation-skipping transfer tax, check here ▶ ☐ and enter those gifts also on Schedule C, Part 1.	4	
5	Total gifts (add lines 3 and 4)	5	25,000
6	Total annual exclusions for gifts listed on Schedule A (including line 4, above) (see instructions) . .	6	20,000
7	Total included amount of gifts (subtract line 6 from line 5)	7	5,000

Deductions (see instructions)

8	Gifts of interests to spouse for which a marital deduction will be claimed, based on items _____ of Schedule A . . .	8		
9	Exclusions attributable to gifts on line 8	9		
10	Marital deduction—subtract line 9 from line 8	10		
11	Charitable deduction, based on items _____ to _____ less exclusions .	11		
12	Total deductions—add lines 10 and 11	12	
13	Subtract line 12 from line 7	13	5,000
14	Generation-skipping transfer taxes payable with this Form 709 (from Schedule C, Part 4, col. H, Total)	14	
15	Taxable gifts (add lines 13 and 14). Enter here and on line 1 of the Tax Computation on page 1 . .	15	5,000

(If more space is needed, attach additional sheets of same size.)

115

SCHEDULE A	Computation of Taxable Gifts (continued)

16 Terminable Interest (QTIP) Marital Deduction. (See instructions.)

☐ ◄ Check here if you elected, under the rules of section 2523(f), to include gifts of qualified terminable interest property on line 8, on page 2. Enter the item numbers (from Schedule A) of the gifts for which you made this election ► --

SCHEDULE B	Gifts From Prior Periods

Did you (the donor) file gift tax returns for prior periods? (If "Yes," see instructions for completing Schedule B below.)   ☐ Yes   ☐ No

A Calendar year or calendar quarter (see instructions)	B Internal Revenue office where prior return was filed	C Amount of unified credit against gift tax for periods after December 31, 1976	D Amount of specific exemption for prior periods ending before January 1, 1977	E Amount of taxable gifts
	NONE			

1 Totals for prior periods (without adjustment for reduced specific exemption) **1**

2 Amount, if any, by which total specific exemption, line 1, column D, is more than $30,000 . . . . . **2**

3 Total amount of taxable gifts for prior periods (add amount, column E, line 1, and amount, if any, on line 2). (Enter here and on line 2 of the Tax Computation on page 1.) **3**

SCHEDULE C	Computation of Generation-Skipping Transfer Tax

Note: *Inter vivos direct skips which are completely excluded by the grandchild exclusion and/or the GST exemption must still be fully reported (including value and exclusions and exemptions claimed) on Schedule C.*

Part 1.—Generation-Skipping Transfers

A Item No. (from Schedule A, Part 2, col. A)	B Value (from Schedule A, Part 2, col. E)	C Split Gifts (enter ½ of col. B) (see instructions)	D Subtract col. C from col. B	E Annual Exclusion Claimed	F Subtract col. E from col. D	G Grandchild Exclusion Claimed	H Net Transfer (subtract col. G from col. F)
1							
2							
3							
4							
5							
6							
7							
8							

If you elected gift splitting and your spouse was required to file a separate Form 709 (see the instructions for "Split Gifts"), you must enter all of the gifts shown on Schedule A, Part 2, of your spouse's Form 709 here. In column C, enter the item number of each gift in the order it appears in column A of your spouse's Schedule A, Part 2. We have preprinted the prefix "S-" to distinguish your spouse's item numbers from your own when you complete column A of Schedule C, Part 4. In column D, for each gift, enter the amount reported in column C, Schedule C, Part 1, of your spouse's Form 709.	Split gifts from spouse's Form 709 (enter item number)	Value included from spouse's Form 709					
	S-						
	S-						
	S-						
	S-						
	S-						
	S-						
	S-						
	S-						
	Total grandchild exclusions claimed on this return. Must equal total of column D, Schedule C, Part 2						

(If more space is needed, attach additional sheets of same size.)

SCHEDULE C   Computation of Generation-Skipping Transfer Tax (continued)

Part 2.—Grandchild Exclusion Reconciliation

Name of Grandchild	A Maximum Allowable Exclusion	B Total of Exclusions Claimed on Previous Returns	C Exclusion Available for This Return (subtract col. B from col. A)	D Exclusion Claimed on this Return	E Exclusion Available for Future Returns (subtract col. D from col. C)
	$2,000,000				
	$2,000,000				
	$2,000,000				
	$2,000,000				
	$2,000,000				
	$2,000,000				
	$2,000,000				
	$2,000,000				

Total grandchild exclusions claimed on this return. Must equal total of column G, Part 1

Part 3.—GST Exemption Reconciliation (Code section 2631)

1	Maximum allowable exemption	1	$1,000,000
2	Total exemption used for periods before filing this return	2	
3	Exemption available for this return (subtract line 2 from line 1)	3	
4	Exemption claimed on this return (from Part 4, col. C total, below)	4	
5	Exemption allocated to transfers not shown on Part 4, below. You must attach a Notice of Allocation. (See instructions.)	5	
6	Add lines 4 and 5	6	
7	Exemption available for future transfers (subtract line 6 from line 3)	7	

Part 4.—Tax Computation

A Item No. (from Schedule C, Part 1)	B Net transfer (from Schedule C, Part 1, col. H)	C GST Exemption Allocated	D Divide col. C by col. B	E Inclusion Ratio (subtract col. D from 1.000)	F Maximum Gift Tax Rate	G Applicable Rate (multiply col. E by col. F)	H Generation-Skipping Transfer Tax (multiply col. B by col. G)
1					55% (.55)		
2					55% (.55)		
3					55% (.55)		
4					55% (.55)		
5					55% (.55)		
6					55% (.55)		
7					55% (.55)		
8					55% (.55)		
					55% (.55)		
					55% (.55)		
					55% (.55)		
					55% (.55)		
					55% (.55)		
					55% (.55)		
					55% (.55)		

Total exemption claimed. Enter here and on line 4, Part 3, above. May not exceed line 3, Part 3, above . . . . . .

Total generation-skipping transfer tax. Enter here, on line 14 of Schedule A, Part 3, and on line 20 of the Tax Computation on page 1 . . . .

(If more space is needed, attach additional sheets of same size.)

☆U.S. Government Printing Office: 1989-242-473/80041

**Department of the Treasury
Internal Revenue Service**

Instructions for Form 709

(Revised December 1988)

United States Gift (and Generation-Skipping Transfer) Tax Return

(For gifts made after December 31, 1986, and before January 1, 1990)
For Privacy Act Notice, see the Instructions for Form 1040
(Section references are to the Internal Revenue Code unless otherwise noted.)

If you are filing this form solely to elect gift-splitting for gifts of not more than $20,000 per donee, you may be able to use Form 709-A, United States Short Form Gift Tax Return, instead of this form. See the Instructions for "Who Must File" on page 2.

If you made gifts before January 1, 1982, do not use this Form 709 to report these gifts. Instead, use the November 1981 revision of Form 709. For gifts made after December 31, 1981, and before January 1, 1987, use the January 1987 revision of Form 709.

Paperwork Reduction Act Notice.—We ask for this information to carry out the Internal Revenue laws of the United States. We need it to ensure that taxpayers are complying with these laws and to allow us to figure and collect the right amount of tax. You are required to give us this information.

The time needed to complete and file this form will vary depending on individual circumstances. The estimated average time is:

Recordkeeping	40 min.
Learning about the law or the form	51 min.
Preparing the form	1 hr., 50 min.
Copying, assembling, and sending the form to IRS	1 hr., 3 min.

If you have comments concerning the accuracy of these time estimates or suggestions for making this form more simple, we would be happy to hear from you. You can write to the **Internal Revenue Service,** Washington, DC 20224, Attention: IRS Reports Clearance Officer, TR:FP; or the **Office of Management and Budget,** Paperwork Reduction Project, Washington, DC 20503.

Changes You Should Note

• The scheduled decline in gift tax rates is deferred until 1993.
• The benefit of the unified credit and graduated rates is phased out for transfers exceeding $10,000,000 for gifts made after 1987.

General Instructions

Purpose of Form.—Form 709 is used to report transfers subject to the Federal gift and certain generation-skipping (GST) taxes and to figure the tax, if any, due on those transfers.

All gift and GST taxes are computed and filed on a calendar year basis regardless of your income tax accounting period.

Transfers Subject to the Gift Tax.—Generally, the Federal gift tax applies to any transfer by gift of real or personal property, whether tangible or intangible, that you made directly or indirectly, in trust, or by any other means to a donee.

The gift tax applies not only to the gratuitous transfer of any kind of property, but also to sales or exchanges, not made in the ordinary course of business, where money or money's worth is exchanged but the value of the money received is less than the value of what is sold or exchanged. The gift tax is in addition to any other tax, such as Federal income tax, paid or due on the transfer.

The exercise or release of a power of appointment may be a gift by the individual possessing the power.

The gift tax may also apply to the forgiveness of a debt, to interest-free (or below market interest rate) loans, to the assignment of the benefits of an insurance policy, to certain property settlements in divorce cases, and to certain survivorship annuities.

Bonds that are exempt from Federal income taxes are not exempt from Federal gift taxes.

Publication 448, Federal Estate and Gift Taxes, contains further information on the gift tax.

Transfers Not Subject to the Gift Tax.—Three types of transfers are not subject to the gift tax. These are transfers to political organizations and payments that qualify for the educational and medical exclusions. These transfers are not "gifts" as that term is used on Form 709 and its instructions. You need not file a Form 709 to report these transfers and should not list them on Schedule A of Form 709.

*Political organizations.—*The gift tax does not apply to a gift to a political organization (defined in section 527(e)(1)) for the use of the organization.

*Educational exclusion.—*The gift tax does not apply to an amount you paid on behalf of an individual to a qualifying domestic or foreign educational organization as tuition for the education or training of the individual. A qualifying educational organization is one that normally maintains a regular faculty and curriculum and normally has a regularly enrolled body of pupils or students in attendance at the place where its educational activities are regularly carried on. See section 170(b)(1)(A)(ii) and its regulations.

The payment must be made directly to the qualifying educational organization and it must be for tuition. No educational exclusion is allowed for amounts paid for books, supplies, dormitory fees, board or other similar expenses that do not constitute direct tuition costs. To the extent that the payment to the educational institution was for something other than tuition, it is a gift to the individual for whose benefit it was made, and may be offset by the annual exclusion if it is otherwise available.

*Medical exclusion.—*The gift tax does not apply to an amount you paid on behalf of an individual to a person or institution that provided medical care for the individual. The payment must be to the care provider. The medical care must meet the requirements of section 213(d) (definition of medical care for income tax deduction purposes). Medical care includes expenses incurred for the diagnosis, cure, mitigation, treatment, or prevention of disease, or for the purpose of affecting any structure or function of the body, or for transportation primarily for and essential to medical care. Medical care also includes amounts paid for medical insurance on behalf of any individual.

The medical exclusion does not apply to amounts paid for medical care that are reimbursed by the donee's insurance. If payment for a medical expense is reimbursed by the donee's insurance company, your payment for that expense, to the extent of the reimbursed amount, is not eligible for the medical exclusion and you have made a gift to the donee.

To the extent that the payment was for something other than medical care, it is a gift to the individual on whose behalf the payment was made, and may be offset by the annual exclusion if it is otherwise available.

The medical and educational exclusions are allowed without regard to the relationship between you and the donee. For examples illustrating these exclusions, see Regulations section 25.2503-6.

*Disclaimers.—*For the rules governing when a disclaimer is a qualified disclaimer and not subject to the gift tax, see Publication 448.

Transfers Subject to the Generation-Skipping Transfer Tax.—The GST tax to be reported on Form 709 is that imposed on inter vivos direct skips made after September 25, 1985. (See Temporary Regulations section 26.2662-1(b), for instructions on how to report other generation-skipping transfers.) An *inter vivos direct skip* is a transfer of an interest in property that is: (1) subject to the gift tax; and (2) made to a skip person. (See page 4.)

A transfer is *subject to the gift tax* if it is required to be reported on Schedule A of Form 709 under the rules contained in the gift tax portions of these instructions, including the split gift rules. Therefore, transfers made to political organizations, transfers that qualify for the medical or educational exclusions, transfers that are fully excluded under the annual exclusion, and most transfers made to your spouse are not subject to the GST tax.

Transfers subject to the GST tax are described in further detail in the instructions for Schedule A, on page 3.

Who Must File

Only individuals are required to file gift tax returns. If a trust, estate, partnership, or corporation makes a gift, the individual beneficiaries, partners, or stockholders are considered donors and may be liable for the gift and GST taxes.

If a donor dies before filing a return, the donor's executor must file the return.

A married couple may not file a joint gift tax return. However, see "Split Gifts" on page 3.

If a gift is of community property, it is considered made one-half by each spouse. For example, a gift of $100,000 of community property is considered a gift of $50,000 made by each spouse, and each spouse must file a gift tax return.

Citizens or Residents of the United States.—If you are a citizen or resident of the United States you must file a gift tax return (whether or not any tax is ultimately due) in the following situations:

Gifts to your spouse.—**Except as described below, you do not have to file a gift tax return to report gifts to your spouse regardless of the amount of these gifts and regardless of whether the gifts are present or future interests.**

However, you must file a gift tax return if your spouse is not a U.S. citizen and you made the gift after July 13, 1988, or if you made any gift of a terminable interest that does not meet the "Life Estate With Power of Appointment" exception described on page 5. You must also file a gift tax return to make a QTIP (Qualified Terminable Interest Property) election described on page 5.

Gifts to donees other than your spouse (including charitable donees).—You must file a gift tax return if you gave gifts to any such donee that are not fully excluded under the $10,000 annual exclusion (as described below). Thus, you must file a gift tax return to report any gift of a future interest (regardless of amount) or to report gifts to any donee that total more than $10,000 for the year.

Gift splitting.—You must file a gift tax return to split gifts (regardless of amount) with your spouse as described in the Specific Instructions for Part 1 on page 3.

The term *citizen of the United States* includes a person who, at the time of making the gift:

- was domiciled in a possession of the United States;
- was a U.S. citizen; and
- became a U.S. citizen for a reason other than being a citizen of a U.S. possession or being born or residing in a possession.

Annual Exclusion.—The first $10,000 of gifts of present interests to each donee during the calendar year is subtracted from total gifts in figuring the amount of taxable gifts.

All of the gifts made during the calendar year to a donee are **fully excluded under the annual exclusion** if they are all gifts of *present interests* and if they total $10,000 or less.

A gift of a *future interest* cannot be excluded under the annual exclusion.

A gift is considered a *present interest* if the donee has all immediate rights to the use, possession, and enjoyment of the property and income from the property. A gift is considered a *future interest* if the donee's rights to the use, possession, and enjoyment of the property and income from the property will not begin until some future date. Future interests include reversions, remainders, and other similar interests or estates.

Note: *Beginning with gifts made after July 13, 1988, to spouses who are* **not** *U.S. citizens, the annual exclusion has been increased from $10,000 to $100,000.*

In the case of transfers for the benefit of a minor and for the transitional rules for certain trusts with a power of appointment referenced to the annual exclusion, see Publication 448.

Nonresident Aliens.—Nonresident aliens are subject to gift and GST taxes for gifts of tangible property situated in the United States. Under certain circumstances they are also subject to gift and GST taxes for gifts of intangible property. (See section 2501(a).)

If you are a nonresident alien who made a gift subject to gift tax, you must file a gift tax return if: (1) you gave *any* gifts of future interests; or (2) your gifts of present interests to *any* donee (including your spouse) total more than $10,000.

When To File

Form 709 is an annual return.

Generally, you must file Form 709 on or after January 1 but not later than April 15 of the year following the calendar year when the gifts were made.

If the donor of the gifts died during the year in which the gifts were made, the executor must file the donor's Form 709 not later than the *earlier* of (1) the due date (with extensions) for filing the donor's estate tax return, or (2) April 15 of the year following the calendar year when the gifts were made. Under this rule, Form 709 may

be due before April 15 if the donor died before July 15 of the year in which the gifts were made. If the donor died after July 14, the due date for Form 709 (without extensions) will always be April 15 of the following year. If no estate tax return is required to be filed, the due date for Form 709 (without extensions) is April 15. For more information, see Regulations section 25.6075-1.

Extension of Time To File.— There are two methods of extending the time to file the gift tax return. *Neither method extends the time to pay the gift or GST taxes.* If you want an extension of time to pay the gift or GST taxes, you must request that separately. (See Regulations section 25.6161-1.)

(1) By letter.—You can request an extension of time to file your gift tax return by writing to the district director or service center for your area. You must explain the reasons for the delay; or

(2) By form.—Any extension of time granted for filing your calendar year Federal income tax return will also extend the time to file any gift tax return. Income tax extensions are made by using Form 4868, 2688, or 2350, which have check boxes for Form 709.

Where To File

File Form 709 with the Internal Revenue Service center where you would file your Federal income tax return. See the Form 1040 instructions for a list of filing locations.

Penalties

The law provides for penalties for both late filing of returns and late payment of tax unless you have reasonable cause. There are also penalties for valuation understatements that cause an underpayment of the tax, willful failure to file a return on time, and for willful attempt to evade or defeat payment of tax.

Joint Tenancy

If you buy property with your own funds and the title to such property is held by yourself and the donee as joint tenants with right of survivorship and if either you or the donee may give up those rights by severing your interest, you have made a gift to the donee in the amount of half the value of the property. If you create a joint bank account for yourself and the donee (or a similar kind of ownership by which you can get back the entire fund without the donee's consent), you have made a gift to the donee when the donee draws on the account for his or her own benefit. The amount of the gift is the amount that the donee took out without any obligation to repay you. If you buy a U.S. savings bond registered as payable to yourself or the donee, there is a gift to the donee when he or she cashes the bond without any obligation to account to you.

Transfer of Certain Life Estates

If you received a qualifying terminable interest (see page 5) from your spouse for which a marital deduction was elected on your spouse's estate or gift tax return, you will be subject to the gift (and GST, if applicable) tax if you dispose of (by gift, sale, or otherwise) all or part of your life income interest.

The entire value of the property involved less: (1) the amount you received on the disposition, and (2) the amount (if any) of the life income interest you retained after the transfer will be treated as a taxable gift. That portion of the property's value that is attributable to the remainder interest is a gift of a future interest for which no annual exclusion is allowed. To the extent you made a gift of the life income interest, you may claim an annual exclusion, treating the person to whom you transferred the interest as the donee for purposes of computing the annual exclusion.

Specific Instructions
Part I.—General Information
Gifts by Husband or Wife to Third Parties—Split Gifts

A married couple may not file a joint gift tax return.

If you and your spouse agree, all gifts either of you make to third parties during the calendar year may be considered as made one-half by each of you if:

- you and your spouse were married to one another at the time of the gift;
- you did not remarry during the rest of the calendar year;
- neither of you was a nonresident alien at the time of the gift; and
- you did not give your spouse a general power of appointment over the property interest transferred.

If you transferred property partly to your spouse and partly to third parties, you can only split the gifts if the interest transferred to the third parties is ascertainable at the time of the gift.

If you meet these requirements and want your gifts to be considered made one-half by you and one-half by your spouse, check the "Yes" box on line 11, page 1; complete lines 12 through 16; and have your spouse sign the consent on line 17. If you are not married or do not wish to split gifts, skip to Schedule A.

Line 14.—If you were married to one another for the entire calendar year, check the "Yes" box and skip to line 16. If you were married for only part of the year, check the "No" box and go to line 15.

Line 15.—Check the box that explains the change in your marital status during the year and give the date you were married, divorced, or widowed.

Consent of Spouse

To have your gifts (and generation-skipping transfers) considered as made one-half by each of you, your spouse must sign the consent. The consent may generally be signed at any time after the end of the calendar year. However, there are two exceptions. They are:

1. The consent may not be signed after April 15 following the end of the year in which the gift was made. (But, if neither you nor your spouse has filed a gift tax return for the year on or before that date, the consent must be made on the first gift tax return for the year filed by either of you.)
2. The consent may not be signed after a notice of deficiency for the gift or GST tax for the year has been sent to either you or your spouse.

The executor for a deceased spouse or the guardian for a legally incompetent spouse may sign the consent.

The consent is effective for the entire calendar year; therefore, all gifts made by both you and your spouse to third parties during the calendar year (while you were married) must be split.

If the consent is effective, the liability for the entire gift and GST taxes of each spouse is joint and several.

When the Consenting Spouse Must Also File a Gift Tax Return.—If the spouses elect gift splitting (described under "Split Gifts," above), then both the donor spouse and the consenting spouse must each file separate gift tax returns unless all the requirements of either Exceptions 1 or 2 below are met.

Exception 1.—During the calendar year:
- Only one spouse made any gifts;
- The total value of these gifts to each third-party donee does not exceed $20,000; and
- All of these gifts constitute present interests.

Exception 2.—During the calendar year:
- Only one spouse (the donor spouse) made gifts of more than $10,000 but not more than $20,000 to any third-party donee;
- The only gifts made by the other spouse (the consenting spouse) were gifts of not more than $10,000 to third-party donees other than those to whom the donor spouse made gifts; and
- All of the gifts by both spouses constitute present interests.

If either Exception 1 or 2 is met, only the donor spouse needs to file a return and the consenting spouse signifies consent on that return. This return may be made on **Form 709-A, United States Short Form Gift Tax Return**. This form is much easier to complete than Form 709, and you should consider filing it whenever your gifts to each third-party donee are not more than $20,000 for the year.

Schedule A.—Computation of Taxable Gifts

Do not enter on Schedule A any gift or part of a gift that qualifies for the political organization, educational, or medical exclusions. In the instructions below, "gifts" means gifts (or parts of gifts) that do not qualify for the political organization, educational, or medical exclusions.

Gifts to Donees Other Than Your Spouse.—You must always enter all gifts of *future interests* that you made during the calendar year regardless of their value.

If you do not elect gift splitting.—If the total gifts of *present interests* to any donee are more than $10,000 in the calendar year, then you must enter *all such gifts* that you made during the year to or on behalf of that donee, including those gifts that will be excluded under the annual exclusion. If the total is $10,000 or less, you need not enter on Schedule A any gifts (except gifts of future interests) that you made to that donee.

If you elect gift splitting.—Enter on Schedule A the entire value of every gift you made during the calendar year while you were married, even if the gift's value will be less than $10,000 after it is split on line 2 of Part 3.

Gifts to Your Spouse.—If you were a citizen or resident during the entire calendar year, you do not need to enter any of your gifts to your spouse on Schedule A unless you gave a gift of a terminable interest to your spouse or you gave a gift of a future interest to your spouse as described below.

Terminable interest.—If you gave your spouse any terminable interest that does not qualify as a life estate with power of appointment (defined on page 5), you must report on Schedule A *only* gifts of terminable interests you made to your spouse during the year. You should not report any gifts you made to your spouse that are not terminable interests; however, you must report all terminable interests, whether or not they can be deducted.

Future interest.— If you gave a gift of a future interest to your spouse and you are required to report the gift on Form 709 because you gave the present interest to a donee other than your spouse, then you should enter the entire gift, including the future interest given to your spouse, on Schedule A. You should use the rules under "Gifts Subject to Both Gift and GST Taxes," below, to determine where to enter the gift on Schedule A.

Charitable remainder trusts.—If you make a gift to a charitable remainder trust and your spouse is the only noncharitable beneficiary (other than yourself), the interest you gave to your spouse is not considered a terminable interest and therefore should not be shown on Schedule A. For definitions and rules concerning these trusts, see section 2056(b)(8)(B) and Regulations section 20.2055-2.

Nonresident aliens.—If you were a nonresident alien at any time during the year, you must enter *all* gifts you made to your spouse during the year.

If you need more space than that provided, attach a separate sheet, using the same format as Schedule A.

How To Complete Schedule A.—After you determine which gifts you made are subject to the gift tax and therefore should be listed on Schedule A, you must divide these gifts between those subject only to the gift tax (gifts made to non-skip persons—see page 4) and those subject to both the gift and GST taxes (gifts made to skip persons—see page 4). Gifts made to non-skip persons are entered on Part 1. Gifts made to skip persons are entered on Part 2.

Gifts Subject to Both Gift and GST Taxes.—

Direct Skip.—The GST tax to be reported on Form 709 is imposed only on inter vivos direct skips. An "inter vivos direct skip" is a gift that: (1) is subject to the gift tax; (2) is an interest in property; and (3) is made to a skip person. All three requirements must be met before the gift is subject to the GST tax. A gift is "subject to the gift tax" if you are required to list it on Schedule A of Form 709

Page 3

120

(as described above). To determine if a gift "is of an interest in property" and "is made to a skip person," you must first determine if the donee is a "person" or a "trust" as defined below.

Trust.—For purposes of the GST tax, "trust" includes not only an explicit trust, but also any other arrangement (other than an estate) which although not explicitly a trust, has substantially the same effect as a trust. For example, "trust" includes life estates with remainders, terms for years, and insurance and annuity contracts.

Person.—A "person" is any donee that is not a trust.

Interest in Property.—If a gift is made to a "person," it is always considered a gift of an interest in property for purposes of the GST tax.

If a gift is made to a "trust," a person will have an interest in the property transferred to the trust if that person either has a present right to receive income or corpus from the trust (such as an income interest for life) or is a permissible current recipient of income or corpus from the trust (e.g., possesses a general power of appointment).

Skip Person.—A donee who is a "natural person" is a "skip person" if that donee is assigned to a generation which is two or more generations below the generation assignment of the donor. See "Determining the Generation of a Donee," below.

A donee who is a "trust" is a "skip person" if all the interests in the property transferred to the trust (as defined above) are held by skip persons.

A trust will also be a "skip person" if there are no interests in the property transferred to the trust held by any person, and future distributions or terminations from the trust can be made only to skip persons.

Non-Skip Person.—A non-skip person is any donee who is not a skip person.

Determining the Generation of a Donee.—Generally, a generation is determined along family lines as follows:

(1) A lineal descendant of a grandparent of the donor is assigned to the generation that results from comparing the number of generations between the grandparent and the descendant with the number of generations between the grandparent and the donor.

(2) A lineal descendant of a grandparent of a spouse (or former spouse) of the donor (other than the spouse; see (3), below) is assigned to the generation that results from comparing the number of generations between the grandparent and the descendant with the number of generations between the spouse (or former spouse) and the grandparent.

(3) A person who at any time was married to a person described in (1) or (2) above is assigned to the generation of that person. A person who at any time was married to the donor is assigned to the donor's generation.

(4) A relationship by adoption or half-blood is treated as a relationship by whole-blood.

(5) A person who is not assigned to a generation according to (1), (2), (3), or (4) above is assigned to a generation based on his or her birth date as follows:

(a) A person who was born not more than 12½ years after the donor is in the donor's generation.

(b) A person born more than 12½ years, but not more than 37½ years, after the donor is in the first generation younger than the donor.

(c) Similar rules apply for a new generation every 25 years.

If more than one of the rules for assigning generations applies to a donee, that donee is generally assigned to the youngest of the generations that would apply.

If an estate or trust, partnership, corporation, or other entity (other than certain charitable organizations and trusts described in sections 511(a)(2) and 511(b)(2) and governmental entities) is a donee, then each person who indirectly receives the gift through the entity is treated as a donee and is assigned to a generation as explained in the above rules.

Generation Assignment Where Intervening Parent Is Dead.—If you made a gift to your grandchild and at the time you made the gift, the grandchild's parent (who is your or your spouse's or your former spouse's child) is dead, then for purposes of generation assignment your grandchild will be considered to be your child rather than your grandchild. Your grandchild's children will be treated as your grandchildren rather than your greatgrandchildren. (However, gifts to your greatgrandchildren under these circumstances would not qualify for the grandchild exclusion.)

This rule is also applied to your lineal descendants below the level of grandchild. For example, if your grandchild is dead, your greatgrandchildren who are lineal descendants of the dead grandchild are considered your grandchildren for purposes of the GST tax.

Charitable organizations and trusts described in sections 511(a)(2) and 511(b)(2) and governmental entities are assigned to the donor's generation. Transfers to such organizations are therefore not subject to the GST tax. These gifts should always be listed in Part 1 of Schedule A.

Charitable Remainder Trusts.—Gifts in the form of charitable remainder annuity trusts, charitable remainder unitrusts, and pooled income funds are not considered made to skip persons and therefore are not direct skips. You should always list these gifts on Part 1 of Schedule A even if all of the life beneficiaries are skip persons.

The rules above can be illustrated by the following examples:

Example 1.—You give your house to your daughter for her life with the remainder then passing to her children. This gift is made to a "trust" even though there is no explicit trust instrument. The interest in the property transferred (the present right to use the house) is transferred to a non-skip person (your daughter). Therefore, the trust is not a skip person because there is an interest in the transferred property that is held by a non-skip person. The gift is not a direct skip and you should list it on Part 1 of Schedule A.

Example 2.—You give $100,000 to your grandchild. This gift is a direct skip that is not made in trust. You should list it on Part 2 of Schedule A even if you will later use part of your grandchild exclusion to exempt it from the GST tax.

Example 3.—You establish a trust that is required to accumulate income for 10 years and then pay its income to your grandchildren for their lives and upon their deaths distribute the corpus to their children. Since the trust has no current beneficiaries, there are no present interests in the property transferred to the trust. All of the persons to whom the trust can make future distributions (including distributions upon the termination of interests in property held in trust) are skip persons (i.e., your grandchildren and greatgrandchildren). Therefore, the trust itself is a skip person and you should list the gift on Part 2 of Schedule A.

Example 4.—You establish a trust which pays all of its income to your grandchildren for 10 years. At the end of 10 years, the corpus is to be distributed to your children. All of the interests in this trust are held by skip persons. Therefore, the trust is a skip person and you should list the entire amount you transferred to the trust on Part 2 of Schedule A even though some of the trust's ultimate beneficiaries are non-skip persons.

Part 1.—List gifts subject only to the gift tax on Part 1. Generally, all of the gifts you made to your spouse (that are required to be listed, as described earlier), to your children, and to charitable organizations are not subject to the GST tax and should, therefore, be listed only on Part 1.

Group the gifts in four categories: gifts made to your spouse; gifts made to third parties that are to be split with your spouse; charitable gifts (if you are not splitting gifts with your spouse); and other gifts. If a transfer results in gifts to two or more individuals (such as a life estate to one with remainder to the other), list the gift to each separately.

Number and describe all gifts (including charitable, public, and similar gifts) in the columns provided in Schedule A. Describe each gift in enough detail so that the property can be easily identified, as explained below.

For real estate provide:
● a legal description of each parcel;
● the street number, name, and area if the property is located in a city; and
● a short statement of any improvements made to the property.

For bonds, give:
● the number of bonds transferred;
● the principal amount of each bond;
● name of obligor;
● date of maturity;
● rate of interest;
● date or dates when interest is payable;
● series number if there is more than one issue;
● exchanges where listed or, if unlisted, give the location of the principal business office of corporation; and
● CUSIP number, if available. The CUSIP number is a nine-digit number assigned by the American Banking Association to traded securities.

For stocks:

- give number of shares;
- state whether common or preferred;
- if preferred, give the issue, par value, quotation at which returned, and exact name of corporation;
- if unlisted on a principal exchange, give location of principal business office of corporation, state in which incorporated, and date of incorporation;
- if listed, give principal exchange; and
- give CUSIP number, if available. The CUSIP number is a nine-digit number assigned by the American Banking Association to traded securities.

For interests in property based on the length of a person's life, give the date of birth of the person.

For life insurance policies, give the name of the insurer and the policy number.

Donor's Adjusted Basis of Gifts.—Show the basis you would use for income tax purposes if the gift were sold or exchanged. Generally, this means cost plus improvements, less applicable depreciation, amortization, and depletion.

For more information on adjusted basis, please see **Publication 551**, Basis of Assets.

Date and Value of Gift.—The value of a gift is the fair market value of the property on the date the gift is made. The fair market value is the price at which the property would change hands between a willing buyer and a willing seller, when neither is forced to buy or to sell, and when both have reasonable knowledge of all relevant facts. Fair market value may not be determined by a forced sale price, nor by the sale price of the item in a market other than that in which the item is most commonly sold to the public. The location of the item must be taken into account wherever appropriate.

Stock of close corporations or inactive stock must be valued on the basis of net worth, earnings, earning and dividend capacity, and other relevant factors.

Supplemental Documents.—To support the value of your gifts, you must provide information showing how it was determined.

For stock of close corporations or inactive stock, attach balance sheets, particularly the one nearest the date of the gift, and statements of net earnings or operating results and dividends paid for each of the five preceding years.

For each life insurance policy, attach **Form 712**, Life Insurance Statement.

Note for single premium or paid-up policies: *In certain situations, for example, where the surrender value of the policy exceeds its replacement cost, the true economic value of the policy will be greater than the amount shown on line 56 of Form 712. In these situations, you should report the full economic value of the policy on Schedule A. See Rev. Rul. 78-137, 1978-1 C.B. 280 for details.*

If the gift was made by means of a trust, attach a certified or verified copy of the trust instrument.

Also attach appraisal lists, such as any appraisal used to determine the value of real estate.

If you do not attach this information, you must include in Schedule A full information to explain how the value was determined.

Part 2.—List on Part 2 only those gifts that are subject to both the gift and GST taxes. **You must list the gifts on Part 2 in the chronological order that you made them.** Number, describe, and value the gifts as described in the instructions for Part 1, above.

If you made a gift in "trust," list the entire gift as one line entry in Part 2. Enter the entire value of the property transferred to the "trust" even if the "trust" has non-skip person future beneficiaries.

Part 3.—Gift Tax Reconciliation

Line 1.—Add the value of all your gifts shown on column E, Parts 1 and 2. Enter the total on line 1.

Line 2.—If you are not splitting gifts with your spouse, skip this line and enter the amount from line 1 on line 3. If you are splitting gifts with your spouse, show half of the gifts you made to third parties on line 2. On the dotted line indicate which numbered items from Parts 1 and 2 of Schedule A you treated this way.

Line 4.—If you are not splitting gifts, skip this line and go to line 5. If you gave all of the gifts, and your spouse is only filing to show his or her half of those gifts, you need not enter any gifts on line 4 of your return, or include your spouse's half anywhere else on your return. Your spouse should enter the amount from Schedule A, line 2, of your return on Schedule A, line 4, of his or her return. If both you and your spouse make gifts for which a return is required, the amount each of you shows on Schedule A, line 2, of his or her return must be shown on Schedule A, line 4, of the other's return.

Line 6.—Enter the total annual exclusions you are claiming for the gifts listed on Schedule A (including gifts listed on line 4). See "Annual Exclusion" on page 2. If you split a gift with your spouse, the annual exclusion you claim against that gift may not be more than your half of the gift.

Deductions

Line 8.—Enter on line 8 all of the gifts to your spouse which you listed on Schedule A and for which you are claiming a marital deduction. **Do not enter any gift that you did not include on Schedule A.** On the dotted line on line 8, indicate which numbered items from Schedule A are gifts to your spouse for which you are claiming the marital deduction.

Nonresident aliens.—If you were a nonresident alien for the entire calendar year, enter "-0-" on line 8. If you were a citizen or resident of the U.S. for part of the calendar year, you may claim a marital deduction for gifts you made to your spouse while you were a citizen or resident of the U.S. even if your spouse was a nonresident alien. You may deduct all gifts of nonterminable interests made during this time that you entered on Schedule A regardless of amount, and certain gifts of terminable interests as outlined below. **Do not enter on line 8 any gifts to your spouse that were made while you were a nonresident alien.**

Note: *Beginning with gifts made after July 13, 1988, no marital deduction is allowed for any gifts to a spouse who is not a U.S. citizen. The annual exclusion for such gifts (and only those gifts) has been increased from $10,000 to $100,000, however.*

Citizens or residents of the U.S.—You may deduct all gifts to your U.S. citizen spouse of nonterminable interests that you entered on Schedule A regardless of their amount, and regardless of whether they are future interests. Terminable interests are deducted according to the rules below.

Terminable Interests.—Generally, you cannot take the marital deduction if the gift to your spouse is a terminable interest. Some examples of terminable interests are:

- a life estate;
- an estate for a specified number of years; or
- any other property interest that after a period of time will terminate or fail.

If you transfer an interest to your spouse as sole joint tenant with yourself or as a tenant by the entirety, the interest is not considered a terminable interest just because the tenancy may be severed.

Life Estate With Power of Appointment.—You may deduct, without an election, a gift of a terminable interest if all four requirements below are met:

1. your spouse is entitled for life to all of the income from the entire interest;
2. the income is paid yearly or more often;
3. your spouse has the unlimited power, while he or she is alive or by will, to appoint the entire interest in all circumstances; and
4. no part of the entire interest is subject to another person's power of appointment (except to appoint it to your spouse).

If only part of the property interest meets the above requirements, see Publication 448 for the part that qualifies for the marital deduction.

Election To Deduct Qualified Terminable Interest Property (QTIP).—You may elect to deduct a gift of a terminable interest if it meets requirements 1, 2, and 4 above, even though it does not meet requirement 3.

Make the election by checking the box on line 16 of Schedule A and entering the appropriate item numbers from Schedule A. You may not make the election on a late filed Form 709.

Note: *A recent amendment to section 2523 provides an automatic QTIP election for gifts of certain joint and survivor annuities. The donor spouse may elect out of QTIP treatment by attaching a letter to the Form 709 indicating which annuity(ies) is not being treated as QTIP property. For details, see section 2523(f)(6).*

Line 9.—Enter the amount of the annual exclusions that were claimed for the gifts you listed on line 8.

Line 11.—You may deduct from the total gifts made during the calendar year all gifts you gave to or for the use of:

- The United States, a State or political subdivision of a State or the District of Columbia, for exclusively public purposes;

- Any corporation, trust, community chest, fund, or foundation organized and operated only for religious, charitable, scientific, literary, or educational purposes, or to prevent cruelty to children or animals, or to foster national or international amateur sports competition (if none of its activities involve providing athletic equipment (unless it is a qualified amateur sports organization)), as long as no part of the earnings benefits any one person, no substantial propaganda is produced, and no lobbying or campaigning for any candidate for public office is done;

- A fraternal society, order, or association operating under a lodge system, if the transferred property is to be used only for religious, charitable, scientific, literary, or educational purposes, including the encouragement of art and the prevention of cruelty to children or animals;

- Any war veterans organization organized in the United States (or any of its possessions), or any of its auxiliary departments or local chapters or posts, as long as no part of any of the earnings benefits any one person.

On line 11, show your total charitable, public, or similar gifts (minus exclusions allowed). On the dotted line indicate which numbered items from the top of Schedule A are charitable gifts.

See Publication 448 for more information.

Line 14.—If you did not list any gifts on Part 2, enter "-0-" on line 14. If you entered gifts on Part 2, or if you and your spouse elected gift splitting and your spouse made gifts subject to the GST tax that you are required to show on your Form 709, complete Schedule C, and enter on line 14 the total of Schedule C, Part 4, column H.

Line 16.—If you make the election under section 2523(f), the terminable interest property involved will be included in your spouse's gross estate upon his or her death (section 2044). If your spouse disposes (by gift or otherwise) of all or part of the qualifying life income interest, he or she will be considered to have made a transfer of the entire property that is subject to the gift tax (see "Transfer of Certain Life Estates" on page 2).

Schedule B.—Gifts From Prior Periods

If you did not file gift tax returns for previous periods, check the "No" box at the top of Schedule B and skip to the Tax Computation on page 1. (However, be sure to complete Schedule C, if applicable.) If you filed gift tax returns for previous periods, check the "Yes" box and complete Schedule B by listing the years or quarters in chronological order as described below. If you need more space than that provided, attach a separate sheet, using the same format as Schedule B.

If you filed returns for gifts made before 1971 or after 1981, show the calendar years in column A. If you filed returns for gifts made after 1970 and before 1982, show the calendar quarters.

In column B, identify the Internal Revenue Service office where you filed the returns. If you have changed your name, be sure to list any other names under which the returns were filed. If there was any other variation in the names under which you filed, such as the use of full given names instead of initials, please explain.

In column E, show the correct amount (the amount finally determined) of the taxable gifts for each earlier period.

Schedule C.—Computation of Generation-Skipping Transfer Tax

Part 1.—Generation-Skipping Transfers
You must enter on Part 1 all of the gifts you listed on Part 2 of Schedule A in that order and using those same values.

Column C.—If you elected gift splitting, enter half the value of each gift entered in column B. If you did not elect gift splitting, enter "-0-" in column C.

Column E.—You are allowed to claim the gift tax annual exclusion with respect to your generation-skipping transfers, using the rules and limits discussed earlier for the gift tax annual exclusion. However, you must allocate the exclusion on a gift by gift basis for GST computation purposes. Be sure that you do not claim a total exclusion of more than $10,000 per donee (or $100,000 if applicable; see instructions for "Annual Exclusion" on page 2).

Column G.—For any gift that was not made to your grandchild(ren), enter "-0-" in column G. If you made gifts to your grandchild(ren), complete columns A–C of Schedule C, Part 2, to determine your available exclusion amount(s), before completing column G. An aggregate grandchild exclusion of $2,000,000 per grandchild is allowed for transfers made before January 1, 1990. This exclusion is not optional. You must allocate it to gifts to your grandchildren in the chronological order that the gifts were made until the $2,000,000 per grandchild limit is reached. Note that in column E, Part 2 of Schedule C, you will compute the remaining exclusion for each grandchild, while in column G, Part 1, you will enter the exclusion on a gift by gift basis. A gift may be made to more than one grandchild, and more than one grandchild's exclusion may therefore be combined on each entry of column G. The total of all the entries in column G must equal the total of all the entries in column D, Part 2, Schedule C.

If you transferred property to your grandchild in trust, you may claim a grandchild exclusion only if the following conditions are met:

(1) during the life of the grandchild, the corpus and income of the trust may only be distributed to the grandchild;

(2) if the grandchild dies before the trust is terminated, the assets of the trust will be included in the grandchild's gross estate for Federal estate tax purposes (e.g., the grandchild had a general power of appointment over the trust); and,

(3) all trust income after the grandchild reaches the age of 21 will be distributed to the grandchild at least annually (applies only to transfers after June 10, 1987).

Part 2.—Grandchild Exclusion Reconciliation
Enter on Part 2 the name of each grandchild to whom you made gifts listed on this Form 709. If you elected gift splitting, also enter the name of each grandchild to whom your spouse made gifts that you are reporting on this Form 709.

Part 3.—GST Exemption Reconciliation
Line 5.—You may wish to allocate your exemption to transfers made in "trust" that are not direct skips. For example, if you transferred property to a trust that has your children as its present beneficiaries and your grandchildren and greatgrandchildren as future beneficiaries, the transfer was not a direct skip because the present interests in the trust are held by non-skip persons. However, future terminations and distributions made from this trust would be subject to the GST tax. You may elect to reduce the trust's inclusion ratio by allocating part or all of your exemption to the transfer. Since this transfer would be entered on Schedule A, Part 1, it will not be shown on Schedule C. In other cases you may wish to allocate your exemption to a trust which is not involved in a transfer listed on Schedule A or C.

To allocate your exemption to such a transfer, you should attach a statement to this Form 709 and entitle it "Notice of Allocation." You may file one Notice of Allocation and consolidate on it all of your Schedule A, Part 1, transfers to which you wish to allocate your exemption. The notice should contain the following for each "trust":

- The trust's EIN, if known;
- The item number(s) from column A, Schedule A, Part 1, of the gifts to that trust;
- The values shown in column E, Schedule A, Part 1 for the gifts;
- The annual exclusion claimed against each gift;
- The net value of each gift after the reduction for the annual exclusion, if applicable; and
- The amount of your GST exemption allocated to each gift.

Total the exemption allocations and enter this total on line 5.

Part 4.—Tax Computation
You must enter on Part 4 every gift you listed on Part 1 of Schedule C.

Column C.—Unlike the grandchild exclusion, you are not required to allocate your available exemption. You may allocate some, all, or none of your available exemption, as you wish, among the gifts listed in Part 4 of Schedule C. However, the total exemption claimed in column C may not exceed the amount you entered on line 3 of Part 3 of Schedule C.

You may enter an amount in column C that is greater than the amount you entered in column B.

Column D.—Carry your computation to three decimal places (i.e., "1.000").

Page 6

123

Part 2.—Tax Computation (Page 1)

Lines 5a–c and 8a–c.—If you are reporting gifts made before January 1, 1988, skip lines 5a–c and lines 8a–c. Enter the amount from line 4 on line 6. Enter the amount from line 7 on line 9.

Line 11.—If you are a citizen or resident of the United States, you must take any available unified credit against gift tax. Nonresident aliens may not claim the unified credit. If you are a nonresident alien, delete the 192,800 entry and write-in "-0-" on line 11.

Line 14.—Enter 20% of the amount allowed as a specific exemption for gifts made after September 8, 1976, and before January 1, 1977. (These amounts will be among those listed in column D of Schedule B, for gifts made in the third and fourth quarters of 1976.)

Line 17.—Gift tax conventions are in effect with France, the United Kingdom, Australia, West Germany, and Japan. If you are claiming a credit for payment of foreign gift tax, figure the credit on an attached sheet and attach evidence that the foreign taxes were paid. See the applicable convention for details of computing the credit.

Line 23.—Make your check or money order payable to "Internal Revenue Service" and write the donor's social security number on it. You may not use an overpayment on Form 1040 to offset the gift and GST taxes owed on Form 709.

Signature.—You, as a donor, must sign the return. If you pay another person, firm, or corporation to prepare your return, that person must also sign the return as preparer unless he or she is your regular full-time employee.

Table for Computing Tax

Column A	Column B	Column C	Column D
Taxable amount over—	Taxable amount not over—	Tax on amount in Column A	Rate of tax on excess over amount in Column A
--------	$10,000	--------	18%
$10,000	20,000	$1,800	20%
20,000	40,000	3,800	22%
40,000	60,000	8,200	24%
60,000	80,000	13,000	26%
80,000	100,000	18,200	28%
100,000	150,000	23,800	30%
150,000	250,000	38,800	32%
250,000	500,000	70,800	34%
500,000	750,000	155,800	37%
750,000	1,000,000	248,300	39%
1,000,000	1,250,000	345,800	41%
1,250,000	1,500,000	448,300	43%
1,500,000	2,000,000	555,800	45%
2,000,000	2,500,000	780,800	49%
2,500,000	3,000,000	1,025,800	53%
3,000,000	----------	1,290,800	55%

7 BORROW THE DOWNPAYMENT FROM FAMILY OR FRIENDS

INTRODUCTION

The prices of homes, particularly new homes, have soared in recent years. For many young couples or others attempting to enter the housing market for the first time, the cost of a new home, particularly the downpayment, is elusively out of reach. An approach that many first-time home buyers have resorted to is obtaining assistance from their parents. Chapters 6, 7, and 8 present a number of ways in which parents can help their children come up with the cash necessary to close on a house. The parents can make an outright (no legal strings attached) gift of money to the children (Chapter 6); they can lend their children money, at least initially expecting (this may later change) that the money will be repaid (see below); or the parents may participate in some form of co-ownership (equity sharing and the like) in the house with their children (Chapter 8). In some cases the parents may wish to use a hybrid or combination of these various alternatives to assist their children.

CAUTION: Because of the complexities that can arise, it is important at the outset to determine which type of arrangement the parents wish to have. The income tax, estate-planning, and cash-flow consequences can be dramatically different. The legal documents that must be prepared for each type of arrangement are also completely different. For example, there are important legal differences between making a loan to a child where part (or all) of the interest is based on the appreciation in the value of the house (an equity kicker), versus an equity-sharing arrangement, where the parent actually owns an interest in the house. If you're not absolutely positive which approach is the correct one, consult your attorney, accountant, and financial planner. At a minimum you should discuss the issues with the attorney you've hired to complete the necessary legal documents. Review Chapters 6, 7, and 8 first. An understanding of the different options will help you reach a conclusion with your adviser faster and thus keep fees lower.

In most cases, the rules applicable to parents making loans to their children will apply if another relative, friend, or even investor is involved. The notable exception is that where an unrelated investor is involved, the gift and estate tax considerations will obviously be different. In addition, the IRS tends to be somewhat less suspicious of transactions between unrelated taxpayers. However, for simplicity, it will be assumed in this chapter that the lender (at least for a portion of the money) will be the parent, and the borrowers will be their children.

TIP: An unrelated investor, perhaps one found with the assistance of your broker or through a newspaper advertisement, shouldn't be overlooked as a potential source of money. Investors other than the seller can also benefit from the higher interest rates they can earn on a loan to a homeowner, as compared with what they can earn on many alternative investment opportunities.

While the important personal and emotional issues involved in a decision by parents to lend their children money to buy a home can be paramount for many, the legal, tax and financing consequences—for example how the loan affects the children's ability to qualify for additional mortgage financing—shouldn't be overlooked. This chapter will highlight a number of the factors to be considered when parents help their children by lending them money for the downpayment (or closing costs, moving expenses, furniture, or other needs) on their first (or other) home.

THE BASIC OPTIONS FOR THE LOAN ARRANGEMENT

There are a number of important possibilities to consider when parents lend their children money, even before the legal, tax, and other considerations can be reviewed, because they have implications for all these other factors.

Interest Rate: What interest rate will the parents charge on the loan?

- No interest charged—an interest-free loan. The children will have to repay only the principal amount of money borrowed. The parents aren't concerned about the income and merely want to protect themselves should the children become divorced, be sued by creditors, or have some other unforeseeable financial problem. Perhaps the parents have sufficient income now but want to protect their ability to obtain the money back in case of a financial setback of their own later, or a desire to use the money during their retirement. Interest-free loans have important tax consequences discussed below.

- Low interest rate. If the rate of interest a typical home buyer would have to pay for mortgage money is, say, 11.5 percent, and the parents decide to charge the children only 5 percent, there will be important tax consequences that are discussed below.

- Market-rate interest. The parents may decide to charge the children about the same rate of interest that they would pay to get a mortgage loan elsewhere. Paying parents the same interest rate that would be required with two unrelated people negotiating a fair loan (called "arm's-length" in tax jargon) eliminates some of the thorny tax problems. There will still be important tax considerations, however (discussed below). A loan at market-interest rates is an approach that can benefit both parents and children. The interest rate the parents receive can be higher than the one at which the parents borrowed, or, more likely, if the parents are taking money out of a money market fund, higher than the rate they're earning. It can also be a great deal for the children, because the interest rate the parents charge can still be much lower than the rate the children would have to pay for a comparable mortgage loan on their own, particularly if they have short or no job histories. These advantages may make good ammunition for children trying to convince their parents to help out with a loan.

Loan Term: The term of the loan is also important. The term is the period of time before the loan is due (matures). At this time, the principal amount (the amount borrowed without considering interest) and any remaining unpaid interest must be paid. There are generally three types of terms that are used:

- A demand loan. A demand loan doesn't have any set due date. The parents can require the children to repay the loan anytime they want to. All they have to do is demand the money back. While this sounds frightening—where do you get the money in one day to repay the loan?—remember that the lenders are your parents and not an insensitive, unfeeling financial institution. Nevertheless, the parents legally have the right to insist on repayment at anytime, and if they are not repaid and the legal documents permit, take the house and sell it to obtain their money. Many parents lending money to their children use a demand loan because it gives them this important element of control. If they see things happening they don't like, they can always get their money back quickly. If the children indicate the possibility of divorce, if creditors are on the children's backs, if the son-in-law develops a penchant for drinking and gambling, or if there is any other concern, the parents have control. This control is often an important consideration that encourages parents to make the loan. There can be important tax consequences to some demand loans, and these are discussed below.

- A loan for a fixed term. If the loan isn't due on demand, a fixed due date should be stated in the loan documents. At the due date all principal and interest payments will have to be repaid. Some parents may want to link the maturity date of the loan to when they begin retirement and will want the money, or some other time that has particular financial significance to them. A common approach is to use a relatively short term such as five years. This is because the parents and children generally anticipate that the children's earnings will increase and they will be able to repay the small (relative to the bank mortgage) loan to the parents, or if it is a large loan, to refinance the house and repay the parents.

CAUTION: It is important to consider the due date carefully when the loan is initially made. If the loan is made due in three years, and the couple have two children and one of them gives up working to raise the children in the interim, repayment could be a tremendous hardship, and refinancing with only one wage-earning spouse impossible. If the lender is anyone other than the parent this may be one of the most important considerations in negotiating a loan—an unrelated investor may not be the least bit concerned about your financial predicament.

- Balloon loan. In a balloon loan there is a large payment owed when the loan comes due. The best way to understand a balloon loan is to compare it to a regular (self-amortizing) loan. In a regular loan you make payments each month of the same amount of money. At the end of the loan term the entire loan, including interest, has been repaid through the equal monthly installments. A balloon loan, on the other hand, may require a very large payment at the end. This means that you will typically have to refinance the loan when the balloon payment is due.

EXAMPLE: In Chapter 5, the sellers provided financing of $105,000 for the buyer at 13-percent interest with monthly payments of $971.21. At the end of 10 years the buyer will have a balloon payment due. The reason is simple: the sellers agreed to finance the buyer and not pull all of their money out of the house, but they didn't want to wait more than 10 years to be paid. The buyer couldn't afford to make the $1,550.96 monthly payments required to pay off (amortize) over this 10-year period. This is $579.75 more per month than he is paying now. Instead, the buyer arranged the loan with installments that would repay the entire loan over 25 years, and only the balance remaining after 10 years of payments will have to be repaid.

Miscellaneous Matters: There are a number of other terms or provisions of the loan that require consideration.

- Collateral or security. When a bank lends you money to buy a home, you give the bank a mortgage on your home. This gives the bank certain rights (interests) in the house if you don't make the mortgage payments as agreed. Thus, the bank's interest in your house provides it security against default. Parents making a loan to their children may or may not want any security other than the children's promise to repay the money. In fact, some parents may not even want the children's agreement to repay the money but obtain it to avoid certain gift tax problems discussed below. The most common security is the house itself. Careful attention must be given to the requirements of the bank (or other lender) where the children are getting their mortgage. The children's attorney should review the loan documents with the bank to be certain there are no problems with the parents taking a second mortgage on the house. At a minimum, the bank is certainly going to want disclosure of the fact that the parents have made the loan.

CAUTION: If the bank wants the parents to sign a Gift Certification Letter, which states that the money was an outright gift by the parents to the children and not a loan, they can't do it. If proper legal documents for a loan are used it would be fraud for the parents to sign anything saying the money was a gift. In such a situation, if the bank relies on the parents' Gift Certification Letter in determining to make the loan, the bank could sue the parents if the children later default on the loan. Signing such a letter would also compromise the parents' position with the IRS that the transaction was a loan and not a gift. This could have adverse gift tax consequences as well. The IRS may also assess interest and penalty charges.

There is another very important implication to the security. If the children's home doesn't serve as security for the loan, the children may not be able to deduct the interest paid (see below).

- Notice. An important right that the children (or others) borrowing money for the purchase of a home should understand is the notice and opportunity to cure provision. If you fail to make a payment on the loan when required, you don't want the lender (whether your parents or an unrelated investor) to have the legal right to immediately declare you in default on the loan and be able to begin legal proceedings to take your house. You may have mailed the check, and the mail is simply late. In short, you want a couple of days (at least!) to try to make good on the payment you owe for that month (a grace period). If somehow you violated some other requirement in the loan agreement, you would at least like a letter or phone call from the lender (notice) telling you the problem and giving you some time to correct it. Examples of problems are: you may have missed a property tax payment or not insured the home for a sufficient amount of money.

- Assignability. If your parents make a loan to you to buy a house, the loan probably won't be assignable by either of you. You don't want your parents to be able to sell or assign to a bank, investor, or anyone else, the loan they made to you, particularly if it's a demand loan. Similarly, if your parents make a loan to help you buy a house, they may not want you to be able to sell the house and let another buyer assume their loan.

If an unrelated investor is involved, the situation is somewhat different. The investor is unlikely to allow you to assign the loan to someone else, since the investor may want to be able to check out the credit of whoever is responsible for the payments. The investor, however, may be willing to let you assign the loan if the value of the house (i.e., the security for the loan) is substantial, and if the investor has an opportunity to approve the assignment before it can be made. The investor may insist on keeping you liable on the loan even if your buyer assumes the primary responsibility to repay the loan.

It is common for many lenders to require that loans be due on sale. (If due on sale, the loan can't be assigned.) This is the lender's insurance that if interest rates rise, the money can be reloaned at the current higher rates. Still another possibility is that the investor will insist that he or she can assign the loan. If in a year or two the investor needs money, he or she can sell your loan to another investor. If you had no personal relationship with the first investor, you should not be that concerned if the loan is assigned so long as you receive adequate notice that it is being assigned.

- Acceleration. For any kind of loan other than a demand loan, the lender, even if it's your parents, will usually require a provision that allows the lender to make the entire loan due immediately if you miss a payment. The reason is that if the loan agreements didn't give the lender this right, the lender would have to sue separately to obtain each monthly payment owed. If a payment is missed and the lender can accelerate all payments under the loan, only one suit need be brought. Further, if you're late paying, the lender should have the right to get out of the loan.

There are a number of other important provisions in loan agreements. Many of these are contained in the sample loan documents contained in the For Your Notebook section in this chapter and in Chapter 5. The attorney you hire to put together the legal documents can review these, and other, provisions with you.

TAX CONSEQUENCES TO PARENTS/LENDERS OF LENDING MONEY FOR A DOWNPAYMENT

When parents, or an unrelated investor, make a loan to help you buy a house there are a number of important tax consequences to both you and the lender.

- The interest received is taxable.

- The interest the parents (or lender) pay to get the money they lend children may or may not be tax deductible. The limitations on deducting home-equity loans and the investment interest rules may curtail the parents' tax deductions. If the parents charge the children the going interest rate, and this rate is higher than the rate the parents pay to borrow the money they lend the children, then the parents' interest expense should be a tax deduction. The investment interest limitation rules discussed below should apply to this type of investment loan by the parents. The parents may borrow the money on their home-equity line and lend it at a modest interest rate (or no interest) to their children. The interest expense the parents pay on their home-equity loan should be deductible for tax purposes if the parents' loan meets the requirements of the home mortgage interest rules described below.

- If the interest rate on the loan is too low, there may be both gift tax and income tax implications to the parents.

- The gift and estate tax considerations of the parents may make a gift rather than a loan a better choice (assuming the personal considerations don't make a gift inappropriate).

TAX CONSEQUENCES TO CHILDREN/BORROWERS OF RECEIVING A LOAN FOR A DOWNPAYMENT

For the children, or other borrowers, there are also special tax consequences to consider when receiving a loan for a downpayment on a home.

- Is the interest paid to the parent or other lender deductible for tax purposes? The home-mortgage interest deduction rules must be considered. If these requirements are met, the interest paid should provide the children a tax deduction.

- If the loan is made by a parent at a low interest rate, there may be surprising income tax consequences.

The basic rules applicable to each of these tax consequences are reviewed in the discussions following.

THE HOME MORTGAGE INTEREST RULES

As noted above, if the loan the children receive from their parents meets the requirements of the home mortgage interest rules, the children will be able to deduct the interest they pay. In addition, if the parents borrow the money they lend the children on their home-equity line, the parents will qualify to deduct the interest on their loan if they meet the requirements for deducting home-equity loan interest (but see the investment limitation rules discussed in a later section).

There are a number of rules that limit the maximum amount of home mortgage interest that can be deducted. One factor is when the home mortgage was made. The following rules apply where a new home mortgage was taken out after October 13, 1987.

There are two parts to figuring out the maximum mortgage interest that can be deducted:

(1) The maximum amount of home mortgage on which you can deduct interest is $1 million used to acquire, construct, or substantially improve your primary home (principal residence) or your qualifying second home. One second home or vacation home qualifies if, in a year, you use it the greater of either 14 days or 10 percent of the number of days the second home is rented at a fair rental. This minimum-use test is waived if the vacation home sat idle all year. Your principal residence and qualifying second or vacation home are called "qualifying residences." The mortgage debt used to acquire your qualifying residences is called "acquisition indebtedness." The $1-million limit applies to both your principal residence and second home combined: you can't deduct interest on mortgages up to $1 million on each. The mortgages must be secured by a qualified first or second residence at the time the interest is paid.

(2) In addition to the acquisition indebtedness in (1), you are allowed to take out an additional amount of debt up to $100,000—which must be secured by a lien on your residence—and deduct the interest on it. This debt is called home-equity indebtedness and can be used for any purpose. It's common for parents to tap the equity in their home to get money to help their children break into the housing market. The tax deduction the parents may get for their loan will help defray the cost of helping their children.

The rules are a bit different if you took out a home mortgage or equity loan before October 13, 1987. Prior to the 1987 Tax Act (these rules are still important because they affect how much interest you can deduct now), you could take out mortgages and equity loans on your home up to the original purchase price of your home plus any amounts used to pay for qualifying tuition and medical expenses and deduct the interest. The total loans could not exceed the fair market value of your home.

There is one final wrinkle. If you took out your mortgages prior to August 17, 1986, you have even fewer restrictions. Mortgages taken out before this date, which are secured by a qualified residence, are generally not subject to any rules of the Tax Reform Act of 1986 or the 1987 Tax Act.

To qualify, the debt must be secured by an instrument (mortgage or loan agreement) that makes your ownership in the residence (your principal residence or qualified second home) specific security for the payment of the loan. The lender's security interest in your residence must be recorded (filed with the appropriate government agency) in accordance with applicable state law. The lender's security interest will be sufficient for the loan to be a qualified residence mortgage even if local laws make the security interest ineffective or only partially enforceable.

CAUTION: Well-meaning parents may decide that they trust the children and don't need to go through the formality and expense of placing a mortgage on their children's home. This act of kindness may end up costing the children important tax benefits. The interest they pay their parents may not qualify for the favorable home-mortgage interest deduction rules.

The parents may also jeopardize their own protection if they don't record their mortgage on the children's home, notes New York City real estate attorney Richard Hofflich. "If the parents' mortgage isn't recorded, the parents' lien on the children's home won't be protected from subsequent liens of record." This means that other creditors can foreclose on the children and collect on the value of the home before the parents.

The situation regarding cooperatives is that owners of cooperative apartments (or townhouses) are really tenant-shareholders. A cooperative corporation actually owns the building and other real estate, so that the owner is really a shareholder in the cooperative corporation and gets the right from the cooperative corporation to use a specific apartment (a proprietary lease). Even though you own stock you can treat it as a principal residence for the home mortgage interest rules.

THE INVESTMENT INTEREST LIMITATION

If the parents charge a reasonable interest rate on their loan to their children, the interest the parents incur on borrowing the money to lend to their children should be treated as investment interest subject to the investment interest expense limitation.

This rule generally limits the deductions you can claim for interest expense on debt used to buy and carry (hold) investment property to the amount of "net investment income" you have (see below). If the parents are charging the going interest rate to their children (as noted above, this can still be a great benefit for the children), the loan should be considered an investment asset of the parents.

TIP: There is an important advantage to parents who can successfully claim that their loan to their children is an investment asset. As noted previously, there is a limit of $100,000 on the amount of home-equity loans on which interest is deductible by the parents. While $100,000 sounds like a lot of money, if there are a number of children with college educations to finance, or a number of children who will need a hand buying their first homes, the $100,000 may not be enough. If the loans to the children are investment assets, then the money the parents borrow needn't be home-equity loans for the parents to be allowed to deduct interest. The parents may be able to deduct interest on their loans under the investment interest deduction rules. This will enable the parents to save their $100,000 home-equity borrowing for college loans and other transactions.

Net investment income refers to income from dividends, interest on bonds, and gains from selling investment property less expenses incurred to generate that income (to the extent these expenses exceed 2 percent of your adjusted gross income). In addition, a small allowance above the amount of investment income you have is permitted subject to complicated phase-out rules. Finally, any passive losses that you deducted, using the phase-out rules provided by the 1986 Tax Act, must be applied to reduce your net investment income. The most common interest expense subject to this limitation is the expense on a margin account used to buy stocks and bonds.

TAX CONSEQUENCES OF A LOAN WITH NO INTEREST OR LOW INTEREST CHARGED

If the parents lend money to their children and decide to give them a break by charging them only, say, 5 percent interest, Uncle Sam may have some unpleasant surprises. Fortunately, these nasty surprises don't apply for small loans. If all of the loans between the parents and children total no more than $10,000, there won't be any complications so long as the children use the money to buy a house (or any other nonincome-producing asset). If the loan exceeds this amount and the interest rate is too low, the IRS may find that the parents have made what's called a "gift loan."

The IRS will then impute an interest charge (calculate interest where there actually was none), using a realistic market rate of interest, which the children as borrowers should have paid the parents, and which the parents as lenders should have reported as income. The amount of this imputed interest charge will be treated as a gift made from the parents to the children, possibly creating a gift tax cost as well. Although these rules are rather complex, parents making low-interest loans to help their children out, and the children receiving those loans, will have to deal with them. The complexity means it's going to be essential to get the help of a qualified professional.

The gift tax consequences of a low- (or no-) interest loan will depend on whether it is a term loan (due in a certain number of years) or a demand loan (must be repaid whenever the parents say). For a term loan, the excess of the amount lent by the parents to the children over the present value (the value in today's dollars, considering the time value of money) of all the payments required to be made by the children to the parents, is treated as the amount transferred by the parents as a gift to their children.

EXAMPLE: The concept of present value can best be illustrated with a simple example. If you put $1 in a bank for one year, receiving 5 percent simple interest, you will have $1.05 in one year from today. The value today of the right to receive $1.05 one year from now, if the going interest rate is 5 percent, is $1.00. Thus, the present value of $1.05 is $1.00.

If the parents lend $50,000 for 10 years at a low interest rate they really save their children the difference between the low and going interest rates for the 10 years the children have the use of the $50,000. The excess of the $50,000 lent over the present value of the payments the children must make under the loan is considered a gift.

EXAMPLE: Phil and Pauline Parent lent their daughter and son-in-law Chip and Chris Children $50,000 to use as a downpayment on their first home. The Parents want to give the kids a break and charge them only

5 percent interest. The Children must pay interest on December 31 of each year and repay the $50,000 in 10 years. Assume that the proper interest rate to charge should have been 9 percent. The Children will pay the Parents $2,500 in interest [5% × $50,000]. The IRS would say that they should have paid $4,500 [9% × $50,000]. It's as if the Children paid an additional $2,000 of interest to the Parents (which the Parents may report as interest income) and the Parents gave the Children this additional $2,000 of legitimate interest back as a gift.

The excess of the $50,000 lent over the present value of the payments the Children will make is a gift by the Parents. The Children will actually be making two types of payments to the Parents. The first type is the annual interest payment of $2,500. The second is the repayment of the $50,000 after 10 years.

The interest payments for the 10 years will total $25,000 [10 years × $2,500 per year]. The present value of the $2,500 payments for 10 years, using a 9 percent interest rate, is $16,044. The present value of the $50,000 payment to be made in 10 years is $21,120. The sum of the two present values is $37,164 [$16,044 + $21,120]. The amount of the gift is therefore $12,836 [$50,000 − $37,164]. Your accountant can advise you of the actual interest rate the IRS will require for these calculations.

CAUTION: The above example is merely intended to illustrate the general concept of gift loans. The rules are much more complicated. Some of these complications are explained below. It's best, however, to review the tax consequences with your accountant.

The amount of the loan in the above example will not result in a gift tax to the parents if both have made the loan (because the gift amount is under $20,000). If one parent had made the loan, or if the loan amount were larger, or the interest charged were lower, the parents could have to pay a gift tax. (See Chapter 6.)

If the parents make a demand loan to their children instead of a term loan, the tax consequences are somewhat different. For a term loan the gift was treated as if made in the year the loan was made. For a demand loan, since it isn't possible to know when the loan will be repaid until it is actually repaid, the gift will be calculated at the end of every year in which the loan remains unpaid. The amount deemed as the gift when a demand loan is used is based on interest calculations for the amount of unpaid imputed interest for each day in the year for which the loan remains outstanding.

In case the gift tax consequences of a low- (or no-) interest loan weren't confusing enough, there are also income tax consequences to be dealt with. Again, the complexity of these rules means the help of a professional tax adviser is critical.

For income tax purposes an interest amount (called foregone interest) may have to be treated as if it were transferred from the parents/lenders to the children/borrowers. Since this transfer is a gift, there will be no income tax consequences to the parents or children (but there was a gift tax consequence as discussed above). This foregone interest (based on interest rates set monthly by the IRS) is then treated as if it were retransferred by the children/borrowers to the parents/lenders. The children will be able to deduct this interest "paid" to the parents if they meet the regular home interest deduction rules described above. The parents, unfortunately, may have to report this "interest" as income (even though they didn't actually receive any money!).

There is an exception that will limit the impact of these rules for many parental loans. Where the total gift loans are less than $100,000, the amount treated as interest transferred from the children/borrowers to the parents (and to be reported as income by the parents) each year will be limited to the amount of the children's net investment income for that year. Net investment income, as stated above in relation to the investment interest limitation rules, is income from stock dividends, bond interest, savings account interest, and so forth, less expenses incurred in earning this income. If the children's net investment income is less than $1,000, it will be assumed to be zero. However, if the parents make the loan for the purpose of avoiding taxes, this special rule won't apply.

OTHER GIFT AND ESTATE TAX CONSIDERATIONS

To have a family loan transaction respected by the IRS, the loan must be treated like a real loan by both the parents and the children. It is critically important that you have a legally binding loan agreement drafted by an attorney and signed by all the people involved. The children must then make all of the payments they are required to make according to the loan agreements. If this is not done, the IRS may claim that the transfer of money by the parents to the children was really a gift and not a loan. This could result in the parents incurring a gift tax, where they would not have owed any tax if the loan were really treated as a loan. (See Chapter 6 for an explanation of the gift and estate taxes.)

From an estate tax perspective, if the parents are very well-to-do, an outright gift may make more sense than a loan, if the parents are comfortable making a gift. The loan will be treated as an asset in the parents' estate and will be subject to estate tax on their eventual death. A compromise solution may be for the parents to make a loan and each year forgive some portion of the loan. You must exercise great care in using such a plan, so as to avoid the appearance of never intending the children to repay the loan.

ESTATE-PLANNING CONSIDERATIONS

One of the most important estate-planning considerations that parents must consider when making a gift or a loan is the fairness to the other children involved. Many times the parents prefer to treat all of their children approximately equally. If this is the case, and one child receives a loan at a favorable interest rate, the parents may want to provide some additional benefit to their other children in their wills. If the loan is made at market interest rates, it is reasonable to say that the child hasn't received any special economic benefits, and special treatment need not be afforded to the other children to compensate them. In any event, it may be important to inform all of the children of the loan (or other assistance) to avoid any jealousy or hurt feelings.

Another estate-planning consideration of lending one child money to buy a home may not be as easily dealt with, and some instructions in your will may be necessary. What is to happen to the loan if the parents die before it is repaid? If the parents provide nothing in their wills, it will be up to the administrator of their estates to handle the matter.

CASE STUDY: According to New York City attorney Richard Hofflich, doing nothing can be a big mistake. "The parents may assume that the administrator of their estate will handle affairs as they would. However, where an estranged older brother was serving as the executor, his wife, jealous over perceived favoritism of the other siblings, convinced her husband in his capacity as executor to call due the demand loan the parents had made to a younger brother. This created a substantial hardship to the younger brother, all to the delight of the older brother's wife."

One solution is for the parents to state in their wills when the loan should be repaid, or to give additional consideration to the payment schedule and the possible enforcement of the note by their estate, when their lawyer draws up the loan documents originally.

The parents could even provide in their wills that the loan will be forgiven as part of the inheritance of the child who borrowed the money.

LEGAL AND OTHER DOCUMENTS THAT MAY BE USED

The legal documents will depend on the nature of the transaction. If the parents lend the money for a set period of time, a "promissory note," where the children promise to repay the money borrowed at a specified time, will be used. If the loan is made so that the parents can require it to be repaid whenever they choose, a "demand note" will be used. If the parents wish to secure the repayment of their money, the note used will be a "secured promissory note," or a "secured demand note," in which the children will pledge their ownership of their home to repay the loan.

If the parents wish to secure their loan, a mortgage will be used. The mortgage will give the parents an interest in the children's home to secure the repayment of the loan. This mortgage will have to be recorded in the appropriate governmental office for the children to qualify for their tax deduction on the interest paid to the parents, so that later creditors can't get in line ahead of them should the children have financial problems.

As discussed above, the parents may wish to have their wills amended to make certain provisions to equalize their children's inheritances, or to prevent the premature call for the repayment of a loan. If the will is being changed, be certain to have it done by a qualified attorney. Very specific procedures must be followed for a change in a will to be valid. The slightest failure in following these strict requirements could make the intended change ineffective.

A sample loan document is included in the For Your Notebook section of this chapter to illustrate some of the provisions that may be included in the legal documents used when parents make a loan to their children. This document is for illustration only and should not be used without an attorney's assistance. As stated, it is generally advisable also to have a mortgage that the children give the parents on the home. If the children have borrowed money from a bank as well, the mortgage to their parents will be a second mortgage.

CAUTION: If parents (or any relative or even an unrelated investor) lend money to their children (or anyone buying a home), it's always the safest approach to have a lawyer draw up the appropriate legal documentation. This will protect everybody's interest in case there are problems. If there is no proper legal agreement, what happens if one of the children dies or the couple divorce, or if the relationship between lender and home buyer sours? The potential for problems is endless. Be safe and do it right. The fee for this should be modest.

Have the attorney verify that the interest rate charged is sufficient, to avoid any tax problems, and not excessive under local usury laws.

If an unrelated investor is serving as a lender, there is no doubt that the house will have to be pledged as security. The legal documents are likely to be more lengthy and contain numerous protections for the investor/lender. The investor may also require that the children's parents guarantee the loan. If the children fail to make the required loan payments (they default) their parents would be obligated to pay the investor. Depending on the terms of the guarantee agreement, the lender may or may not have to foreclose on the house and sell it before looking to the parents for money. The legal documentation that the lender will use will be similar to those documents at the end of Chapter 6.

CHAPTER SUMMARY

This chapter has reviewed one of the most common techniques for young couples and other first-time home buyers to break into the housing market—a loan from their families. A loan from the parents not only can help the children get the necessary financing; it can also be a great investment for the parents.

Unfortunately, legal, tax, estate-planning, and other complications make what many people think should be a very simple transaction complex. To safeguard everyone's interests, and to avoid unnecessary tax costs, you should discuss the planning ideas in this chapter with your lawyer and accountant before completing any such loan.

FOR YOUR NOTEBOOK

For the following form relating to a secured, interest-free demand loan, assume that Pete and Pat Parent, and the children, Chad and Carrie Child, don't have to be concerned about the many tax and legal considerations outlined in this chapter. Since there is no interest, the Childs aren't concerned about meeting the requirements to qualify for a home mortgage deduction. And since the amount lent is small, only $10,000, the Parents are not worried about the Childs' ability or desire to repay them. They trust their daughter, Carrie, to repay the money whenever she is able to. They *are* concerned about the stability of the Childs' marriage, however; all the talk they hear about divorce rates has them somewhat nervous. So the Parents prefer to have legal documentation, like the protection of a demand note secured by the Childs' house, in case the marriage later starts to falter. The Childs aren't worried about their home mortgage interest deduction, because they don't itemize deductions and the Parents agreed to make an interest-free loan. When the Parents and Childs went to the family lawyer, she suggested that the following legal document could be sufficient for them.

FORM: *SECURED DEMAND NOTE*

$10,000   June 1, 1990

FOR VALUE RECEIVED, Chad Child and Carrie Child (the "Borrowers"), who reside at 456 Lovers' Lane, Bigtown, Onestate, jointly and severally, promise to pay on DEMAND, to the order of Pete Parent and Pat Parent (the "Lenders"), at 123 Main Street West, Bigcity, Onestate, or such other place as the Lenders may designate in writing to the Borrowers, the sum of Ten Thousand Dollars and 00/100's ($10,000.00), in lawful money of the United States, without interest, except as provided for below.

The Borrowers do hereby pledge, transfer and grant to the Lenders, as security for the payment of their obligations under this Demand Note ("Note"), all their right, title and interest in the house, improvements, land and fixtures located at 456 Lovers' Lane, Bigtown, Onestate, more specifically described as Lot 12, Block 454A:5 on the tax map of Onetown.

This note shall be payable in full upon the receipt by the Borrowers of Lenders' written demand for payment of any part or all of the principal hereof. Lenders' demand may be made at any time. Demand shall be deemed made Four (4) days after the Lenders mail a written demand via certified mail, return receipt requested, postage prepaid, or the day following personal service on the Borrowers. No further demand or notice of any kind shall be required, all of which are hereby expressly waived. Payment shall be made by cash, Borrowers' personal check, money order, or bank check. Upon payment of all principal (and any other costs or interest) provided for under this Note, Lenders shall return all copies of this Note marked "CANCELED/ PAID IN FULL" and Borrowers' obligations hereunder shall be terminated.

Borrowers may prepay this Note at any time without penalty.

In the event the Borrowers fail to make payment in full within Five (5) days of any demand hereunder, then this Note shall bear interest at the lesser of: (i) Eighteen percent (18%), or (ii) the maximum rate allowed by law, and the Lenders may take any legal action they deem necessary or appropriate to collect the amounts due them hereunder.

If the Lenders shall institute any action to enforce collection of this Note, there shall become due and payable from the Borrowers, in addition to the principal and interest provided hereunder, all costs and expenses of that action (including reasonable attorney's fees) and the Lenders shall be entitled to judgment for all such additional payments.

This Note shall be governed according to the laws of Onestate.

This Note cannot be changed except in a writing signed by the Borrowers and Lenders.

Borrowers:

_____

Chad Child

_____

Carrie Child

8 EQUITY SHARING

INTRODUCTION

Equity-sharing arrangements have been hyped and promoted by a host of magazines and real estate writers and consultants. For a person trying to break into the housing market and get his or her first home, equity sharing may provide an important opportunity. However, there is a lot of confusion about what "equity sharing" really is—and about the true merits of some forms of equity sharing as compared with alternative arrangements for someone trying to buy a home. In many instances the tax benefits that were touted as an important advantage of an equity-sharing arrangement may no longer be available. This chapter will review equity sharing and suggest some viable alternatives that may be easier to use.

WHAT IS EQUITY SHARING?

There is no exact definition of what equity sharing is with respect to residential housing. The factors common to most equity-sharing arrangements include the following:

- An individual or couple need to raise money to purchase a home.
- An investor, who may or may not be a parent, will assist in the acquisition of the home.
- The investor, or parent, in exchange for providing financial assistance to the home buyer, will have the opportunity to share in the value of the house purchased.

In spite of these common factors, equity-sharing arrangements can have substantial differences. However, almost all equity sharing,

145

when analyzed by a lawyer, will be seen as a variation on one of the following three types of relationships, or some hybrid combination of them:

- Partnership type.
- Lease option.
- Mortgage with an equity kicker.

Each of these three basic formats will be examined in more detail, and then some suggestions can be made as to which approach is best to use.

PARTNERSHIP FORM OF EQUITY SHARING

In the partnership type of equity sharing, the home buyer and the investor own the house in a manner similar to partners. The agreement that they sign can be a variation of a partnership agreement where the home buyers have the right to live in and use the property. It is critical to note, however, that the parties generally don't want to be partners, and the agreement should so state. Partners can legally bind each other to agreements, and the parties to an equity-sharing arrangement don't want this. The legal documentation, however, should still contain some of the basic provisions commonly found in real estate partnership agreements. This is the most common approach to equity sharing advocated in the financial news and "how to" real estate books.

EXAMPLE: Phil and Pauline Parent will provide their daughter and son-in-law Chris and Chip Children with the money for the downpayment on the home the Children want to buy—money that the Children, just starting out on their own after college, don't have. In return for their cash downpayment the Parents will own 50 percent of the house. The Children will live in the house, maintain and repair the house, and make all monthly payments for mortgage principal and interest, property taxes, and insurance. The Children will own the remaining 50 percent of the house.

The Parents will actually lease the Children the portion (undivided interest) of the house that the Parents own so that the Children will have full use of the entire home.

Some time later, say 5 to 10 years after they have established a sufficient job history to carry a large mortgage, the Children will refinance their home and buy out the Parents' interest. If the Children can't refinance, or simply don't want to, the Parents and Children together will sell the house. The Parents will, if all goes well, receive back their downpayment plus an agreed percentage of the profits—50 percent of the appreciation on the home during the time it was owned.

This type of an equity-sharing arrangement is often touted as the great solution for both the parents/investors and the children/home buyers. The parents supposedly get significant tax breaks and a portion of the appreciation. The children get a chance to break into the housing market and start building equity.

CASE STUDY: Years ago, before equity sharing became popular, Norman Kailow, a real estate broker in Wayne, New Jersey, got interested. His daughter was going to the American University in Washington, DC; dormitory space was expensive, and his daughter preferred to have her own place. So together they bought a condominium. He made the downpayment; she paid the closing costs. She paid him rent; he took tax deductions. When she graduated, they sold the condo and split the profits. "Everyone came out ahead," Kailow reports. As it turned out, they sold the place to a woman and her two daughters—and Kailow persuaded the three of them to enter an equity-sharing arrangement.

The daughter who graduated from American University later moved to Arlington, Va., where she bought a house, sharing the expense with her sister and brother-in-law. The brother-in-law wanted a tax shelter.

It's important to further analyze these purported benefits. The investor may be able claim depreciation deductions on the half of the house rented to the home buyer. Depreciation is calculated on a 27.5 year period, on the investor's share in the house rented to the home buyers.

EXAMPLE: Irma Investor entered into a partnership-type equity-sharing arrangement with Harry Homebuyer. They bought the house in January, 1988 for $160,000, with Irma putting up a downpayment of $35,000. Irma owns 45 percent of the house, and Harry owns 55 percent of the house. Harry is responsible for all monthly payments. Irma is responsible for mortgage payments that Harry fails to make. Irma's depreciation deduction for 1989 is calculated as follows:

Purchase Price	$160,000
Less Price Allocable to Land	45,000
Depreciable Basis	$115,000
Investor's Share	× 45%
Investor's Depreciable Basis	$ 51,750
Depreciation Period	÷ 27.5
Depreciation for the Year	$ 1,882
Tax Rate	× 28%
Tax Benefit*	$ 527

* Tax benefit assumes that the entire amount of depreciation can be used to offset income of the investor's other than rental income from the same property, and that the passive loss rules and other restrictions don't limit the benefits involved.

The many tax limitations enacted in recent years make the tax benefits of the partnership type of shared equity arrangements shown in the above example of very limited value.

In addition to depreciation, the investor may have other tax deductions, depending on whether the investor is responsible for and actually makes a portion of the monthly mortgage payments. Interest and property taxes, to the extent they are paid, and certain other expenditures (repairs, utilities, and so forth) may be deductible. Expenditures for repairs that prolong the useful life of the property, or that add to its value (a new porch, aluminum siding, and so forth), can't be deducted immediately even if paid for by the investor. These expenditures (called capital improvements) must be added to the investment in the property and depreciated over the 27.5 year period.

If these deductions offset the rental income the investor receives from the home buyer sufficiently, there may be a tax loss. This loss, since it is attributable to a rental property, will be subject to the passive loss limitation rules. These rules, explained more fully below, may prevent the investor from getting any tax benefit from the deductions until the property is sold. Thus, the passive loss limitations can effectively eliminate all the tax benefits that the investor hoped to gain from participating in the partnership type of shared-appreciation arrangement. This makes the other two approaches to equity sharing, particularly the equity-kicker-mortgage approach, far more important as viable alternatives.

There is another very important tax implication to the use of the partnership form of shared equity appreciation where parents serve as the investors and the children as the home buyers. The IRS may raise a number of questions about the transaction, particularly if the parents are able to claim tax benefits. If the IRS determines that the transaction was largely set up for tax benefits and lacks economic reality, they may seek to disallow the parents' tax deductions. It is critical that the children pay a fair rent to the parents for the portion of the house that they live in. Don't assume that the monthly mortgage interest, insurance, and tax payments equal a reasonable rent. They may or may not. The legal documents must be realistic and must be followed. If the children sign a lease but don't make timely rental payments (by check), the IRS could question whether there was a real rental situation. The family relationship alone will make the IRS suspicious and should be expected to increase the chance of an audit.

Finally, there is another tax benefit to the use of the partnership form of equity sharing. If the house appreciates, the profit the investor realizes will be a capital gain. This may have some modest benefit if the investor has capital losses that can offset the capital gains. If Congress reinstates the favorable taxation of capital gains, this tax benefit could be tremendous, especially when compared with the mortgage form of equity sharing.

CAUTION: Considering the gift and estate taxes, as well as the income tax savings, if any, the IRS is likely to carefully scrutinize any such arrangement to see if the parents and children are engaging in a transaction designed to benefit all of them at the IRS' expense. If any terms of the arrangement are suspect, problems could follow. If the profit percentage is obviously too low or too high compared with the investment, the IRS may claim that the parties have tried to disguise a gift from the parents to the kids or vice versa.

Because of the substantial tax risks, never enter into a partnership-type equity-sharing arrangement before having your tax adviser review the tax aspects of the transactions. Also, because of the many restrictions on benefiting from tax deductions on rental real estate, don't count on tax benefits to make the investment worthwhile unless you've checked with your tax adviser.

CAUTION: Unless you have a qualified real estate attorney draft all of the necessary documents you'll be looking for trouble from the IRS, and possibly elsewhere. As a general rule, the simpler a transaction is, the more it is likely to avoid tax and legal problems. The partnership form of equity sharing is really a bit more complicated than many proponents let on. What if the parents want the money for their retirement and the

kids don't want to sell or refinance to pay the parents out? The legal
documents must deal with a lot of uncertainties to protect everybody,
and there is still the risk of family friction. A simple loan or gift may
work just as well.

When entering into a partnership type of equity sharing, have a
knowledgeable real estate attorney prepare an equity-sharing agreement and a lease. Some of the many points that should be considered
when you meet with your real estate lawyer include the following:

- What payments will the investor (parent) be primarily responsible
  for and what payments will the home buyer be primarily responsible for?
- How much cash must each put into the house?
- How much of the house will each own?
- How much rent must the home buyers pay the investor (parent)?
- How long will the agreement continue before the home buyers
  have to buy out the investor's interests?
- What kind of access and inspection rights will the investor
  have to the house?
- What happens if the home buyers want to make an improvement,
  such as to finish a basement, add a new room, or remodel the
  kitchen? Will the investor have a right to veto the improvement?
  Will the investor have any say in which contractors do the
  work? Should the investor be afforded an opportunity to review
  or approve the plans? Who should benefit from the cost of the
  improvements when the property is sold?
- Who should pay for repairs?
- What happens if one person wants to sell and the other doesn't?
- Can the home buyers sublet?
- If the home buyers miss payments, what rights should the investor
  have to buy them out, to evict them, and to claim for damages?
  It is important to have an attorney in the area where the house
  is located advise you of any local laws that may affect the
  investor's rights.
- How much insurance must be carried? The investor will want
  to be named on the insurance policies, have a copy of the
  policies, and get notice from the insurance company if the
  investor ever fails to make a required payment.

- What happens if the investor or the home buyer dies?
- If the home buyer wants to keep the house, how does he or she determine the fair price of the house for purposes of buying out the investor? This can be done by establishing a formula in the beginning, or using some form of appraisal procedure. For example, the investor can hire an appraiser. If the home buyer doesn't agree with the appraised amount, he or she can hire his or her own appraiser. If the two appraisers don't agree, they can choose a third appraiser whose opinion must be followed.
- What kind of notification must the investor give the home buyer of the home buyer's default under the agreement (failure to meet the payments or other terms required) before commencing legal actions?
- If the town or city has a special property tax assessment, who should pay it and in what proportion?
- What happens if there is a casualty such as a fire or tornado that destroys the house, or the house is condemned? Should the house be rebuilt or should the investor be paid off? How should the insurance proceeds be allocated between the investor and the home buyer?
- If radon or asbestos is found, who is responsible for the costs that must be incurred?

In some forms of equity sharing, the investor holds an unrecorded mortgage on the house. This raises two problems. First, the existence of the mortgage may encourage the IRS to recharacterize the investor's position as that of a creditor rather than an owner. This could eliminate the investor's depreciation and any other tax benefits. Second, an unrecorded mortgage may not provide any real protection to the investor. Investors wanting the protection of a mortgage should use an equity-kicker mortgage instead of the partnership type of equity-sharing arrangement.

LEASE-OPTION EQUITY SHARING

In the lease-option form of equity sharing, the investor may actually own the home (hold legal title to the property), and the "home buyers," in exchange for paying some or all of the monthly payments and for maintaining the property, have a right to buy the house from the investor after a certain period of time and upon making certain payments. The investor may share in the appreciation of the house if the purchase price that the home buyers will eventually have to pay is somehow tied to the value of the house at some later date when they obtain ownership. These arrangements are often a variation of a lease with a purchase option.

EXAMPLE: Ida Investor buys the house and Harry and Hindy Homebuyer lease the house from Ida Investor. Twenty-five percent of the $1,200 monthly rental payments the Homebuyers make is applied as credit toward the purchase price the Homebuyers will have to pay to acquire the house at some future date. The purchase price is usually based on the fair value of the house when the Homebuyers purchase it. The Homebuyers build equity, since a portion of their rental payments is credited against the amount they will have to pay when they buy the house. Ida Investor has an interest in the appreciation of the home, since the more the home increases in value, the more she will get paid when the Homebuyers purchase it.

This example illustrates how a lease arrangement can be used as a form of equity sharing since the investor shares in the increase in the value of the house while the tenant builds equity. Although the lease-option arrangement has much merit as a form of equity sharing, it is recommended too infrequently. Lease-option arrangements are explained more fully in Chapter 13.

The lease-option arrangement has a number of advantages to the investor over the partnership type of equity sharing. The investor owns the entire house, so that the tax benefits may be greater. For example, the investor can claim depreciation on the entire price (tax basis) of the house, not just a portion of it. The tax consequences should also be clearer, since the investor owns and is renting out the entire house. A lease arrangement, when properly structured, can have more certain tax results than some of the partnership types of equity sharing, which can be more nebulous. A key tax risk that the investor in a lease-option arrangement must consider is whether the IRS will maintain that the house was actually sold to the investor rather than leased. (See Chapter 13.)

The tenant generally has no tax advantages from this lease-option arrangement. Since the tenant is merely a renter, for tax purposes there are no deductions.

The tenant, however, can have other important advantages. If there is a major repair (the boiler breaks, the roof must be replaced, and so forth), the investor is responsible. In addition, compared with the typical renter, the renter under a lease option can build substantial equity long before he or she can come up with a down-payment.

The lease-option arrangement also should have some legal benefits to the investor: if the tenant defaults, it should be easier to get the tenant out than in a partnership-type arrangement where the tenant has an ownership interest as well. From a practical perspective, the courts will have an easier time dealing with a common lease ar-rangement, which will use a form of lease agreement that is standard in the area, than a partnership type of equity-sharing arrangement, which is not likely to be on a standard legal form. The legal relationship between the parties in the partnership type of arrangement may be harder for the court to sort out. Any delays arising from this difficulty could be to the investor's detriment as he or she seeks to evict a nonpaying tenant. The investor using the lease-option method has an important advantage over the typical landlord. As the tenant builds equity in the house, the tenant will view the house as his or her home and is likely to take much better care of it.

MORTGAGES WITH EQUITY KICKERS AS A FORM OF EQUITY SHARING

In some equity-sharing arrangements, the investor providing the assistance actually lends the downpayment money to the home buyers, rather than taking a real equity (ownership) interest in the house. As an additional incentive, or sweetener, to encourage the investor to make the loan, particularly to first-time home buyers, who may not have the best qualifications as borrowers, the home buyers agree to give the lender what is called an equity kicker. When the home is eventually sold, or after a fixed period of time, the lender gets a payment as additional interest on his or her loan, based on the appreciation in the house's value. Because the investor receives a percentage of the appreciation in the house, this relationship is sometimes lumped together with the various equity-sharing arrange-ments. Such shared-equity mortgages are called shared-appreciation mortgages, or SAMs for short.

EXAMPLE: Sam Seller purchased a house that Bob and Betty Buyer wanted for $140,000. Sam then sold the house to the Buyers on the installment method. Sam retains title to the home until the Buyers make the last

payment on the installment contract. Sam gave the Buyers a good deal
on the installment contract (a low downpayment and a favorable interest
rate). The agreement calls for a balloon payment at the end of five years,
and the Buyers can prepay at any time.

In exchange for giving the Buyers a good deal on the downpayment
and interest rate, Sam negotiated a special payment to be made to him
as additional interest equal to a set percentage of the value of the house.
Furthermore, because Sam felt that if the Buyers paid off the installment
contract early he would lose out, he specified that a higher percentage
of the house value be paid to him in the early years. The value of the
house would be determined by the sales price the Buyers would receive
if they sold the house. If they didn't sell the house, a real estate appraiser
would be hired by Sam to value the house. The additional interest the
Buyers would have to pay was based on the following:

Year Sold	Percentage of House Value to Sam as Additional Interest
1st	20%
2nd	18
3rd	15
4th	12
5th	10

There are some very important economic advantages for the investor
that the equity-kicker mortgage has over the other two equity-sharing
methods. One is certainty. In the lease-option arrangement, there is
no guarantee that the house will be sold to the tenant. If the tenant/
home buyer doesn't exercise the option to purchase, the investor
will have to begin the entire sales process again. Under the partnership
equity-sharing method, depending on the agreement between the
parties, there may or may not be certainty. Generally the home buyer
will have to buy out the investor by refinancing or selling the house.
There is some risk that the home buyer won't be able to accomplish
either plan without some assistance from the investor. Further, under
the partnership method the investor has no guaranteed return. Under
the equity-kicker method, the investor is far more certain of his or
her return. At a minimum, the investor will get the interest rate
stated in the mortgage, even if the home doesn't appreciate, while
in the partnership-type, there may be no return at all.

There are a number of important tax considerations with the equity-
kicker mortgage, for both the investor and the home buyer. For the
investor, the interest on the mortgage and the additional (equity-
kicker) interest is all taxable as ordinary income when received.

Prior to the Tax Reform Act of 1986, this taxability was an important disadvantage to the investor when compared with the other two types of equity-sharing arrangements, because the other two kinds of arrangements would generally result in the investor's share of the appreciation being capital gains, which were taxed more favorably. Now, however, with all income, whether ordinary income or capital gains, being taxed at the same rates, there is no penalty to the investor in using the equity-kicker arrangement. Should Congress reinstate favorable treatment of capital gains, the other two equity-sharing methods would have some advantage on this score.

There is another potentially important disadvantage to the equity-kicker approach when compared to the other two methods. The investor, as a lender, has no ownership interest in the property and can't claim depreciation or other deductions. For investors who can qualify for the special $25,000 allowance under the passive loss rules (see below), this could be an important disadvantage. However, with long (27.5 years) depreciation periods and numerous other tax restrictions, this may not be as negative as it first appears. For investors who can't meet the requirements of the $25,000 allowance, there may be no tax disadvantage to the equity-kicker mortgage method.

The interest which the investor (lender) receives on the appreciation of the house can be tax deductible by the home buyer as interest expense when the home buyer actually pays it to the investor. If, however, the contingent interest is paid to the investor as part of some refinancing arrangement, it will only be deductible over the term of the new financing arrangement. This potential deduction constitutes a considerable advantage to the home buyer over the other equity-sharing plans.

TIP: Find an investor/lender willing to lend on a shared-equity mortgage through your real estate broker or advertisements in the real estate sections of the newspapers where you are looking for houses. These mortgages are easier to understand and more secure than other equity-sharing methods. Many of the disadvantages these mortgages once had as compared with other methods have disappeared as a result of the new tax laws.

There is an important tax advantage to home buyers in using a shared appreciation or equity-kicker mortgage arrangement. Some investors/lenders may be willing to accept a lower interest rate in exchange for a greater equity kicker at some future date. This approach can provide an additional and valuable benefit. Millions of Americans don't get much, if any, benefit from mortgage-interest or other itemized deductions. If an equity-kicker mortgage is used, however, a large part of the interest will be deducted in the year the lender is paid the contingent-profits interest. Bunching most of the interest deductions into one tax year could easily enable millions of taxpayers to get big tax deductions, in contrast with paying interest each year under conventional loans, or under equity-kicker mortgages with a higher interest during the years before payment of the equity kicker.

CAUTION: If the interest rate used is too low there may be problems with the IRS. Check with your tax adviser.

EXAMPLE: The following calculations show how a shared-equity mortgage can benefit a homeowner more than a conventional mortgage. A shared-equity mortgage, however, will primarily benefit homeowners with modest mortgages, in states with low tax rates.

Conventional Mortgage

Price	$ 60,000
Downpayment	15,000
Mortgage	$ 45,000
Interest @ 10%	4,500
Property taxes	850
State income taxes	1,000
Total itemized deductions	$ 6,350
Standard deduction	5,000
Extra itemized deductions	$ 1,350
Tax benefit of itemizing[1] (tax @ 15%)	$ 202
Value of house[2]	$186,351
Tax benefit[3]	2,926
Total value	$189,277

[1] Note that $5,000 − ($1,000 + $850) = $3,150 of the mortgage interest provides no tax benefit.
[2] Assumes appreciation at a rate of 12 percent per year, annual compounding.
[3] Future value of $202 tax benefit for 10 years at 8 percent = $2,926. Note that the tax benefit will be higher in later years as the homeowner moves into a higher tax bracket. This has been ignored to simplify the example.

Shared-Equity Mortgage

Assume that no interest payments are made for 10 years but that the lender will receive 59 percent of appreciation. Say the house appreciates at 12 percent per year, and the house is now worth $186,351. Fifty-nine percent of $126,351 [$186,351 value − $60,000 purchase price], or $74,540, is paid to the lender in tax-deductible interest. Assume that $72,690 [$74,540 − ($1,000 + $850)] is deductible at a 28-percent tax rate (because in 10 years the homeowner's income has increased). The tax benefit is $72,690 × 28% = $20,353.

Value of house	$186,351
Interest paid	(72,690)
Tax benefit of interest deduction	20,353
Future value of $4,500 annual interest savings invested @ 8% tax free	70,405
Value	$204,419

Based on the above assumptions, the homeowner would have benefited by $15,142 [$204,419 − $189,277] by using a shared-equity mortgage.

CAUTION: Be sure to use an attorney familiar with this type of loan instrument. If the loan documents are not properly drafted, the lender could be considered an owner of the property from the beginning, and the payment of the profit percentage then may not be deductible.

WHICH EQUITY-SHARING METHOD IS BEST?

There is no simple answer as to which approach is the right one to use. A lot will depend on the relative bargaining strength of the investor as compared with the home buyer. The only way to make the right decision is to go over all of the factors involved with your real estate broker, investment adviser, accountant, and attorney. Some of the considerations involved include the following:

- Will there be any tax benefits for the investor from the partnership or lease-option types of equity-sharing arrangement?
- If there are tax losses on a partnership or lease-option arrangement, will the investor be able to use them, or will the passive loss (or other) limitations prevent the investor from using them? Because of their importance, the passive loss rules are explained in some detail below.
- Even if the investor can use the tax losses, how much benefit will actually be available, with tax rates at the lowest levels in decades?

- How much cost in professional time will be necessary to properly set up the equity-sharing arrangement? In many cases, since forms are readily available to attorneys in most states for mortgage and lease (or even lease-option) arrangements, these should be much less expensive to complete. Partnership-type equity sharing can be a vague and nebulous concept. Many attorneys simply may not want to get involved, or cannot complete the work at a fee the investor or home buyer can justify paying.

- How well-defined is the relationship? Although many equity-sharing proponents (the partnership form of arrangement) argue that equity sharing has been around for a long time, the fact remains that the equity-kicker mortgage and lease with a purchase option are more traditional real estate transactions, for which there exists more case law, tax law, forms, and other materials and sources. The latter two types of relationships are likely to be easier to deal with should a problem arise than many of the residential partnership methods of equity sharing.

- Which form of equity sharing will provide the investor the most protection if the home buyer defaults, damages the house, fails to make the required payments, or just becomes difficult and bothersome? A lot will depend on the specific nature of the legal documents used. In general, however, the partnership form of equity sharing will probably prove to be the most difficult to untangle. Both parties will be listed on the deed to the house and will own a substantial interest in the property.

CAUTION: Some partnership equity-sharing arrangements call for the investor to get a mortgage on the house to protect his or her investment. While this may help protect the investment, it may also create tax problems and tremendous tax uncertainty. A mortgage is used where a loan has been made, not where an ownership interest is purchased. The use of a mortgage could provide the IRS with reason to try to deny the investor any tax benefits. The moral is the same one repeated throughout this chapter: to avoid problems, use a simple and understandable relationship that is commonly used in other real estate transactions.

In contrast with the partnership approach, either under the mortgage with an equity kicker or the lease-option arrangement, the investor has complete ownership (title) to the house and is likely to be in a better position to remove the home buyers. In the partnership arrangement, even where a lease is signed by the home buyers for the investor's portion of the house in which they live, the investor may face difficulties removing the home buyers as tenants; after all, they own some portion of the house as well. These issues must be carefully reviewed with your lawyer. There can be important differences in the real estate laws in the different states. The formalities and expense that the investor as landlord will have to go through to evict the home buyers as tenants can differ substantially from those required of the investor as a lender, to foreclose on a mortgage and collect his or her funds.

NOTE: Stuart M. Saft, a partner with the New York City law firm of Wolf, Haldenstein, Adler, Freeman, Herz prefers the equity-kicker mortgage, since as a lender "you are a secured creditor and if the homeowner goes into bankruptcy, you're not precluded from collecting."

- What will the return be to the investor? Since the major motivation for the investor in entering the transaction is to make a profit, the potential returns using each of the three methods should be evaluated. Rental rates, house prices, real estate inflation rates, and interest rates are all important factors.

PASSIVE LOSS LIMITATION RULES

The passive loss limitation rules have implications in the planning and structuring of any investment transaction. These limitations can be particularly important to an investor hoping to achieve tax benefits on a partnership or lease-option equity-sharing arrangement.

The passive loss limitations can prevent an investor from using the tax losses on equity-sharing real estate investments (from depreciation, interest deductions, and so forth) to offset the income earned from a full-time job or on CDs, stocks, and bonds. In short, these rules can take the tax shelter out of real estate. The best way to achieve a basic understanding of the passive loss rules is to understand first the three general categories into which these rules require investors (and others) to divide their income.

In the illustration on page 160, each of the three baskets contains a different type of income. In addition, there is a limited number of exceptions between the categories of income. The rules aim to prevent (or at least to severely limit) an investor's ability to use losses from the passive category (which include equity-sharing and other rental

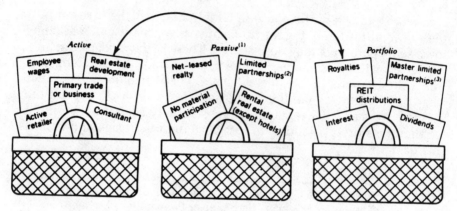

(1) Up to $25,000 of certain passive losses, or up to $7,000 of tax credits on passive investments, can be used to offset any type of income, including active income.
(2) Limited partnerships and other passive activities that have money invested in money market accounts, bonds, or CDs may have a portion of their income categorized as portfolio income instead of passive income. This concept is illustrated in examples later in this chapter.
(3) Income from a master limited partnership will generally be categorized as portfolio income instead of passive income, so it can't be offset by your tax shelter losses. Losses from a master limited partnership generally can't be used to offset income from any investment other than itself, until you sell.

Figure 8-1. Three types of income baskets for passive loss rules. (Reprinted from Martin M. Shenkman, *The Total Real Estate Tax Planner* [New York: John Wiley & Sons, Inc., 1988], p. 133.)

real estate investments, subject to some important exceptions discussed below) to offset income and gains from active (wages) or portfolio (interest and dividends) income categories.

EXAMPLE: Ida Investor has a strong aversion to paying income taxes. As a result she purchased a house and entered into a lease-option equity-sharing arrangement. She seeks to use depreciation deductions from the real estate as a tax shelter to limit the taxes on her other income.

	Income
Salary	$35,000
Dividends	3,000
Interest	2,000
Equity-share real estate loss	(7,000)
Taxable income before exemptions, etc.	$33,000

As a result of the passive loss limitations, Ida Investor will have to treat the income as having fallen into three categories as follows: active ($35,000 salary); portfolio ($3,000 dividends + $2,000 interest); and passive ($7,000 loss on equity sharing). Under the passive loss rules, Ida won't, generally, be allowed to use the losses from the passive category of income to offset the income and gains from the other categories. Unfortunately, her positive income from salary and portfolio earnings will be taxed without benefit of the $7,000 loss.

TIP: Fortunately, however, for Ida Investor in the above example, she may be able to qualify for a special exception to the passive loss limitation that will enable her, as an active investor, to use her tax losses. (See below.)

A business or investment (referred to as an "activity") is considered passive if you do not materially participate in the activity. For example, if you own an interest in an obviously active business but spend all your time on the golf course, this business won't count. You have to materially participate in the business yourself for the income to be considered active. The key rule for you as a real estate investor is that investments in rental real estate (except for a hotel) are usually passive.

Although an involvement in real estate rental will never be considered active business, no matter how materially you participate, there is a very important exception. Without this exception, losses from your rental real estate investments would be available to offset income only from your other passive investments—for example, from other equity-sharing arrangements (except mortgages with equity kickers, which generate portfolio income). This exception permits certain investors to treat some real estate rental losses as losses from an active business. This means these losses can be used to offset income from wages or active businesses in which you materially participate.

To qualify for the real estate loss exception, you must meet both an income and a participation test. For the income test, you must have adjusted gross income (all of your income less certain taxable social security amounts, and after adding back passive losses and IRA deductions) less than $150,000. The $25,000 allowance is granted in full if your adjusted gross income (subject to certain modifications) doesn't exceed $100,000. For adjusted gross income above this amount, up to $150,000, the $25,000 allowance is phased out at the rate of 50 cents for each additional dollar of income.

EXAMPLE: Betty Broker has adjusted gross income of $120,000. Betty also has $32,000 in passive tax losses (in excess of her other passive income) from partnership-type equity-sharing arrangements. These losses should qualify for the special allowance. How much can she use? First, the loss in excess of $25,000 is clearly in excess of the allowance. Thus, $7,000 [$32,000 − $25,000] can immediately be treated as a loss carryover (suspended loss) to future years. Next, a portion of Betty's allowance will have to be reduced because her adjusted gross income exceeds the $100,000 hurdle. The $20,000 excess will reduce her allowance at a rate of 50 cents for each dollar of excess, or $10,000. Thus, Betty can use only $15,000 of her equity-sharing real estate losses to offset income from her wages as a real estate broker.

The other requirement for this $25,000 allowance is an "active participation" test, which includes the following:

(1) You must own at least 10 percent of the value of the activity (i.e., there cannot be more than 10 equal investors).

(2) You must make management decisions or arrange for others to provide services (such as repairs) in a significant and bona fide sense. For example, you could approve new tenants, decide on rental terms, or approve repairs of large ("capital") improvements. You don't even have to do these directly—you can hire a rental agent and repairman.

(3) The management decisions you make in (2) must not be contrived to meet this active participation test.

Make sure the lawyer preparing the legal documents is aware of the requirements to meet this standard. What is treated as a real estate rental activity? A real estate rental receives payments that are principally for the use of tangible property, rather than for the performance of substantial services. Renting property under net leases, where the tenants bear the responsibility for most expenses, or where the landlord is guaranteed a specified rate of return or is guaranteed against loss, will generally be treated as rental activity.

What happens to the losses that you couldn't use? They are not lost forever. Rather, they are carried forward to future years (suspended losses). If you have passive income in future years (including gains from sales of passive investments, such as partnership or lease-option equity-sharing arrangements), your unused passive-loss carry-forwards from prior years can be applied against the current income to obtain a tax savings. If you can't use up your undeducted passive-loss carry-forwards from prior years before you sell your equity-sharing investment, you can use these losses to offset the gain you would otherwise have to recognize on the sale of your investment.

EXAMPLE: Ivan Investor owns a number of houses under the partnership type of equity-sharing arrangement. The investments were made in 1986, when 19-year depreciation write-offs were still available. As a result of these favorable depreciation deductions, Ivan realizes losses each year of $25,000. Since this is Ivan's only passive investment, the losses are suspended and remain unused. By 1990, Ivan will have accumulated unused losses of $125,000 [$25,000 per year for five years]. Suppose at the end of 1990 Ivan sells all of his equity-share interests in the houses for a $200,000 profit. This profit will be reduced by the $125,000 in losses not yet used. Thus, the gain that should be taxed will be only $75,000.

LEGAL AND OTHER DOCUMENTS

Before your lawyer can decide what legal documents to prepare, you and your advisers must determine the form the equity-sharing transaction will take. The types of documents needed will then be as follows:

- For partnership type of equity-sharing arrangement: An equity-sharing agreement and a lease for the portion of the house the home buyers must lease from the investor.
- For lease-option arrangement: The home buyers will sign a lease with the investor. The lease should have at least two

special sections dealing with the equity-sharing arrangement. One section should provide that a portion of the monthly rental payments will be credited against the purchase price that the home buyers will have to pay for the house. The second section should describe the home buyers' option to purchase the house. In some instances the investor's lawyer may insist on the signing of some additional documents that will make it easier for the investor to evict the home buyers for failing to make the monthly payments. Home buyers are cautioned to have their own lawyers carefully review all agreements before signing.

● For equity-kicker mortgage: The home buyers will own the house, and the investor will make a loan that will require a note and mortgage document to be signed. See Chapter 5 for information concerning these documents. These documents will each contain a special section stating that the home buyers will pay the investor at a certain time a portion of the appreciation in the value of the house as additional interest.

CHAPTER SUMMARY

This chapter has reviewed some of the many considerations of using a form of equity sharing to acquire a house, when there is little or no money available for the downpayment. The methods discussed provide tremendous opportunity for a creative home buyer, with the proper legal, tax and business advice, to arrange a method of buying a home. Equity sharing clearly has the most interesting and creative possibilities of any method available to buy a home. However, the tremendous opportunities for creativity also require the exercise of proper caution.

FOR YOUR NOTEBOOK

Documents for two of the three equity-sharing approaches discussed in the chapter are presented here. These documents—a Home Purchase Equity Sharing Agreement, and an Equity Kicker Note—are for illustration only; they are not complete. In addition, there are a number of important alternatives and provisions that have not been included. Local laws vary considerably with respect to rentals of residential property. To properly protect your interests, be certain to consult an attorney.

FORM: *HOUSE PURCHASE EQUITY SHARING AGREEMENT*

THIS AGREEMENT entered into this 1st day of July, 1988 between Ira Investor, who resides at 789 Golden Road, Anytown, Onestate ("Investor") and Harry Homebuyer and Heidi Homebuyer, his wife, who reside at 123 Apartment Street, Centerville, Onestate (the "Homebuyers").

WHEREAS, Investor and the Homebuyers shall purchase the property located at 456 Wonder Lane, Centerville, Onestate, as TENANTS-IN-COMMON, described more fully as:

ALL that tract or parcel of land and premises, situated, lying and being in the City of Centerville, in the County of Oakland, and State of Onestate. BEING known and designated as Lot No. 3 in Block No. 13 on a certain map entitled "Map of Elmora Manor, Centerville, Onestate, O.L.P. Jones, Surveyor, dated June 10, 1812" and filed in the Register's Office as Case #38-CH-4.

BEGINNING at a stake in the Northeasterly side of Wonder Lane, at a point therein distant 50 feet Southeasterly from the intersection formed by the said Northeasterly side of Wonder Lane and the Southeasterly side of Glenwood Road; thence running (1) North 36 degrees 01 minutes East, a distance of 100 feet to a stake for a corner; thence running (2) South 54 degrees 18 minutes East a distance of 48.02 feet to a point for

165

another corner; thence running (3) South 35 degrees 42 minutes West a distance of 100 feet to a point in the aforesaid line of Wonder Lane; thence running (4) North 54 degrees 18 minutes West a distance of 48.57 feet to the point or place of BEGINNING. BEING also known as 456 Wonder Lane, Centerville, Onestate.

BEING known as Lot 3 in Block 13, Account No. 10-504B on the official tax map of the City of Centerville, Oakland County, Onestate (the "House").

WHEREAS, Investor and Homebuyers each wish to purchase an undivided Fifty percent (50%) interest in the House as TENANTS-IN-COMMON.

WHEREAS, Homebuyers desire Investor's assistance to purchase the House.

WHEREAS, the parties desire to provide for financing, ownership, management, maintenance, and sale of the House and the division of any profits realized therefrom.

THEREFORE, based on the mutual premises herein contained, the parties hereto agree as follows:

1. *PURCHASE OF HOUSE.*
   The Investor has contracted to purchase the House pursuant to a Contract dated June 15, 1988 between Investor and Sam Seller, a copy attached hereto as Exhibit A (the "Contract"). Investor hereby sells, assigns, and transfers to Homebuyers, and Homebuyers purchase Fifty percent (50%) of Investor's interest in the contract to purchase the House for the consideration, for One Dollar ($1) and other good and valuable consideration, and on the terms and conditions, set forth in this Agreement. The assignment is attached hereto as Exhibit B (the "Assignment"). The Investor and the Homebuyers shall purchase the House pursuant to the terms and conditions of the Contract.

2. *TERM.*
   This Agreement shall terminate at the earlier of: (i) Sixty (60) months from the date the House is acquired; (ii) Sixty (60) days from the scheduled closing date for the House in the Contract if the closing does not occur, unless the closing date is extended in accordance with the terms of the Contract; (iii) upon the sale of the House; (iv) upon

the refinancing of the House and payment of the Investor of the amounts due hereunder; (v) by written agreement between the parties; or (vi) the termination of the Contract in accordance with its terms prior to closing on the House.

3. VALUE OF PROPERTY.
The value of the House is agreed to be not less than the purchase price and closing costs, which the parties agree is One Hundred Fifty-Two Thousand Dollars ($152,000).

4. INVESTOR'S INVESTMENT.
The Investor's investment, including cosing costs, in the House shall be Thirty-Five Thousand Dollars ($35,000.00), which shall be paid by Investor at the signing of this Agreement to Investor's attorney to hold in escrow ("Investor's Investment"). Such funds shall be applied towards the downpayment on the closing of the Contract. Title to the House shall be taken in the name of both the Investor and the Homebuyers as equal tenants-in-common (with the Homebuyers owning title to their interest as tenants-by-the-entirety), subject to required financing and security documents, and conditioned upon full compliance by the Investor and the Homebuyers with all terms of this Agreement. The Investor and the Homebuyers shall each own a Fifty Percent (50%) undivided interest in the House, respectively.

5. LEASE.
The Homebuyers and the Investor shall execute a lease agreement granting Homebuyers with the exclusive right to use and occupy the Investor's Fifty percent (50%) undivided interest in the House for the term of this Agreement (the "Lease"). The Lease is attached hereto as Exhibit C and its terms and provisions fully incorporated herein. Should there be any conflict between a provision of this Agreement and the Lease, the provision in this Agreement shall control.

6. REPRESENTATIONS, COVENANTS AND WARRANTIES OF HOMEBUYERS.
(a) Homebuyers agree to pay to State Savings & Loan (the "Bank") at 2468 Financial Lane, Richtown, Onestate, monthly payments in advance of One Thousand Thirty-Six Dollars and 32/100s ($1,136.32) for mortgage interest and principal payments on the first mortgage, and upon accepting and signing this Agreement, monthly payments in advance for property taxes and casualty insurance, as necessary. The monthly payments are, at the date of this Agreement, estimated to be One Hundred Three Dollars ($103.00) for property taxes and Fifty-Six

Dollars ($56) for casualty insurance, for total initial monthly payments aggregating One Thousand Two Hundred Ninety-Five and 32/1000s ($1,295.32). These payments shall be based on the actual amount of payments due, and Homebuyers acknowledge that such payments may increase. The above payments may increase or decrease in amount, depending on the type of existing financing or any variations in property taxes or insurance. Payments are due on the first day of the month and shall be delinquent if not received by the Bank by the fifth day of every month.

(b) Homebuyers agree to execute any additional documents deemed necessary by Investor's attorney for the purpose of securing:

(i) Payment to Investor for Investor's Investment as set forth in Section 4 above.

(ii) The performance of each agreement of the Homebuyers incorporated by reference or contained herein.

(c) Homebuyers acknowledge that their Fifty percent (50%) interest in the House is subject to Notes and Mortgages securing the House in the amount of One Hundred Seventeen Thousand Dollars ($117,000) to the Bank, plus any and all investments made by the Investor as defined in this Agreement.

(d) Homebuyers agree to maintain the House at their sole expense and to be responsible for any and all repairs or improvements up to One Thousand Five Hundred Dollars ($1,500.00). Homebuyers shall not make, or allow to be made, any major repairs or capital improvements to the House without having first obtained the written consent of the Investor, which consent shall not be unreasonably withheld. A major repair or capital improvement shall be defined as any improvement in excess of Five Hundred Dollars ($500.00) in value. The fair value of the Homebuyers' labor shall be considered in this calculation. Notwithstanding anything herein to the contrary, Homebuyers may make any reasonable emergency repair necessary to preserve and maintain the House. Any repair expense in excess of One Thousand Five Hundred Dollars ($1,500) shall be paid according to each party's ownership in the House. When the House is sold at the termination of this Agreement, or Investor purchases Homebuyers' interests pursuant to Section 10, Homebuyers shall be entitled to recover the lesser of the actual amount they expended on any approved capital improvement, or the increase in the value of the House due to such capital improvement prior to the allocation of any profit between them resulting from such sale.

(e) Homebuyers shall not dispose of any real or personal property, other than furniture and personal effects not acquired as part of the purchase, connected with the House without written consent of the Investor, which consent shall not be unreasonably withheld.

(f) Upon signing this Agreement, the Homebuyers shall pay for a homeowners insurance policy naming the Investor as a co-insured. Fire and casulty insurance coverage shall be a replacement value policy with the amount not less than One Hundred Fifty Thousand Dollars ($150,000) for property. In the event of total loss, Homebuyers shall first assign their interest in monies paid by the insurance company to the investor to cover his Investment. Any excess monies shall then be divided equally based on each party's ownership interest. In the event of a loss of the Homebuyers' personal property, Investor shall assign his interest of any monies paid by the insurance company on account of Homebuyers' personal property, to the Homebuyers.

(g) Term life insurance in an amount not less than Fifty Thousand Dollars ($50,000) paid by the Homebuyers, shall be purchased on Harry Homebuyer's life, payable to the Investor. The payment of insurance proceeds to the Investor shall be applied to reduce the amount due the Investor by Homebuyers on the sale of the House or the repurchase of the Investor's interests.

7. ENCUMBRANCES AND ASSIGNMENTS.

The Homebuyers shall not sell, assign, transfer, mortgage, or encumber the Contract, the House, this Agreement, or the Lease without the prior written consent of the Investor, which consent may not be unreasonably withheld.

8. DEFAULT BY THE HOMEBUYERS.

The occurrence of any of the following shall constitute a default by the Homebuyers:

(a) Failure to make any payment under Section 5 and 6(a) when due, which failure continues for Ten (10) days;

(b) Abandonment of the House;

(c) Failure to perform or violation of any provision of this Agreement other than as specifically, provided herein, not cured within Ten (10) days after Notice has been given by the Investor;

(d) Default under the Lease;

(e) Filing of a petition in bankruptcy or the appointment of a receiver or trustee in bankruptcy.

Notice given under this Section shall specify the alleged default and the applicable Agreement provisions, and shall demand that Homebuyers perform the provisions of this Agreement or the Lease within the applicable period of time, or quit the premises. No such Notice shall be deemed a forfeiture or termination of this Agreement unless Investor so states in the Notice.

9. INVESTOR'S REMEDIES IN CASE OF DEFAULT.

The Investor shall have the following remedies if the Homebuyers Default. These remedies are not exclusive and are in addition to any other remedies allowed by law or in equity.

(a) If the Homebuyers default under Section 7, Investor may terminate the Lease and regain possession of the House in any manner provided by law, the law of unlawful detainer notwithstanding, of the Investor's interest in Fifty percent (50%) of the House. At Investor's option, the Lease may remain in effect for so long as Investor does not terminate Homebuyers' right to possession of the House by Notice.

(b) If the Homebuyers fail to make any payment within Ten (10) days as set forth in Section 6(a) above, or default on any of their obligations under Section 6(b) or 6(c) above, the entire amount of past due payments and charges, plus the entire amount of monthly payments due throughout the term of the lease, plus the entire value of Investor's Investment, shall become immediately due and payable to Investor. Upon the sale or repurchase by Investor of Homebuyers' Fifty percent (50%) interest in the House, Homebuyers shall be deemed month-to-month tenants as to the entire House and shall be obliged to pay to Investor as rent an amount equal to all principal, interest, insurance, tax and assessment payments due on such property, until Homebuyers' leasehold interest in the House is terminated as set forth in the Lease.

(c) The Homebuyers acknowledge that if any monthly payment due to be made by the Homebuyers is not made when due, Investor will incur costs the exact amount of which is extremely difficult and impractical to fix. Therefore, the Homebuyers shall pay to Investor an additional sum of Eight percent (8%) of the unpaid or late paid amounts as a late charge. The parties agree that this late charge represents a fair and reasonable estimate of the costs that Investor shall incur by reason of late payment by the Homebuyers. Acceptance of any late charge shall not constitute a waiver of the Homebuyers' default with respect to the overdue amount, or prevent the Investor from exercising any of the other rights and remedies available to him.

10. OPTIONS TO PURCHASE OR SELL.

Each party shall have the right to purchase the interest of the other party in the House under the following terms and conditions:

(a) At any time during the first Twelve (12) months after the closing of the purchase of the House, the Homebuyers may purchase the Investor's interest in the House for the sum of Forty-Five Thousand Dollars ($45,000.00).

(b) At any time during the period from the Thirteenth (13th) through the Twenty-Fourth (24th) month after the closing of the purchase of the House, the Homebuyers may purchase the Investor's interest in the House or this Agreement for the sum of Sixty-Five Thousand Dollars ($65,000.00).

(c) At any time after the Twenty-Fourth (24th) month anniversary date of this Agreement, the Homebuyers may purchase the Investor's interest based on Appraised Value.

(d) If the Homebuyers should elect not to purchase Investor's interest as set forth in Section 10(a), (b), or (c), the Investor shall then have the right to purchase the Homebuyers' interest in the House for the Appraised Value of the Homebuyers' share after the Twenty-Fourth (24th) month anniversary date of this Agreement. To exercise this right Investor must give Homebuyers Notice of his intent and Thirty (30) days within which they may exercise their right under Section 10(c) to purchase the House. If the Homebuyers do not elect to purchase the House within this period, the Investor may then exercise his right to purchase.

(e) If neither the Investor nor the Homebuyers elect to purchase the other's interest in the House after the Sixty (60) month anniversary date of this Agreement, the parties agree to offer the House for sale at Appraised Value, and to accept a valid cash offer in the amount of the Appraised Value. If an offer has not been accepted within Sixty (60) days after listing, the parties agree to exercise good faith and business judgement in reducing the offering price as then may be necessary to sell the House without undue delay.

(f) The Appraised Value for determining the sale or purchase price of the home pursuant to this Section 10 shall be determined as follows. The party wishing to exercise its option to purchase the other party's interests in the House shall retain a qualified independent appraiser to appraise the House. The party retaining the appraiser shall give the other party hereto Notice of the appraised amount, and a copy of the appraiser's report within Five (5) days following its receipt of the appraisal. The other party, if it does not accept the appraisal, may within Thirty (30) days from the date of the Notice obtain its own independent appraisal, which it shall furnish to the other party in accordance with the terms of this Section. If the parties do not agree on an appraised value for the House, they shall direct the two appraisers to hire a third appraiser whose opinion shall be binding. The cost of this third appraiser shall be borne equally by both parties. Any party not objecting to the Notice it receives of an appraised value within Ten (10) days shall be deemed to have accepted such appraised value and shall be bound to buy or sell based on such value. The value for the House determined in accordance with these provisions, less the amounts to be allocated to either party on account of major repairs or capital improvements in accordance with Section 6(d), shall be the Appraised Value.

(g) The closing for any purchase pursuant to an option exercised under this Section shall take place Sixty (60) days following the Notice fixing the Appraised Value for such sale, or in the case of a purchase pursuant to Section 10 (a) or (b), Sixty (60) days following the Notice given by Homebuyers that they wish to exercise such option. If the Sixtieth (60th) day is a Saturday, Sunday or legal Holiday, the closing shall take place on the first business day thereafter. The closing shall take place at the offices of the Investor's attorney. All payments due at closing shall be made in accordance with the same terms contained in the Contract.

11. SALE OF THE HOUSE.

Upon the sale of the House, the net proceeds shall be distributed as follows:

(a) The Investor shall first receive an amount equal to the Investor's Investment, and any other monies expended by the Investor on major repairs pursuant to Section 6(d).

(b) The Homebuyers shall then receive an amount equal to their investment in the House, including the cost of any major repairs or capital improvements.

(c) The remainder of the sales price shall be divided between Investor and Homebuyers, based on their percentage of ownership.

(d) Selling party shall furnish Buyer with a marketable Title free of Liens and Judgments evidenced by a policy of Title Insurance.

11. NO PARTNERSHIP.

The Investor and the Homebuyers do not intend to be partners. The Investor may not bind or commit the Homebuyers, and the Homebuyers may not bind or commit the Investor without the prior written consent of the other. Neither party is the agent of the other.

12. NOTICES.

Any and all notices and other communications required or permitted by this Agreement shall be served on or given to either party by the other party in writing and shall be deemed duly served and given when personally delivered to any of the parties to whom it is directed, or in lieu of such personal service, when deposited in the United States Mail, using a registered or certified letter with a return receipt, postage prepaid, addressed to Investor at the address noted above, or to the Homebuyers at the House address, or such forwarding address that either party gives the other in accordance with these requirements ("Notice"). Notice shall be effective Four (4) days after mailing or on the day personally delivered.

IN WITNESS WHEREOF, the parties have signed this Agreement as of the date first above written.

_____

Ira Investor

_____

Harry Homebuyer

_____

Heidi Homebuyer

STATE OF ONESTATE   )
                         : ss.:
COUNTY OF OAKLAND   )

On this _____ day of _____ , 19 ___ , before me personally came IRA INVESTOR, to me known and known to me to be the individual described in and who execute the forgoing instrument, and he duly acknowledged to me that he executed the same.

_____

Notary Public

STATE OF ONESTATE   )
                         : ss.:
COUNTY OF OAKLAND   )

On this _____ day of _____ , 19 ___ , before me personally came HARRY HOMEBUYER, to me known and known to me to be the individual described in and who execute the forgoing instrument, and he duly acknowledged to me that he executed the same.

_____

Notary Public

STATE OF ONESTATE   )

                          : ss.:

COUNTY OF OAKLAND   )

On this _____ day of _____ , 19 __ ,
before me personally came HEIDI HOMEBUYER, to me known and
known to me to be the individual described in and who execute the
forgoing instrument, and he duly acknowledged to me that he
executed the same.

                          _____

                                  Notary Public

FORM: *EQUITY SHARING (EQUITY KICKER) NOTE*
[To be used with Equity Kicker Mortgage]

$95,000

Big City, Onestate
February 1, 1989

1. *UNDERSIGNED'S PROMISE TO PAY.*

In consideration for a loan the undersigned have received, they jointly and severally, promise to pay to Ivan Investor or any assignee or transferee thereof ("Lender"), or order, at 111 Financial Plaza, Big City, Onestate, or such other place as Lender may from time to time designate in writing, in lawful money of the United States, the principal sum of Ninety-Five Thousand Dollars ($95,000) plus interest thereon from this date on the unpaid principal balance at the rate of Ten percent (10%) per annum ("Fixed Interest"). The undersigned shall pay the principal sum and Fixed Interest calculated using a Twenty-Five (25) year amortization period, in monthly installments of Eight Hundred Fifty-Six Dollars and 13/00s ($856.13) on the first day of each month. Payments shall begin on March 1, 1989, and continue until February 1, 1996 ("Maturity"), at which time the entire amount of principal, Fixed Interest, Contingent Interest (as defined below), and any other charges set forth herein shall be due and payable.

2. *CONTINGENT INTEREST.*

Contingent Interest shall be Forty percent (40%) of the net appreciation in the value of the House from the date of this Note until Maturity. Net appreciation is the adjusted fair market value of the House on Maturity less the sum of the undersigned's cost of the House and the cost of capital improvements ("Appreciation"). Fair market value shall be determined by the actual sales price in the case of a bona fide sale made in good faith prior to Maturity (but excluding any sale upon a foreclosure or trustee's sale), or in all other cases, an appraisal performed as described below.

3. *COST OF HOUSE.*

The undersigned's cost of the House is the total cost to the borrower incident to the purchase of the House, including documentary transfer taxes, escrow and recording fees, and title insurance premiums. The undersigned's cost of the House is agreed to be One Hundred Two Thousand Dollars ($102,000).

4. CAPITAL IMPROVEMENTS.

The cost of improvements which materially prolong the useful life or increase the value of the House ("Capital Improvements") made by undersigned having an appraised value greater than Two Thousand Five Hundred Dollars ($2,500) shall be excluded from the Appreciation for purposes of calculating Contingent Interest under this Note if the following procedures are followed: (i) No improvements shall be made without the Lender's advance written permission, not to be unreasonably withheld; (ii) Within Thirty (30) days following the completion of the improvements, the undersigned shall send Notice of completion of the improvements, with proof of their cost, and undersigned's estimated increase in value of the House as a result of such improvements to the Lender; (iii) If the Lender disputes the value of such improvements and the parties cannot agree as to the value of such improvements then the Lender shall select a qualified independent appraiser to determine the increase in value of the House, if any, by reason of the improvements. The value assigned to such Capital Improvements by the appraiser shall be conclusive proof of their contribution to the increase (if any) in the value of the House and shall constitute the conclusive determination of the increase in the value of the House by reason of the Capital Improvements for purposes of computing the Appreciation. If the undersigned's estimate of the increase in the value of the House as a result of the Capital Improvements exceeds the value determined by Lender's appraiser by more than Fifteen percent (15%), then the undersigned shall bear the cost of such appraisal and the undersigned shall pay the cost of Lender's appraisal within Thirty (30) days of mailing to them of an invoice therefor. The undersigned's failue to promptly pay this cost will constitute a default under this Note.

If the undersigned dispute the Lender's Appraisal, they may at their own expense and within Thirty (30) days of the receipt of Lender's appraisal, secure a qualified independent appraiser to determine the increase in value of the House, if any, by reason of the Capital Improvements, and undersigned shall give to the Lender Notice of same.

If undersigned's appraisal is higher than the Lender's the value of the improvements will be taken to be one-half (½) the sum of the two appraisals. If Undersigned's Appraisal is not higher, Lender's Appraisal will govern.

5. SECURITY.

This loan is secured by a mortgage of even date on the House. The undersigned certify that they shall occupy the House as their principal residence. The undersigned do hereby pledge, transfer and grant to the Lender, as security for their obligations under this Note, their entire right, title and interest in the House, improvements and land described more fully in Exhibit A attached hereto (the "House").

6. APPRAISAL.

The Lender shall seclect a qualified independent appriaser to appraise the House if required pursuant to Section 2. The appraisal shall be performed within Thirty (30) days before the Maturity date of this loan, and the Lender shall give the undersigned Notice of that appraisal no later than Five (5) days following the Lender's receipt of the appraisal. The undersigned may procure an independent appraisal if they dispute the Lender's appraisal, otherwise, the Lender's appraisal shall constitute a final determination as to the value of the House.

Undersigned shall provide reasonable exterior and interior access to the House to Lender's appraiser. If undersigned fail to provide access, Lender's appraiser may choose to conduct an appraisal based only upon exterior view.

If undersigned's appraisal is lower than Lender's, the value of the House shall be taken to be one-half (½) the sum of the two appraisals. The Lender, however, in his sole discretion and at his sole expense may choose a third appraiser whose conclusions shall be binding. If undersigned's appraisal is not lower, than the Lender's appraisal shall govern.

7. PREPAYMENT.

The undersigned shall have the right to prepay, at any time, in full, the principal loan balance together with accrued Fixed Interest, Contingent Interest, and appraisal costs, if applicable. All amounts prepaid shall be credited first to appraisal or other costs, next to Fixed Interest, then to Contingent Interest, and only after all such debts have been satisfied, shall be applied to the principal loan balance.

No charge will be imposed for prepayment of the Contingent Interest after Twenty-Four (24) months from the date hereof. There will be a prepayment charge upon the prepayment of the principal amount and the Contingent Interst prior to the expiration of this time. The prepayment charge shall equal the result of the following formula (24 − number of months elapsed from the date of this Note) × 1% × the principal balance. If the maximum amount of interest allowed by law is less than the result of the above formula, such lesser amount shall be used.

8. DEFAULT/ACCELERATION.

The entire unpaid balance of principal, Fixed Interest, Contingent Interest, attorney fees, and appraisal costs provided for in this Note shall be due and payable upon Maturity, or when the House is sold (including a sale pursuant to a land sale contract), exchanged, or if title is transferred in any manner other than to or from the undersigned, a lease with an option to purchase is executed, upon a foreclosure sale, or at the time the loan is prepaid in full, whichever shall occur first.

If the undersigned fail at any time to occupy the House as their principal residence, or if they fail to make any payment due under this Note, or fail to perform any other obligation under this Note or the mortgage that secures it, then the Lender may, at his election, declare all amounts owed hereunder including the unpaid balance of principal, Fixed Interest, Contingent Interest, attorney fees, and appraisal costs, to become immediately due and payable.

9. ATTORNEY FEES AND COSTS.

The undersigned agree to pay, in addition to the amounts owned hereunder, all costs and expenses of collection and reasonable attorney fees actually incurred by the Lender in enforcing their obligations under this Note or the deed of trust that secures it, whether or not a lawsuit is filed.

10. ASSIGNMENT.

Lender may freely assign or transfer this Note and the mortgage which secures it. The undersigned may not assign or transfer this Note.

11. LATE CHARGES.

If the undersigned do not promptly pay within Ten (10) days after due, the full amount of all sums owing under this Note, including the amount due upon Maturity, interest shall accrue at the rate of Eighteen percent (18%) per annum (or the highest rate permitted by law).

12. NOTICE.

Any notice that must be given to the undersigned under this Note shall be given by certified or registered mail. All notices shall be addressed to undersigned at the House. Notice to the Lender shall be made by certified mail to the Lender at 111 Financial Plaza, Big City, Onestate. Any party hereto may change its address for notice by providing the other party hereto notice of such change in accordance with this Section ("Notice").

IN WITNESS WHEREOF, the undersigned jointly and severally intend to be legally bound by this Note and executed their signatures as of the date first above written.

_____

Betty Borrower

_____

Bob Borrower

Address for Communication:
789 Center Street
Big City, Onestate

9 FHA-INSURED MORTGAGES: THE 0.5% TO 4.6% SOLUTION

HOW FHA-INSURED MORTGAGES WORK

If you want to buy a house but can scrape up only a 3 percent to 5 percent downpayment, your first thought should be: the Federal Housing Administration. (The 0.5 percent to 4.6 percent in the chapter title is explained later on.) Yet some real estate agents bad-mouth FHA-insured loans. They aren't aware of how efficient the FHA program has become in recent years. "Brokers and lawyers," reports Robert A. Jordan, Jr., vice-president of the County Mortgage Company in West Caldwell, New Jersey, "still have a bad image of FHA- and VA-backed loans."

You should know, first of all, that the FHA—which is a branch of the U.S. Department of Housing and Urban Development—won't lend you, or anyone else, any money. But it may promise your mortgage lender (bank, savings and loan association, mortgage banker, insurance company) that if you default, the FHA will keep the lender from losing a penny: the FHA will pay off the lender and take over the house.

That's how mortgage lenders are able to give you a mortgage with only a 3 percent to 5 percent downpayment; if—because of illness, divorce, loss of your job, whatever—you stop making those mortgage payments and your house is foreclosed, Uncle Sam is ready to pay off the lender.

FHA-insured mortgages are tailor-made for first-time home buyers and low-income families. In fact, around three out of every five FHA clients are first-time home buyers. But don't despair if you're fairly well-to-do. As we shall see, the FHA insures lots of mortgages for prosperous people, too. And apparently Congress wants it that way.

FHA-insured mortgages aren't strange, complex contraptions. Since 1934, the FHA has helped over 17 million American families buy homes, and 10 percent to 12 percent of all homes bought in the United States have FHA-backed mortgages. And, yes, condominiums qualify, as do cooperatives and manufactured homes—so long as you're going to live in them, not rent them out. As for new houses, if a house under construction is less than a year old, your down-payment must be 10 percent, not just 3 percent to 5 percent. Not eligible for FHA insurance are loans for recreational vehicles, house-boats, and yachts.

TOP LIMITS ON FHA MORTGAGE INSURANCE

The most obvious benefit of an FHA-insured mortgage, of course, is the 3 percent to 5 percent downpayment. Naturally, you won't pay just a pittance down if you buy a luxurious house with an astronomical mortgage. The FHA has limits on how much of a mortgage it will insure.

The highest-priced home mortgage that the FHA will normally insure—in high-income areas—is $101,250. (In figuring out the mortgage amount, oddly enough, the FHA includes estimated closing costs, if the buyer pays them.) But the FHA is flexible, and the mortgage amount may be even greater in areas with unusually high house prices. The proposal has even been floated that the FHA be allowed to insure 95 percent of the mortgage on the median house sales price in any area—which would mean dizzying amounts in pricey places like Beverly Hills or Greenwich, Connecticut.

The top mortgage amount that the FHA will insure in all other areas is $67,500. The average FHA-insured mortgage for a single-family home is $60,000.

So, what's the top price on an FHA-insured home? Theoretically, you could buy a $1-million or $10-million house with a $900,000- or $9-million mortgage and still get FHA insurance on a relatively small part of it—$101,250. You would have to borrow the remainder from the lender, with probably a 20 percent downpayment. Practically, however, this is unlikely.

HOW MUCH OF A DOWNPAYMENT?

The downpayment the FHA requires—if you intend to live in a house, not rent it or sell it—is 3 percent of the first $25,000 of the mortgage, and 5 percent of the next $50,000. For a house valued under $50,000, the downpayment remains 3 percent. If it's over $50,000, the 5 percent rate kicks in after $25,000. (Many excellent manufactured houses and houses in remote areas, by the way, do sell for less than $50,000.) Thus, no one pays a full 5 percent downpayment on an FHA-insured mortgage, because part of the downpayment will be at 3 percent.

The chart below should make matters clearer. Keep in mind that for every extra $1,000 above $50,000 you spend for an owner-occupied, existing, or proposed one-family home, you must pay $50 in cash.

Mortgage Maximums and Minimum Downpayments

FHA-Appraised*	Maximum Mortgage	Minimum Downpayment**
$30,000	$29,100	$ 900
40,000	38,800	1,200
50,000	48,500	1,500
60,000	57,500	2,500
70,000	67,000	3,000

* Value plus closing costs.
** Not including mortgage insurance, explained below.

For a home appraised at $71,000, including closing costs, you'll need a $3,050 downpayment. For a home appraised at $100,000, including closing costs, you must pay $750 for the first $25,000, and for the remaining $75,000, $3,750 [75 × $50]. Total: $4,500. You need a downpayment of $750 on the first $25,000 and 5 percent on the rest if your home sells for over $50,000. And the total can't normally be more than $101,250, or your downpayment may be much higher. That works out so that the highest price you can normally pay for a home including closing costs, and get the official maximum FHA mortgage insurance, is around $103,000—4.5 percent more than $101,250 minus $2,800 estimated closing costs. The 4.5 percent rate represents a merger between 3 percent and 5 percent.

Earlier, it was noted that the downpayment on an FHA mortgage is 3 percent to 5 percent. Now you know that 5 percent is too high. What about that 0.5 percent?

Look at the $30,000 in the chart above. The $30,000 includes closing costs, which the FHA estimates at $1,650 in some areas. So the house costs $28,350. The mortgage is for $750 more than that. Subtract $750 from the $900 downpayment and you get $150. And $150 is 0.529 percent of $28,350, the house price. On a $48,000 mortgage, the real downpayment is only 2.1 percent. On a maximum $101,250 mortgage, the real downpayment is about 4.6 percent. Still, because good houses below $50,000 are not plentiful, and because 4.6 percent is close to 5 percent, we have used the somewhat misleading 3 percent to 5 percent.

OTHER BENEFITS OF FHA-BACKED MORTGAGES

Other advantages of an FHA-insured mortgage, besides the low downpayment are:

- The interest rate is usually below the going rates for conventional (nongovernmental) mortgages.
- The lender—not you—deals with the FHA. You save time and effort.
- These days, you can get fairly rapid approval of an FHA-insured mortgage: 45–60 days is typical.
- You're more likely to get an FHA-insured mortgage than a conventional mortgage—and for a higher-priced house. For a conventional mortgage, your housing expenses can't exceed 25 percent to 28 percent of your total monthly income. The FHA permits 35 percent. For a conventional mortgage your total debts can't exceed 33 percent to 36 percent of your total monthly income. The FHA permits 50 percent.
- You can, nonetheless, obtain a variety of FHA-insured mortgages—fixed-rate, adjustable rate, graduated payment. You can make monthly payments over a term of 10, 20, 25, or 30 years—and in special cases, 35 years.
- FHA-insured mortgages are assumable: they can be taken over by the person who eventually buys your house, at the original interest rate (or current rate, in the case of an adjustable or graduated-payment mortgage) and on the original terms. This makes a house with an FHA-insured mortgage easier to sell. Buyers don't have to pay closing costs or undergo a credit check, and if interest rates have risen, they may be getting a fixed-rate mortgage with a bargain interest rate.

CAUTION: The FHA has a new rule that if an FHA-insured mortgage is less than two years old, the new buyer must undergo a credit check with the FHA-approved lender. The same rule applies if it's been less than two years since another buyer assumed the mortgage.

Of course, if your house has soared in value, a buyer who assumes your mortgage will have to come up with the difference between the sales price, minus the remaining mortgage, and his or her downpayment—which could be quite a lot. You could face the same problem if you want to buy a house that already has an FHA-insured mortgage. (Ideally, you'll assume an FHA-insured mortgage a little over two years after it's been in effect, and the house won't have appreciated much.)

- You can even borrow money for the small downpayment, providing that the downpayment loan is backed by real assets other than the property being bought. Examples are a car or securities. For an exception made for people 60 or over, see below.

CAUTION: You cannot qualify for an FHA-insured mortgage if a builder who sells you a new house lowers your downpayment by more than 3 percent (which a builder might do, as an incentive for you to buy the house).

- Finally, you can get an FHA-insured loan even if you buy a mansion or if your income is in the stratosphere. A study commissioned by the FHA's archenemy, the private mortgage insurance industry, reported (in 1987) that between 1982 and 1986, 60 percent of FHA-insured mortgages went to borrowers earning over 120 percent of the typical national income, while 44 percent went to borrowers earning over 140 percent of the typical national income. During that same period, 35 percent of FHA-insured mortgages went to borrowers earning over $40,000, while 9 percent went to borrowers earning over $60,000.

THE DRAWBACKS OF AN FHA-BACKED MORTGAGE

One of the disadvantages of an FHA-insured mortgage is that you must now obtain mortgage insurance, and it's not cheap—3.8 percent of the amount insured by the FHA. On a $60,000 mortgage insured by the FHA, that's $2,280, payable at the closing. (In real life, many lenders allow buyers to spread out the mortgage insurance payment over the course of the regular mortgage payments.) Also, you'll have to make a higher downpayment if you're buying a house for more than the HUD or the Veterans Administration estimate of the property's value. Still, these are minor blemishes compared with the benefits of an FHA-insured mortgage.

HOW TO QUALIFY

These are the general criteria you need to qualify for an FHA-backed mortgage:

- You must have a "satisfactory" credit record.
- You must have the money to pay for closing costs—typically, 2 percent to 3 percent of the cost of the house, not including any points you must pay to the lender. But remember: the closing costs are included in the purchase price, so your downpayment is even lower than you might have calculated—and you may have some cash left over.
- You must have a steady income, to assure the FHA that you can keep up those mortgage payments.
- The residence must "at least meet the objectives of HUD minimum standards, which require that the house be liveable, soundly built, and suitably located as to site and neighborhood." A hovel condemned by the local board of health won't do.

Some important points:

- You can get an FHA-insured mortgage even if you buy a foreclosed home; if you buy a house with experimental design and methods; if you're a disaster victim; if you live in rural areas, or special urban areas; if you work for the Coast Guard or the National Oceanic and Atmospheric Administration.
- The FHA is fair and open-minded. It does not discriminate with regard to creed or sex. You can be single or divorced. Likewise, your race or color don't matter. Nor does age: you can be as old as Methusaleh and qualify for an FHA-insured mortgage. In fact, older people get a special break. A buyer 60 years or older can borrow the money for the downpayment from a person or corporation approved by HUD. Nor is there

a certain income you must have to buy a house at a certain price—though income is one of the factors that the FHA considers in deciding whether someone can repay a mortgage.

Veterans also get special favors. If they get a "certificate of eligibility" from the Veterans Administration, they can obtain FHA-insured mortgages with lower-than-normal qualifications, higher mortgage amounts, and lower downpayments. And because there are more FHA lenders than VA lenders, many veterans are steered toward the FHA. (But VA-backed mortgages have important advantages. See the next chapter on VA-guaranteed mortgages.)

Veterans who don't qualify for VA-guaranteed loans can get favored treatment from the FHA. But they must obtain a "certificate of veteran status" by filing VA Form 26-8261a. All vets except those dishonorably discharged may be eligible. Qualifications:

- You served at least 90 days of service, beginning before September 8, 1980.
- You must have served at least 24 months before being discharged if you are a vet of enlisted service in a regular component of the armed forces, beginning after September 7, 1980—or if you are an officer or reservist who entered into active duty after October 13, 1982. Exception: You need not have served 24 months if the discharge was for hardship or disability.

OBTAINING THE LOAN

To find a lender who makes FHA-insured mortgages, look in the Yellow Pages under "Mortgages," and check for lenders with display advertisements that specify "FHA." Or telephone a local FHA office (under U.S. Government, Housing and Urban Development). Or phone the FHA in Washington, DC, at (202) 755-6600.

Don't go to just one lender. Check out several. See what interest rate each one charges (and how long it's guaranteed before the closing), the number of points, the length of the mortgage, and closing costs. Keep a checklist to compare the various offers. (See Chapter 14.)

Lenders will ask you to fill out an application. You'll have to show your most recent savings statement and your salary stub. And you'll have to produce identification with a photograph of yourself that the lender can copy (a photo driver's license will do), along with proof of your Social Security number.

You'll have to pay the cost of an appraisal (a few hundred dollars) and a credit report fee ($10-$15). You'll also have to pay for mortgage insurance. In many areas, at the closing you must pay the mortgage insurance premium (MIP) in one lump sum. You can pay it in cash or finance it—borrow the money to pay. (In the old days, you could pay off MIP every month, but that's against the official rules now.) If you pay off your mortgage in a few years, you'll be entitled to refunds from MIP. You can pay off the entire mortgage balance any time, or make extra payments of principal. But you should give the lender written notice at least 30 days in advance that you intend to do so.

To make sure that the application process doesn't take longer than 45 to 60 days, check whether a lender on a one-family house can approve the loan, or whether the lender must have FHA endorsement to approve the loan. "Direct endorsement" processing means that the lender can approve loan commitments without submitting the paperwork to the FHA. Around 90 percent of all FHA lenders have the direct-endorsement privilege. "HUD processing" means that the lender must first submit the paperwork to the FHA to get approval. Obviously, you'll save time by dealing with a lender authorized to make loan commitments without first getting approval from the FHA.

CHAPTER SUMMARY

If you qualify for an FHA-insured mortgage, you can make a down payment of less than 5 percent of the house's value. But if the house you buy costs more than around $103,000, you'll have to boost your downpayment by quite a lot. And in any case, you'll have to pay for mortgage insurance—at 3.8 percent of the mortgage, a significant cost. But qualifying for an FHA-insured mortgage is far easier than qualifying for any other kind of mortgage. That's why first-time home buyers, or anyone else who will have trouble raising the traditional 20 percent downpayment, should first think of FHA-insured mortgages. Unless, of course, they happen to be veterans.

10 VA-GUARANTEED LOANS: THE 0% SOLUTION

WHY NONVETERANS SHOULD BE INTERESTED

Even if you're not a veteran, you may benefit from mortgages guaranteed by the Veterans Administration. ("Guaranteed" means that if the homeowner defaults, the VA will pay the lender the amount of the mortgage that the VA "guaranteed.")

You might buy a house from a seller who has a VA-guaranteed mortgage, take over the mortgage, and have to pay him or her only for the appreciation on the house. If the seller hasn't lived in the place long, or if the house simply hasn't grown much in value or has actually declined, your downpayment could be tiny. After all, the owner probably bought the house with no downpayment, and thus has little or no equity (free-and-clear ownership) in the place. By assuming the mortgage, you would also escape closing costs, and your interest rate might be unusually low if rates have risen recently.

CAUTION: You cannot assume a VA-guaranteed loan (as of March 1, 1988) without undergoing a credit check by either the VA or whoever now holds the mortgage.

WHY SOME VETERANS IGNORE VA-GUARANTEED MORTGAGES

Of course, if you happen to be one of the 20 million Americans (just since World War II) who are veterans, the VA will bend over backward to help you buy a house—beyond just enabling you to buy the place with no downpayment.

Yet many veterans don't take advantage of VA-guaranteed mortgages. The number of mortgages backed by the VA in 1988 was way down from the year before. Why? Some possibilities are:

- Veterans—and lenders—may not know that the VA has simplified and speeded up its approval process. The bureaucratic old days are over. Now, getting a VA-backed mortgage takes no longer than obtaining an FHA-insured mortgage or getting private mortgage insurance—45 to 60 days.

- Veterans may not be aware that the VA has increased the maximum percentage of a mortgage it will guarantee. The new limit is $36,000, or 50 percent of the total (whichever is smaller), on a mortgage up to $45,000. Above $45,000, the VA will guarantee 40 percent to a maximum of $36,000. But whatever the amount above $45,000, the VA will guarantee at least $22,500. Otherwise, someone with a $45,000–$56,250 mortgage would have less of it guaranteed than a person with a $44,999 mortgage [$56,250 × .40 = $22,500].

Thus you can buy a house valued at $144,000 with no downpayment—$36,000 is 25 percent of $144,000, and lenders are happy with 25 percent guaranteed. If you buy a house with a mortgage of more than $144,000 and need to borrow more money from a conventional (nongovernmental) lender, you may have to make a sizable downpayment on that second mortgage. If your mortgage is $45,000 or less, the VA will guarantee up to $22,500, or 50 percent of the loan.

What the VA Will Guarantee

Total Mortgage Amount	Amount Guaranteed
Up to $45,000	50%
$45,000–$144,000	Up to $36,000 or 40%, whichever is less; but not less than $22,500

- Veterans themselves may not know that they are entitled to VA-guaranteed loans forever. "I encounter a lot of veterans who wrongly think their benefits have lapsed," reports Robert Jordan,

Jr. of County Mortgage Co. in West Caldwell, New Jersey. Recently, a 72-year-old veteran of World War II, who had long ago paid off the old VA-backed mortgage he had once taken out, was delighted to learn that he could still obtain a VA-guaranteed mortgage.

- Veterans may not know that they are eligible for a partial mortgage guarantee, the amount of the guarantee having increased since they last took out a VA-backed loan. Years ago, the amount guaranteed was only $2,000. (But most lenders insist that any remaining partial guarantee entitlement, plus any cash downpayment, must equal at least 25 percent of the property's value.) Another reason a vet may have a partial guarantee is that the vet sold a house to someone who assumed the mortgage, and the new owner has paid down much of the mortgage. So the vet still has some of the $36,000/40 percent remaining.

OTHER BLESSINGS OF VA-BACKED MORTGAGES

- No downpayment. VA-guaranteed mortgages resemble FHA-insured mortgages and especially PMI (see Chapter 12), except that if you're eligible for a VA-guaranteed mortgage, you need not make any downpayment. The exceptions are if the purchase price is more than the appraised value; if you get a graduated-payment mortgage (the downpayment is to prevent negative amortization, whereby you could eventually owe more than the house is worth); or if the lender you use insists on a downpayment. In that case, try another lender.

- Low interest rate. The VA itself sets the maximum mortgage rate, which is usually lower than on conventional mortgages, and lenders must go along—or charge points to the seller (see below). The FHA accepts the market rate.

- Wide range. You can obtain VA-guaranteed financing to buy a townhouse or condo in a project approved by the VA; to buy a manufactured home, or a lot for one; to build a new home; to repair or improve a home; to purchase a home; or to refinance an existing loan. But usually you cannot get a VA-guaranteed loan to buy a cooperative—it's too complicated to work out such a deal. Recreational vehicles, houseboats, and yachts are out.

- Flexibility. VA-guaranteed loans are also flexible. You can get one to pay off the mortgage on your home, plus additional money "for any purpose which is acceptable to the lender." You can refinance an existing VA-guaranteed loan to get a lower interest rate.

- Leniency. If a veteran has trouble making a mortgage payment, the VA may be tolerant. "Forbearance (leniency)," states the VA, is "extended to worthy VA homeowners experiencing temporary financial difficulty."

- Prepayment. Finally, you can prepay the loan without penalty, though lenders may insist that you prepay only specified amounts, like a monthly installment of $100.

THE DOWNSIDE OF VA-BACKED MORTGAGES

VA-guaranteed loans have negative aspects, too. While they are, strictly speaking, no-downpayment loans, veterans must pay the government a "funding fee" of 1 percent of the mortgage. This is due at the closing, but the amount may be included in the loan and paid from loan proceeds. (Certain people are exempt from the funding fee: those receiving VA compensation for service-connected disabilities, or who would be entitled to such compensation if they weren't receiving retirement pay, or who are surviving spouses of vets who died in service or from a service-connected disability.)

Also, veterans must pay the lender an "origination fee" of one point—1 percent of the loan. So, in effect, buyers must fork over 2 percent of the mortgage to get a VA-guaranteed mortgage. It's not a "downpayment," because that 2 percent doesn't count toward the ownership of the house. It would be nice if it did. Sellers must then pay any points the lender charges above the one point the buyer pays. If a vet gets a $60,000, VA-guaranteed mortgage ($24,000 is guaranteed), the vet pays $600, or one point. If the lender wants two more points, the seller must fork over $1,200. Sellers aren't thrilled about this, as you might imagine. (Apart from VA-guaranteed loans, the buyers of houses usually don't pay any points.) What sellers may do, once they learn that a buyer will apply for a VA-guaranteed loan, is not lower their offering prices. Most sellers price their houses 5 percent to 10 percent above the amount they would accept, just for bargaining purposes. But sellers rarely bargain with buyers who will apply for VA-guaranteed mortgages—unless they are unusually eager to move out.

Vets may also have to pay extra points with the following VA-backed loans: for refinancing a home, for repairing or improving their property, when building a home on land they already own or will buy from someone other than their builder, and when the seller cannot legally pay any points (the seller might be the executor of an estate, or a sheriff selling a house at foreclosure).

Another negative is that the VA won't guarantee adjustable-rate loans. They will guarantee fixed-interest loans, graduated-payment mortgages, growing-equity mortgages, and buydowns. GPMs are loans in which you make smaller-than-normal monthly payments for the first few years, and eventually make larger-than-normal payments. With GEMs, the monthly payments gradually increase over the years, with all of the increases applied to the principal, so that the mortgage is paid off early. A buydown is where the builder of a new home or the seller of an existing home "buys down" (lowers) the buyer's mortgage payments, usually for three to five years, by making a large contribution. But GPMs, as mentioned, entail a downpayment. And in any case, GPMs and GEMs aren't popular.

Fixed-interest loans are usually better for buyers than ARMs, because buyers will know what they must pay from month to month and won't go into shock if the interest rate suddenly zooms. But lenders prefer ARMs, because they can then shift the risk of an interest-rate increase onto the buyer. So it's not just sellers who may be a bit leery of VA-guaranteed, fixed-rate mortgages. So are many lenders.

A final disadvantage concerns assumability. Even though your mortgage is assumable, you cannot get another VA-guaranteed mortgage until the buyer who assumed your home pays off that mortgage. Exceptions: You're off the hook if your buyer is a veteran, assumes the balance of the loan, and substitutes his or her entitlement for the same amount of the entitlement you originally used to get the loan. Even then, you must apply to get your entitlement restored. Use VA Form 26-1880. Also, you may continue to be liable for the VA-backed mortgage if someone assumes your mortgage. But you can obtain a release of liability—by having the VA approve the buyer and the assumption agreement. Ask for a release of liability from the VA office that guaranteed your loan.

WHICH IS BETTER—VA OR FHA?

The FHA insures the entire amount of a mortgage, up to $101,500. The VA guarantees up to $36,000 of a mortgage over $45,000, or 40 percent, up to $144,000, without a downpayment. So, not only does a veteran have less of a downpayment by going with the VA, the vet can also buy a more expensive house. Further, while a vet must pay the VA a "funding fee"—1 percent of the mortgage—to guarantee the loan, the FHA requires a mortgage insurance premium of 3.8 percent.

Still another difference is that while the VA specifies the interest rate on a VA-backed mortgage, the FHA goes with the market rate. So the VA's rate is usually a little lower. Still, lenders may prefer FHA-backed mortgages; as mentioned, lenders lean toward adjustable-rate mortgages. Finally, in a foreclosure, the FHA must take over a house and pay the lender. But the VA has a choice: it may take over a foreclosed house—or it may decide to pay the lender the mortgage amount guaranteed and let the lender keep the house. Most lenders prefer cash from the FHA to the possibility of having the VA present them with a foreclosed home.

So, if a lender ever suggests that you choose an FHA-insured mortgage over a VA-guaranteed mortgage that you qualify for, you will know why.

WHO IS ELIGIBLE?

To qualify, you must have a good credit record. You must also have enough income to meet the mortgage payments on the loan, cover other obligations, and have sufficient left over to support your family. You must live in your house, or intend to live there, within a reasonable period after closing the loan. (You can't intend to rent it out.)

If you are a veteran and your spouse isn't, your loan still qualifies for the full coverage. But if you're buying a house with another person, not your spouse and not a veteran, you get only half the coverage. That means the arrangement will be complicated and lenders may not be eager to deal with you, so in that situation you might be better off with an FHA-insured mortgage.

Obviously, your age doesn't matter. Nor does your marital status. And there's no problem if your income comes from any public assistance programs.

How long you must have served to qualify is a little complicated. It depends on whether you served in peacetime or wartime, whether you are now on active duty, and so forth. The following rules provide a framework for determining qualification:

(1) Wartime: Did you serve at any time during these periods?

(a) World War II (September 16, 1940–July 25, 1947)

(b) Korean Conflict (June 27, 1950–January 31, 1955)

(c) Vietnam Era (August 5, 1964–May 7, 1975)

To qualify, you must have served for at least 90 days on active duty, and not have been dishonorably discharged or released. If you served fewer than 90 days, you may be eligible if you were discharged because of a disability connected with your service.

(2) Peacetime: Did you serve entirely during any of the following periods?

(a) July 26, 1947–June 26, 1950

(b) February 1, 1955–August 4, 1964

(c) May 8, 1975–September 7, 1980 (if enlisted)

(d) May 8, 1975–October 16, 1981 (if officer)

To qualify, you must have served at least 181 days of continuous active duty and not have been dishonorably discharged or released. If you served fewer than 181 days, you may be eligible if you were discharged because of a disability connected with your service.

(3) Service After:

(a) September 7, 1980 (if enlisted)

(b) October 16, 1981 (if officer)

If your service began after these dates, you must have completed 24 months (730 days) of continuous active duty, and not have been discharged or released dishonorably; completed at least 181 days of active duty, with a discharge for hardship or for the convenience of the government; or you had a disability connected with your service that you were eligible to be compensated for; or you were discharged for a disability connected with your service.

(4) Current Active Service: If you're now on active duty, you're eligible after you've served on continuous active status for at least 181 days.

(5) Other Types Of Service: Also eligible for benefits are the following;

(a) Certain U.S. citizens who served in the armed forces of a government allied with the U.S. during World War II, such as England.

(b) Unmarried widows or widowers of eligible veterans who died as the result of service or because of injuries in the service.

(c) The spouses of any members of the armed forces serving on active duty who are listed as missing in action—or who have been prisoners of war for more than 90 days.

(d) People who served for certain other organizations, programs, or schools, such as the U.S. Public Health Service and the U.S. Military Academy at West Point.

What if husband and wife are both veterans and they buy a house together? Can they get more than $36,000 of the mortgage guaranteed? No, but if they have used up part of their entitlements, they can combine what's left to reach $36,000. For example, they may have used VA financing to buy a house that they are now renting out, or that they sold to someone who took over their mortgage.

WHO ISN'T ELIGIBLE?

You are not eligible for VA financing if you served in World War I, if you served on active duty for training in the Reserves, or if you served active duty for training in the National Guard (unless you were activated). But you might then qualify for a favorable FHA veterans' loan. (See Chapter 9.) Children of deceased veterans are not eligible. Even if you're an eligible veteran, you cannot get a loan for purchasing property in a foreign country. You must confine yourself to the United States and its territories—Puerto Rico, Guam, Virgin Islands, American Samoa, and the Northern Mariana Islands.

HOW TO QUALIFY

The reason it doesn't take as long to get a VA-backed loan these days is that many lenders can approve the guarantees themselves, without the okay of the VA. The VA is also allowing lenders to arrange house appraisals.

TIP: To speed things up, make sure you deal with a lender who can do "automatic" processing—is not restricted to "prior approval" processing. Around 85 percent of VA-backed loans are processed under the automatic procedure.

To obtain a VA-guaranteed mortgage, you must have a "certificate of eligibility" from the VA. If you must request one, complete VA Form 26-1880. Submit it with the original or copies of your most recent discharge or separation papers covering active military duty since September 16, 1940. If you left the service after January 1, 1950, submit DD Form 214. If you are now on active duty, submit a statement of service on military letterhead, signed by the adjutant, personnel officer, or commander of your unit, or higher headquarters. The statement must include the date of your entry into active duty, and the duration of any time you lost.

CHAPTER SUMMARY

Normally, the only way you can buy a home with no money down is to be a qualified veteran and deal with a lender authorized to work with the Veterans Administration. In that case, you can buy a house for up to $144,000 with no downpayment.

But you will have to pay one point (1 percent of the mortgage— $1,440 in the case of a $144,000 house) to the lender. And you will have to pay a one-point "funding fee" to the VA.

VA-guaranteed loans are assumable, even by nonveterans. That may make it easier for you to sell your house—especially if you obtain a fixed-rate mortgage and interest rates rise. But normally you won't be able to buy another house with a full VA-guaranteed mortgage until the buyer pays off your existing mortgage—unless the buyer is a veteran and substitutes for you.

11 THE PERFECT MORTGAGE

THE CASE FOR A 30-YEAR MORTGAGE

Most of the time, a low downpayment will mean you'll be saddled with higher mortgage payments, because (1) you'll be borrowing more money, (2) the interest rate you'll be charged will be slightly higher, and (3) you may be paying for mortgage insurance, perhaps over many years of the life of the mortgage. (See Chapter 1.)

That's one argument for choosing a mortgage with the longest possible term. Your monthly payments will be lower and more affordable, even though the total interest you will wind up paying over the years will be higher. The following table shows the difference between 15- and 30-year mortgages at various interest rates:

15- and 30-Year $50,000 Mortgages

Interest Rate	Monthly Payments		Income to Qualify	
	15 Years	30 Years	15 Years	30 Years
10%	$537.30	$438.79	$31,600	$27,400
10.5	552.70	457.37	32,300	28,200
11	568.30	476.16	32,900	29,100
11.5	584.09	495.15	33,600	29,800
12	600.08	514.31	34,300	30,600

But bear in mind that inflation will probably be with us for many more years. So, if you stay in the house, you'll be paying for your mortgage with cheaper money. You'll probably be getting bigger raises and more generous dividends from your stocks.

Also bear in mind that money you borrow against your house is probably the cheapest loan you can obtain. The interest rate is comparatively low, and your interest is probably fully tax deductible—

unlike the interest you pay on credit card loans, car loans, or student loans. And if tax rates rise, as they probably will sometime in the future, you'll benefit even more from the fact that your mortgage interest may remain deductible.

Finally, keep in mind that most home buyers sell their houses in seven to ten years. Interest payments make up the lion's share of mortgage payments in the early years; principal repayments don't really enter the picture until a mortgage is fairly old. So, for most of the time that you will remain in your house, most of your mortgage payments will be deductible for tax purposes if you can itemize your deductions on Schedule A, Form 1040.

But what if you want to own your house free and clear as soon as possible? A long-term mortgage means you'll pay less every month, have more money to spend on necessities, and more to save for emergencies. But if you're able to finance all of your other necessities and build up a healthy emergency fund, equal to three to six months' income, you can start paying off your principal earlier if you wish. Just mail your lender extra payments, specifying that they're to be applied to your principal. Be careful to check your mortgage agreement to see how prepayments will be treated, however. Also, be aware that you'll be getting a less favorable tax result.

On the whole, to be on the safe side, you're best off seeking a 30-year mortgage.

THE CASE AGAINST BIWEEKLY MORTGAGES

You've probably heard a lot about biweekly mortgages. You pay the mortgage every two weeks instead of every month, and you own your house outright in almost no time at all.

Unfortunately, mortgage lenders report that many people have trouble paying even monthly mortgages on time. If you are one of these people, making biweekly payments would be torture, especially when you add in any late charges you might owe. You need an iron discipline to pay a biweekly mortgage—and no unexpected expenses, such as braces for the kids or a new transmission for your car.

But isn't mortgage interest just like rent? Aren't you throwing money away? No, because you can deduct mortgage interest. Furthermore, you're paying that interest in order to borrow money you can use better elsewhere—on braces and transmissions, for example, if not investments. In addition, as stated, the interest will hurt less and less as inflation inevitably makes money cheaper and cheaper.

DEFINITIONS

A mortgage is a legal document that secures a loan you've made (which is evidenced by a note) for real estate. If you can't pay back the money you've borrowed according to the schedule you've agreed to, that's a "default," and the real estate legally can be taken away from you—"foreclosure." (Usually being 90 days late is considered a default, but the period may vary so check your mortgage and note.) The real estate may be sold and the proceeds used to repay the "mortgagee"—the person or institution that lent you the money in the first place. Depending on local law you may have a period in which to redeem your house. The laws affecting real estate vary considerably from state to state, so check with an attorney.

When you pay your monthly mortgage payments to the lender, you may also be paying property tax and insurance escrow amounts. Most lenders want to make sure you pay the property taxes and casualty insurance, so they collect them from you to send on to the state or county (etc.) tax departments and the insurance company.

How long a time you have to pay off your mortgage is its "term." The longest term is usually 30 years, but 35-year mortgages are sometimes available.

The "principal" is the amount you borrowed. The interest rate is the percentage of the principal you must give the bank every month to reward it for letting you borrow its money. The "annual percentage rate" (APR) is even more important than the interest rate. It's the interest rate plus other costs—particularly the cost of "points." A point is a special charge that the lender assesses you for keeping the interest rate down. One point is equal to 1 percent of the loan amount. The APR includes the points, assuming that you pay them off along with the mortgage, not up front. That's why, when you compare mortgages, you must pay more attention to the APR than to the interest rate itself.

With the most common type of mortgage, the amount of your payments will be the same month after month. (If there's any change, it's because property taxes have gone up or down—not your interest and principal payments.) Your monthly payments go toward paying the interest first. Then, as the years go by, the payments begin to retire more and more of the principal. Near the end of the mortgage's term, you will be paying off far more of the principal than at the beginning. This type of mortgage, which has you pay off both your principal and your interest at the same time, and owe nothing at all at the end of the mortgage's term, is called "self-amortizing."

ARM

In the early 1980s, a new type of mortgage was introduced: the adjustable-rate mortgage (ARM). Here, the interest rate isn't fixed and unchanging over the mortgage's term. Instead, it goes up or down according to how interest rates in general are behaving—and so do your monthly payments. In other words, the lender is shifting onto the borrower much of the risk that interest rates will climb.

To compensate the borrower, the lender sees to it that an ARM has a lower interest rate than a fixed-rate mortgage—for a period of a few months to a few years. The fact that an ARM carries a lower initial interest rate means that your early mortgage payments will be lower—and you can usually qualify for a larger mortgage amount.

The interest rate on an ARM is linked to the interest rate on an index—a marker of interest rates in general. As the index rate goes up or down, the ARM's rate will follow. The change might be made every year, every three years, or every five years.

In a typical case, the rate on an ARM is set at one to one and a half percentage points above the interest rate on a one-year Treasury bill (this is called the margin), and then is adjusted every year. If the Treasury bill rate is 7 percent one year, and 7.5 percent a year later, an ARM's interest rate might go from 8.5 percent to 9 percent a year later.

Commonly used indexes include six-month Treasury bills, one-year Treasury bills, three-year Treasury notes, five-year Treasury notes, the national mortgage contract rate, and the 11th District Cost of Funds (the weighted average cost of all funds that flow into 239 savings institutions in California, Arizona, and Nevada).

The typical ARM carries a 30-year term. The initial interest rate is usually about 2.5 percent below the index rate used, plus the margin for the lender. The most common index is a Treasury bill or note, and the adjustment period is one or three years. Interest increases are usually "capped": there is a limit of two percentage points per adjustment and five or six points over the life of the loan.

FIXED RATE OR ADJUSTABLE RATE?

No doubt about it, for most people, fixed-rate mortgages are the best mortgages of all. You know how much to budget for the expense from month to month. And if interest rates rise, you'll be in the catbird seat. All those homeowners who had been paying so little interest with ARMs will now be screaming in pain.

But for homeowners who can afford only low or no downpayments, ARMs may be the way to go. You're more likely to get a mortgage with a low or no downpayment if you spring for an ARM. The reason is that the interest rate on an ARM starts out low. That means that, for a few years, your mortgage payments will be lower than if you had chosen a fixed-rate mortgage. And that in turn means that the ratio of your available income to the mortgage payments will be higher. The upshot is that most lenders will look upon your application for a loan with more favor. They will consider only your first-year housing costs, with a mortgage reduced because of the ARM.

Another reason to choose an ARM is if you're planning to remain in the house only a few years. The lower initial interest rate is perfect for someone who plans to sell and move in only two or three years. Interest rates would have to skyrocket, even if you have a one-year adjustable, for you to not to come out ahead with an ARM.

CAUTION: Some lenders in certain areas may insist on a high downpayment with an ARM.

HOW TO SHOP

A terrible mistake is to concentrate on a mortgage's interest rate. Far more important, as mentioned, is the annual percentage rate, which includes points. Don't underestimate the power of points.

Also check into other charges—loan origination fees, appraisal charges, legal fees. Check whether the lender will hit you with a fee if you pay off your mortgage early—which you might do if you sell your house. (Many states prohibit prepayment penalties.) Find out whether the lender collects property taxes and insurance payments from you, and, if so, whether the lender will pay you interest on this money put into "escrow." If not, you might want to pay the taxes and insurance yourself, putting your money into a money market fund, where it can earn interest before you must pay the bills.

Inquire whether your mortgage will be assumable by a future buyer. That could be a strong selling point when you put a house on the market, especially if you have a fixed-rate mortgage with a large balance and interest rates have risen. Even an assumable ARM could be a selling point if you've reached the limit on the lifetime cap, or are fairly close.

You should look for an ARM that can be adjusted only seldom—every five years is best, but three is acceptable. A one-year adjustment period should make you nervous. Some ARMs can change their rates every month, and they are to be avoided like the plague.

Also look for an ARM linked to an index that has been stable. The 11th District Cost of Funds has proved especially stable. In 1981, the prime rate (the rate lenders charge their best customers) reached 21 percent. One-year Treasuries exceeded 16 percent. But the highest rate on the 11th District Cost of Funds was 12.6 percent in 1982. Among Treasuries, the longer the maturity, the better. Six-month Treasuries may be much less stable than five-year Treasuries. The very worst of indexes is the cost of funds to a lender itself. A lender using such an index might raise its interest rates on certificates of deposit, just to become more competitive, and rates on its ARM would therefore climb.

Check into the caps, too. While a two-percentage-point cap per change, and five- or six-percentage-point cap over the life of the loan are acceptable, see if you can do better. You'll have to compare the frequency of possible changes with the total amount that can be changed. Be on guard against a cap that doesn't start until after the first rate adjustment.

Beware of ARMs with "teaser" rates—very low initial interest rates. At the first adjustment period, the rate reverts to normal or higher. You may be subject to "interest rate shock" the first time the interest rate is adjusted. And you may wind up paying more in the long run.

Also steer clear of "pay-capped" ARMs, in which your monthly payments are kept level even if the interest rate rises. The interest you haven't paid is added back into the loan balance, which could cause negative amortization after a few years—where you owe more on the mortgage than you started out owing.

TIP: An especially desirable ARM is "convertible"—it can be turned into a fixed-rate loan any time, or at certain set intervals, like every one or three years. But don't pay much extra for convertibility; you can always refinance your mortgage for a few hundred dollars, plus an eighth of a percentage point on the new fixed interest rate. So a convertibility feature should cost only $100–$200. The best time to convert is when interest rates are falling.

WHERE TO SHOP

Your real estate agent or agents can suggest lenders for you to con-sult—lenders whose mortgages are competitive, lenders who are efficient and courteous. Many brokers now use computers to check available mortgages.

CAUTION: Guard against agents who will receive commissions for steering you to a particular lender. While some agents have a wide variety of mortgages to choose from, others may have a limited menu. And while it's true that lenders may lower the number of points they charge, so that some of the points the buyer pays can go to the agent, the lenders may be charging too many points in the first place, just to cover commissions to agents. And bear in mind that agents may refer you to lenders that are models of speed and efficiency—but that also offer expensive mortgages. Don't necessarily reject your broker's suggestions. Some brokerage firms, particularly the larger ones, have outstanding programs for helping home buyers make the best mortgage choice. So, listen to your agent—but do your own research.

Your local newspaper may publish a sampling of mortgages being offered by lenders in your area. For example, a typical newspaper could print the following:

Comparison Shopping for Mortgages

Lender	Term	Type	Rate (%)	Pts.	Downpayment (%)
Samson S&L	1/30	ARM	7.875	2	20
Garden Park S&L	30	CON	10.375	2.5	10
Traveler Mortgage	15	CON	10.125	2.5	10
United Bank	15	CON	10.5	1.5	25
Valley S&L	3/30	ARM	9.75	2.5	20

In this chart, CON—for "conventional"—means a fixed-interest mortgage. (In real estate, the word "conventional" usually means a mortgage made by a nongovernmental lender—not guaranteed by the Veterans Administration or insured by the Federal Housing Administration.)

Under "Term," the number before the 30 in the case of ARMs, indicates how frequently the interest rate is changed. Samson may change its rate every year, Valley every three years.

Missing from this chart is the annual percentage rate on the loans. While you may think, at first glance, that the cheapest fixed-rate mortgage is Traveler, at 10.125 percent, you can't be sure. The downpayment requirement of only 10 percent means that you'll have to pay for mortgage insurance—an extra expense that would be included in the annual percentage rate. Besides, Traveler is charging two and a half points, whereas United Savings is charging only one and a half points. The effect of the difference in points would show up in the APR. Then, too, Traveler is offering a mortgage with only a 15-year term, and the shorter the mortgage, typically the lower the interest rate you may be charged.

As for the adjustable-rate mortgages, it appears that Samson is by far the better buy: its interest rate is way below Valley's, and it is charging fewer points. But Samson can adjust its interest rate every year, whereas Valley gives you three years at its initial interest rate. You must find out how high the interest rate can rise—and over what period of time. And, once again, what is the APR? And what about other fees?

At the least, a newspaper listing like this one will give you the names of local lenders. For names of other lenders and their interest rates, you can send $18 to HSH Associates, 1200 Route 23, Butler, NJ 07405 or call 1-800-UPDATES. You'll receive a two-week subscription to computer printouts of a variety of different types of mortgages offered by lenders in your area. HSH covers 50 metropolitan areas in 36 states. You'll also receive a useful booklet on how to choose a mortgage. Finally, don't overlook the most obvious source of names of lenders: check under "Mortgages," "Real-estate Loans," and "Trust deeds" in the Yellow Pages.

Start your shopping expedition with a savings and loan association or building and loan association, especially one where you have a checking or savings account. You may get better terms. Also check into commercial banks and mortgage bankers. And try mutual savings banks, although not all states have them.

TIP: Don't forget to ask your lawyer for suggestions. Lawyers with substantial real estate practices may be aware of financing options that you as a buyer could not find. Matthew Cohen, a real estate attorney and partner with Soons & Soons in Englewood, New Jersey, has put some buyers in contact with banks willing to provide 100% financing (including closing costs!) in the appropriate circumstances.

One place you shouldn't overlook is a credit union. One in six Americans now belongs to one. And in some parts of the country, you can get a mortgage from a credit union even if you're not a member. Check with the National Credit Union Administration, Office of Public and Congressional Affairs, at (202) 357-1050.

CAUTION: Don't confuse a mortgage banker with a mortgage broker. A mortgage banker puts up money for mortgages; a broker shops for mortgage sources. You may wind up paying extra if you deal with a broker, because the broker is getting paid on top of the cost of the mortgage. On the other hand, a good mortgage broker can not only get you the best deal, but may even help you get the financing where you couldn't arrange financing on your own. For example, Dan Koenigsberg of Interstate Mortgage Service Inc. in Hackensack, New Jersey has arranged equity-sharing financing for buyers with insufficient downpayments to get mortgages elsewhere.

Vary the types of institutions you apply to—S&Ls, mortgage bankers, credit unions. Try one in a big city, another in a small town. Phone or visit at least at least three sources. Mortgage rates can differ by 1 percent and even 2 percent. And even small differences in interest rates or the number of points can translate into big money over the years.

MAKING THE LENDER HAPPY

Here's what you can do to obtain a mortgage on the very best terms—including a low downpayment:

- Ask your parents, or another relative, to cosign the mortgage agreement. That means that the cosigner will be responsible if you default. Make sure that your parents or relative know what they may be in for. They could lose a good deal of money if you can't meet your mortgage payments. But lenders will be far more generous if a mortgage is cosigned.

- Build up a good credit record. If you have never had a credit card, get one, charge a few minor items on the card, and pay off the bills promptly. And if you have any other debts outstanding, try to pay them off before applying for a mortgage. Certainly avoid buying a car or furniture on time just before applying for a mortgage.

- If you've been promised a promotion or a raise, ask your supervisor to write a note to that effect and present the note to the lender. (The note can begin, "To Whom It May Concern.")

- If you've received steady raises, prove it to the lender. Either show the lender your salary stubs, or get another note from your supervisor.

OTHER TYPES OF MORTGAGES

Fixed-rate mortgages and ARMs make up 95 percent of all mortgages given in this country. Among the other 5 percent are:

- Graduated-payment mortgage (GPM). The interest rate and the term are fixed, but your early payments are low. Then your payments rise—typically over a period of five years—at which point you have a standard fixed-rate mortgage. While such a mortgage might seem perfect for the low-downpayment buyer—the person who doesn't have much cash but has a steady income—it hasn't proved very popular. One reason is that the new homeowner may face negative amortization. That can happen if, during the early years of the mortgage, you pay only part of the interest you owe, the remainder being added to your balance. Obviously, owing more than you started with is discouraging. And, for lenders, it's scary: if a homeowner owes more on his or her house after a few years, the homeowner may give up in disgust, stop paying the mortgage, and disappear. In fact, the default rate on GPMs has been very high.

- Growing-equity mortgage (GEM). This is a fixed-rate mortgage, but with increasing monthly payments that are applied to the principal. Such mortgages can be paid off rather quickly. They are ideal for homeowners who expect their incomes to soar.

- Shared-appreciation mortgage (SAM). The lender gives you a big break on the interest rate in return for, say, one-third of the house's appreciation after seven to ten years. The house need not be sold then: it could just be appraised. (See Chapter 8.)

CHAPTER SUMMARY

To obtain a low- or no-downpayment mortgage, aim for a 30-year adjustable-rate mortgage or the mortgage with the longest term you can find. Look for one with low limits on how much the rate can be increased during any adjustment, and over the life of the loan. Try to get an index whose rate tends to change slowly, like the 11th District Cost of Funds. Also look for one that's convertible into a fixed-rate mortgage at any time you choose.

Shop various lenders to get the best rates, keeping in mind that the annual percentage rate is the main course, and the interest rate is only a side dish. The annual percentage rate includes points—and points can cost you.

FOR YOUR NOTEBOOK

The worksheet below will be a useful resource when you are hunting for the best mortgage.

FORM: MORTGAGE WORKSHEET
Fixed-Rate Mortgages

	#1	#2	#3
Lender, phone	————	————	————
Loan amount	————	————	————
Downpayment	————	————	————
Term	————	————	————
Application fee	————	————	————
Loan-origination fee	————	————	————
Appraisal/credit-check fees	————	————	————
Points	————	————	————
Interest rate	————	————	————
Annual Percentage Rate	————	————	————
Escrow	————	————	————
Interest on escrow?	————	————	————
Acceleration clause?	————	————	————

	#1	#2	#3
Assumable?			
Prepayment penalty?			

Adjustable-Rate Mortgages

	#1	#2	#3
Annual Percentage Rate			
Initial rate			
Index used			
Current rate			
Margin			
Adjustment period			
Limit			
Lifetime limit			
Convertible?			
When?			
Cost?			

12 PRIVATE MORTGAGE INSURANCE: THE 5%–19% SOLUTION

INTRODUCTION

Most would-be homeowners know little if anything about private mortgage insurance, called PMI. Worse, even some real estate agents are uninformed. As a result, many home buyers never learn that PMI can permit them to buy a house with only 5 percent to 19 percent down, rather than the standard 20 percent, and the mortgage amount can be very high—$168,700 for a 5 percent downpayment; $250,000 for a 10 percent downpayment; $350,000 for a 15 percent downpayment; $500,000 for up to 20 percent.

This widespread ignorance is partly the fault of the insurers themselves. While it's true that they deal with lenders, not with home buyers or real estate agents, in the past they should have taken steps to familiarize the general public with their activities. This is what they are finally beginning to do, through advertising campaigns.

HOW PMI WORKS

PMI is a rival of the FHA and the VA, in that it backs mortgages for lenders. In theory, the FHA insures mortgages for low-income people, but, as it has turned out, the FHA insures mortgages for all comers, regardless of their income. And PMI has wound up insuring mortgages for many low-income people.

Naturally, the PMI industry would love to see the FHA establish a limit on the income of home buyers whose mortgages it will insure.

Business hasn't been great for the PMI industry in recent years, and a key reason is that the FHA has been luring away customers.

Like the FHA, the PMI industry insures mortgages when the buyer makes only a small downpayment. Whereas the FHA insures mortgages with a 3 percent to 5 percent downpayment (less for low-priced houses), the PMI industry insures them with a 5 percent to 19 percent downpayment. (The Veterans Administration guarantees mortgages with a zero downpayment.) Also, PMI companies insure only part of a mortgage, whereas the FHA insures the whole amount (up to $101,250 in the case of a mortgage in a high-priced area).

Lenders are more willing to offer mortgages to buyers who provide little money down if those buyers pay for mortgage insurance. The lenders are protected if the buyers can't continue making the monthly payments for their houses, and the houses must be sold at a foreclosure. In such cases, PMI kicks in and pays the lender the difference between the buyer's downpayment and 20 percent or 25 percent of the house price.

Let's say that a buyer makes a 5 percent downpayment on an $85,000 house ($4,250) and then defaults. A PMI company may pay the lender the difference between 25 percent of the house price ($21,250) and the $4,250 downpayment—$17,000. Why the extra 5 percent? To pay the lender's other expenses, such as legal costs connected with foreclosure proceedings, delinquent property taxes, premiums advanced for house insurance. (But instead of paying claims, PMI companies may take title to the property.) While the buyer pays for the insurance, it's the lender who deals with the PMI company. PMI companies don't even want buyers to phone them with questions. It's the same with title insurance: you pay for it, and the lender is protected too.

How much will you pay for PMI? It depends on how little a downpayment you fork over, the term of the mortgage, whether the mortgage interest rate is fixed or adjustable, and in which state the property is situated. But, in general, if you make a downpayment of 5 percent to 9 percent of the house price, you'll pay 1 percent of the mortgage the first year, and 0.5 percent of the declining balance in later years.

EXAMPLE: Constance Condo obtains an $80,000 mortgage on an $84,211 condominium, making a $4,211 downpayment (5 percent). The first year, she will pay $800 in mortgage insurance (1 percent). In later years, she will pay 0.5 percent of the remaining mortgage, which will be slowly shrinking. She'll keep paying that 0.5 percent a year until she has paid enough of the principal so that she owes only 80 percent of the balance of the mortgage. That should take about 14 years.

If you make a downpayment of 10 percent to 14 percent of the house price, you'll pay 0.4 percent of the mortgage during the first year, and 0.35 percent in later years.

EXAMPLE: If Constance gets an $80,000 mortgage on an $88,888 house, making a $8,888 downpayment (10 percent), the first year, she'll pay $320 in mortgage insurance. In later years, she will pay 0.35 percent of the declining balance. And she'll keep paying 0.35 percent a year until she owes only 80 percent of the balance. That should take 11 years.

If you make a downpayment of 15 percent to 19 percent of the house price, you'll pay 0.3 percent of the mortgage in both the first year and later years.

EXAMPLE: If Constance gets an $80,000 mortgage on a $94,118 house, making a $14,118 downpayment (15 percent), she'll pay $240 a year in mortgage insurance the first year, and 0.3 percent of the declining balance in later years until she owes only 80 percent of the balance.

CAUTION: Some lenders insist that buyers continue paying mortgage insurance even when their mortgage is less than 80 percent of the original purchase price. This is a point to check with your lender before you spring for a mortgage.

While the amount of the insurance is calculated for a whole year, typically you make the actual payments every month, along with your regular mortgage payments. But instead of paying for mortgage insurance over the years, you could pay it all at once, during the first year. The amount might be 2.95 percent of the mortgage, with a 10 percent downpayment. You may pay your insurance in a single premium and borrow to pay that premium. Of course, if you had the money to spare, you might be wiser to boost your downpayment.

You can borrow to pay either the first year's premium on an annual plan or the entire cost of a single-premium plan. MGIC (Mortgage

Guarantee Insurance Corporation), one of the largest PMI companies, offers such a program. You have the right, at any time, to pay more toward the principal you owe, and reduce or eliminate the mortgage insurance.

Some buyers may be concerned about the health of the PMI industry. In recent years a few PMI companies have gone out of business. One got caught up in a rash of foreclosures on properties in California whose true valuations were far less than their appraised valuations. Another discontinued operations when its parent company was unwilling to continue giving support. But the remaining PMI companies appear to be on firm ground.

The two largest, which hold 70 percent of the PMI market, are MGIC and General Electric Mortgage Insurance Company. MGIC in Milwaukee was the very first PMI company established in modern times, dating back to 1957. It's owned by Northwestern Mutual Life Insurance. MGIC's credit rating is very high: it gets an AA from Standard & Poor's and Aa2 from Moody's, the two leading credit-rating companies. Besides MGIC and General Electric, another big company, PMI Mortgage Insurance Co., is owned by Sears.

Typically, only five out of every 100 houses with mortgages insured by PMI go into foreclosure.

Downpayments of only 5 percent comprise around 20 percent of the business of PMI companies. And the typical customer is a first-time home buyer, aged 25 to 34.

Mortgage Insurance Companies of America, the industry organization, gives the following statistics for 1987:

- The typical PMI downpayment was 9.8 percent of the house price, with an $87,443 mortgage, a home price of $97,848, and a term of 28 years. The buyer's typical housing expenses as a percentage of gross income were 21.8 percent. Of the insured loans, 99.2 percent were for owner-residents, 0.3 percent for investors, and 0.5 percent for buyers of vacation homes and other properties.

- Downpayments of 15 percent and more made up 9 percent of the loans; downpayments of 10 percent to 14 percent, 67.6 percent; downpayments of 5 percent to 9 percent, 23.4 percent. (Some very conservative lenders require insurance for downpayments of less than 25 percent.)

- Loan amounts: $60,000 and over, 71.3 percent; $40,000–$59,999, 19.6 percent; under $40,000, 9.1 percent.

- Buyers' income: less than $27,000, 11.0 percent; $27,000–$39,999, 25.7 percent; $40,000 and over, 63.3 percent.
- Of the insured loans, 85.1 percent were for single-family detached houses, 10.1 percent for condominiums, 2.4 percent for one-family townhouses. The rest were for two-, three-, and four-family units, along with second homes.

PMI VS. FHA

You can obtain a higher mortgage with PMI companies—with MGIC less than $168,700 for a 5 percent downpayment, versus $101,150 for an FHA-insured mortgage in a pricey area. But keep in mind that the "mortgage" for FHA purposes includes closing costs, so the amount is really somewhat higher. Other advantages of PMI are that PMI companies act faster than FHA lenders who don't have "direct endorsement"—the right to decide on applications themselves. But today 90 percent of FHA-approved lenders have direct endorsement. Also, with PMI, you get more flexibility in mortgages—more different kinds to choose from.

If you pay for your mortgage insurance in one single premium, it costs less for PMI than for FHA insurance—2.65 percent versus 3.8 percent. You're probably better off, for a number of reasons, paying the premiums yearly.

MGIC argues that it's cheaper to get its insurance than FHA insurance. It gives an example:

EXAMPLE: You make a downpayment of 10 percent and get a $65,000 fixed-rate loan for 30 years. You choose to pay for the mortgage insurance in a single premium, but borrow the cost from MGIC, through its MGIC PLUS program.

Costs

MGIC Plus	FHA
Single premium for 15 years*	Single premium for life of loan
20% coverage	100% coverage
2.95% rate**	3.8% premium rate
Total premium: $1,918	Total premium: $2,470

* The number of years is based on the time required for the mortgage to sink to 80 percent of the house's original value, at which point the insurance might be dropped.

** Rates may vary by state.

Thus, according to MGIC, you would pay $552 less for its single-premium insurance in this case than FHA insurance.

The cost of the FHA insurance on a $65,000 mortgage includes closing costs, but that doesn't lower your expense. On the other hand, as MGIC notes, its own premium may vary by the state. And it would be higher if the downpayment were less than 10 percent, or if the lender wanted 25 percent coverage of the difference between the downpayment and house price, not 20 percent. On the other hand, the FHA's single premium would not be tax deductible, while a small portion of MGIC's would be deductible in 1989 and 1990, because you're paying interest on the premium. (Consumer interest is totally nondeductible in 1991.) And, of course, with MGIC you're conserving out-of-pocket expenses.

It's a complicated question, and your decision will depend on your particular case.

TIP: The less likely you are to qualify for mortgage insurance, the more likely that the FHA and not the PMI companies will accept you.

NOTE: Some large lending institutions will provide mortgages with 10 percent downpayments and no mortgage insurance. They will then raise the mortgage interest rate they charge you, or raise the number of points (special charges, equal to 1 percent of the mortgage amount). So all of the "insurance" becomes tax deductible, because it qualifies as home-equity debt. In effect, these lenders are insuring the loans themselves. They will do this only with their best prospects.

Because the FHA has streamlined its procedures and is less finicky about whom it accepts, FHA insurance has become more popular than PMI. PMI was the leader from 1977 until 1985, at which time the FHA began writing a greater volume. And this trend has been increasing, as the following chart shows.

Insured Mortgages (Millions)

	FHA	VA	Private	% Private
1983	$28,602	$18,876	$43,360	47.7
1984	16,349	12,093	63,403	69.0
1985	23,872	13,222	50,956	57.9
1986	62,038	30,890	47,358	33.8
1987	81,880	34,783	45,217	27.9

Source: Fact Book and Directory, 1988, Mortgage Insurance Companies of America

WHO IS ELIGIBLE?

To qualify for PMI, your major regular housing costs—repayment of principal, mortgage interest, taxes, house insurance—should make up no more than 28 percent of your income. Your total regular debts—including car payments, student loans, and such—should not make up more than 36 percent of your income. The PMI industry would also like you to have some money in reserve, for emergencies. (MGIC no longer insures mortgages sought by investors, as opposed to owner-occupants.)

MGIC prefers that a house it insures not be in an area with an oversupply of housing (like the glutted southern Florida condominium market), or in an area with a single-industry or single-employer economy—like Oklahoma City—where a downturn might slaughter property values.

PMI companies insist that appraisers not include in the value of the house a jacking up of sales prices by builders, who in turn help buyers with their mortgages by giving them some cash for the down-payment or by lowering their mortgage interest rate ("buydowns").

They also will want to know the source of a downpayment. If your downpayment is 10 percent, for example, they may insist that 5 percent of it come from your own personal sources, not from gifts. And if your downpayment is 5 percent and your seller or builder has given you an amount equal to or more than 5 percent, PMI companies will be dubious. Buyers of new homes are significantly more likely to default on their PMI than buyers of old homes, ap-parently because of those builder buydowns. If your downpayment is less than 10 percent of the house price, some PMI companies will insist that seller contributions or buydowns not constitute more than 3 percent of the house value. The percentage rises to 6 percent if your downpayment is 10 percent to 19 percent of the house value.

In general, PMI companies are skeptical about insuring mortgages with 5 percent downpayments. Although MGIC believes "95 percent (loan-to-value) loans can be a profitable class of business for both lenders and mortgage insurers, MGIC recognizes that these loans represent a higher exposure to risk and therefore require more con-servative underwriting and pricing." PMI companies are especially reluctant to insure such mortgages if the buyer has few other cash reserves, if the seller's contribution is more than 3 percent of the mortgage, if the buyer obtained gifts for the downpayment, and if the mortgage was provided by a real estate broker—not always skilled in choosing good credit risks, and perhaps overeager to earn a com-mission.

If you're seeking an adjustable-rate mortgage, some PMI companies will disallow any buydowns—and insist on your making at least a 10 percent downpayment. Reason: With an ARM, because of its low initial mortgage rate, you can more easily qualify for a mortgage. After all, your monthly housing expenses, at least in the initial years, will be lower than with a fixed-rate mortgage. Then, too, if the interest rate on an ARM goes up, buyers may have trouble making their payments. A 2-percent interest-rate jump in a one-year ARM with a 7.5-percent discount rate results in a thumping 21 percent increase in the buyer's monthly payments.

PMI companies may also forbid the use of cosigners—people who guarantee that they will pay the balance of the mortgage if you default. Of course, PMI companies also want you to have a steady job—one where you have been employed for two years or more. And they want you to have a good credit record.

Many of these rules are being put into effect because lenders may want to sell their mortgages to government agencies—the Federal National Mortgage Association (Fannie Mae) or the Federal Home Loan Mortgage Corporation (Freddie Mac). And those agencies want the new, tighter rules. Just how discriminating are the PMI companies? MGIC rejects 20 percent to 25 percent of all applications.

If you're buying a condominium, you may face special obstacles in obtaining PMI. MGIC is dubious of condos where 30 percent of the units are owned by investors. Absentee owners may let their places deteriorate. MGIC also doesn't like (1) condos in areas where there's lots of competition from apartment houses—where the surrounding land use is greater than 50 percent non-single family; and (2) condos that cost less than $75,000 per unit—perhaps because they may be old and dilapidated, their occupants not being wealthy enough to keep them up. Condos also tend to be more sensitive to local market conditions than traditional housing, so MGIC pays special attention to the area in which a condo is situated.

In all cases, however, check carefully with different companies because each has its own criteria, and criteria do change.

HOW TO APPLY

As in the case with the FHA, lenders can either approve PMI applications themselves, or have a PMI company give the approval. Only 10 percent of lenders can give their own approvals, versus 90 percent of the FHA lenders. But the PMI companies work fast. Whether a buyer deals with a "direct endorsement" lender or not, the buyer can usually get approval in one or two days. At MGIC, 95 percent of the applications are processed within 24 hours.

TIP: Make sure that any lenders you visit can originate both PMI and FHA-insured loans, so you have a choice. Some lenders offer only PMI loans, perhaps because they wrongly think that FHA-insured mortgages take forever, so that home buyers may never learn about FHA-insured mortgages from them.

CHAPTER SUMMARY

If you intend to obtain a mortgage with less than a 20 percent down-payment, the lender will probably require you to obtain mortgage insurance. It's called "private" mortgage insurance if you obtain it from a source other than the FHA, the VA, or another governmental agency. You'll pay an initial fee for such insurance, as well as yearly fees until your house value climbs, or your mortgage principal sinks, so that your mortgage represents only 80 percent of the house's value.

PMI may allow you to purchase a house with a higher mortgage than you could obtain with FHA financing. But it's easier to qualify for FHA financing.

13 LEASE THE HOUSE WITH AN OPTION TO BUY

INTRODUCTION

An option provides you, the home buyer, the right to buy a house you rent at some future date (perhaps five years after the lease-option agreement began) or on the occurrence of some future event (your election). When you analyze all possible ways to get a house when downpayment money is scarce or nonexistent, carefully consider the lease-option method. The first reaction to the idea of leasing a house is usually that you want to get away from being just a renter, and leasing a house is still being a renter. Yes and no. There can be a number of important differences between leasing a house with an option to buy it and renting:

- When leasing a house you still will have obtained much of the lifestyle of a homeowner.
- The option to buy the house, if properly negotiated by your attorney, should give you an edge over any other person seeking to buy the house.
- A properly negotiated lease option gives you an opportunity to begin building equity (ownership) in the house.

CONSIDERATIONS IN NEGOTIATING AN OPTION ARRANGEMENT

One of the problems in the lease-option approach is the difficulty of setting the option price (the price at which the home buyer/renter can later purchase the house). If the price is set too low, two results may follow: First the investor/landlord will soon realize that the home buyer has a windfall and may exhaust every legal means to prevent the home buyer from exercising the purchase option.

CAUTION: Dick Schlott of Schlott Realtors notes that one of the biggest obstacles for home buyers/renters in getting their landlords (the investors owning the houses being rented) to grant purchase options at fixed prices is the landlords' fear of inflation.

Second, the IRS may question the treatment of the arrangement as a lease if the home buyer's purchase is a virtual certainty because of the low option price. On the other hand, if the option price is set too high, the home buyer will feel that there may not have been any benefit to all the years of renting and maintaining the house. One of the best solutions is for the option price to be based on the fair market value of the house at the time when the option is exercised.

The investor will want to terminate the option prior to any condemnation (such as the taking of the house by a government agency to make way for a new highway). If this is not done, the home buyer may get a windfall if the property is condemned. The home buyer could simply choose to exercise the purchase option when the option price is less than the condemnation award, to keep the award.

Consideration also must be given to the terms of the investor's mortgage on the house. The mortgage documents may have restrictions on the granting of a purchase option. The lender may insist that the mortgage be repaid before the property can be transferred to the tenant. The attorneys for the investor and for the home buyer both should be alert to such matters. If the lease is part of the basis on which the lender advanced money to the investor, the lender may preclude cancelation of the lease by the tenant in the event that the investor can't transfer ownership of the house to the tenant when the option is exercised.

The investor and the home buyer also should distinguish between a right of first refusal and an option to purchase. A right of first refusal means that if the investor wants to sell the house, he or she must give the tenant the opportunity to buy it for a specific price before selling it to someone else at that price. If the option is set at a fixed amount, the best situation for the home buyer would be to try to negotiate a right of first refusal as well. If the purchase option price was too high, the home buyer could just match an offer the investor received from another potential buyer. If the option price was a bargain, the home buyer would exercise the option before waiting to use the right of first refusal. Obviously, such an arrangement would not be desirable from the investor's perspective.

CASE STUDY: Dick Schlott, president of Schlott Realtors, cites a case of a homeowner who was assigned to a job in London. He wasn't certain whether or not he would stay in London permanently, so when he rented his home in the states, using Schlott Realtors' rental service, he wouldn't agree to give the tenant an option to buy. After all, he could be returning and want to reoccupy his house. However, the owner did agree to give the tenant a right of first refusal. That way, if the owner decided to stay in London, the tenant would have first shot at the house.

Schlott makes an important point, which many owners overlook when easily consenting to give a tenant a right of first refusal. "A right of first refusal can make it tough to sell the house. The owner will have to tell every prospective buyer that if they make a bid on the house, the owner has to give the tenant the right to buy at that price before he can accept their offer."

USING THE LEASE-OPTION TECHNIQUE TO BUILD EQUITY AND BUY WITHOUT A DOWNPAYMENT

An important use of the lease-option method for hopeful home buyers is to have a portion of the rental payments be applied toward the purchase price of the property. This enables the tenant to build equity without coming up with the money for a downpayment and closing costs to buy a house. When these rental credits have continued for a number of years, the home buyer/tenant may have a much easier time purchasing the house. (See Chapter 8.)

TAX CONSEQUENCES OF A LEASE WITH AN OPTION TO PURCHASE

In a properly structured lease-option arrangement, the investor owns the property until the tenant exercises the option and purchases the house. The investor will generally report rental income received from the tenant when he or she receives the rental payments. If the tenant makes any rental payments in advance of when they are actually due, the investor will still have to report the cash received as income. However, money received in advance to be held by the investor as a security deposit will not be taxable income to the landlord if the security deposit is kept in an account separate from the investor's other bank accounts, and the investor accounts to the tenant for the use of the security deposit. It is also helpful if the security deposit is designated to secure nonrental agreements (covenants) in the lease. The investor should be able to deduct the interest portion of any mortgage payments made on the property. Principal payments are not deductible. Repairs are deductible, but not improvements that prolong the life of the house or enhance its value. If there is a net loss for tax purposes, the investor will have to consider the effects of the passive loss limitations. (See Chapter 8.) The home buyer, as a renter, will generally have no tax benefits.

One of the important tax considerations involved in a lease-option arrangement is whether the IRS will respect the arrangement as a lease or attempt to recharacterize it as a sale. An extreme example can illustrate this risk. The tenant pays $1,200 per month for rent where a comparable house could be rented for $750 per month, and at the end of the lease the tenant can exercise an option and buy the house for a nominal amount, say $500. In this scenario, it is obvious that the tenant is buying the property and the monthly payments are installments to the investor for the house. The tax consequences of having the IRS recharacterize a lease option as a sale can be very detrimental to the investor. The investor will be taxed on a portion of the monthly payments as if the investor had sold the property. And since the house has been sold, the investor won't be permitted to claim depreciation deductions.

To avoid tax problems of recharacterization as a sale, the following factors should be considered by the attorney for the landlord preparing the lease-option agreement:

- If a portion of the monthly payments is applied as credit against the purchase price to be paid by the tenant to buy the house, the portion should not be too large. Obviously, the tenant will want as large a portion as possible. This is a tricky area and should be reviewed by the investor's tax adviser with consideration to all of the other points noted here.

- The legal documents should not provide for an automatic transfer of ownership (title) when the tenant has completed the payments required under the lease agreement.

- The monthly rental payments should not exceed the fair rental amount for comparable properties in the area.

- The price of the purchase option should not be so low that the tenant will unquestionably exercise it.

- No portion of the regular payments made by the tenant should be called interest.

- The tenant shouldn't be required to make substantial improvements to the house that would make it obvious that the tenant will have to exercise the option in order to protect the investment in the improvements made.

LEGAL DOCUMENTATION

The lease-option arrangement will require the investor and tenant to sign a lease. The lease will contain a section discussing the option that the tenant can exercise to buy the property, the price of the option, and when it can be exercised. If the investor agrees to credit a portion of the rental payments against the purchase price, this should also be discussed. The investor's attorney may insist that some additional documents be signed to facilitate the investor's ability to remove the tenant for failing to make the required monthly rental payments. The tenant should be careful to have an attorney review any such documents. If the tenant will build up a substantial equity in the property (by getting credit for a portion of the rental payments), forfeiture provisions that the investor may request may be less acceptable. This is a matter for the attorneys to negotiate.

CHAPTER SUMMARY

A lease with a purchase option, particularly one in which some portion of the monthly rental is credited toward the eventual purchase price, is an excellent technique for home buyers seeking to break into the housing market. There are a number of legal and tax considerations important to both the investor and the home buyer/tenant, so both should consult a real estate attorney.

FOR YOUR NOTEBOOK

The following sample lease clause is illustrative of the type of provision that could be added to a lease agreement to provide the home
buyer/tenant an option to purchase the house. Local laws differ, and
some of the facts of any lease will be unique, so consult an attorney
to prepare the necessary legal documentation.

FORM: *OPTION TO PURCHASE*

The Landlord hereby grants to the Tenant an Option to purchase the
House at any time prior to the expiration of this Lease in accordance
with the terms set forth in this Section.

The Tenant cannot exercise this Option if the Tenant is then in default
under any term or provision of this Lease. The Landlord may elect not
to consummate the sale pursuant to this Option if, after the date of
exercise by the Tenant but prior to the date of closing on such purchase,
the Tenant is in default under any provision in this Lease.

The Tenant must exercise this Option by providing the Landlord written
Notice, as provided in Section 12 of this Lease, Thirty (30) days prior
to the intended date of exercise. The notice must set forth a closing
date for the purchase, which shall be not less then Sixty (60) days from
the date of the Notice and not more than Ninety (90) days from the date
of the Notice.

Upon receiving Notice of Tenant's election to exercise this Option, the
Landlord shall: (i) retain an appraiser at Landlord's expense to value
the House. If the Tenant does not agree with the value set by Landlord's
appraiser then Tenant, at Tenant's expense, shall select another appraiser
to value the property. If the two appraisers cannot agree on a value of
the property they shall select a third appraiser whose determination
shall control. The cost of the third appraiser shall be borne equally by

the Landlord and the Tenant. And (ii) order a title insurance report. The tenant may not object to such title insurance report for any exceptions noted in Exhibit C attached hereto.

The Purchase Price to be paid at closing in bank or certified funds shall be equal to the appraised value of the property as determined in this Section, reduced by the Credit. The Credit shall equal Ten percent (10%) of all of the monthly rental payments paid by Tenant to Landlord on a timely basis as required pursuant to this Lease. The Tenant shall be responsible for the costs of a survey, title insurance policy, transfer and recording fees, and other charges. At the Closing, the Landlord shall deliver a general warranty deed. Tenant shall assume all obligations relating to the House for property taxes and assessments, without pro-ration or adjustment.

14 STILL OTHER SOURCES OF DOWNPAYMENT MONEY

INTRODUCTION

In the previous chapters, you've learned about FHA-insured mortgages, VA-guaranteed mortgages, private mortgage insurance, borrowing from parents and friends, sharing ownership, and buying less expensive residences. In this chapter, you'll find still more ways to buy a house—even by amassing the cash you need for a traditional downpayment.

SWEAT EQUITY

Some sellers may not need cash to buy another residence. They may be preparing to rent, or to live in their summer homes, or they just may be cash-rich. In any case, they might be willing to sell you a house for little or no downpayment—in exchange for services you perform. The services would be in place of the downpayment.

CASE STUDIES: A young lawyer was able to buy a house from a builder with nothing down by offering to provide legal help worth $10,000, based on the lawyer's regular charge per hour. The builder sold him a house and got a promising young lawyer—cheap.

A secretary agreed to work for the seller's business for a year, in return for the seller's taking back a mortgage with no downpayment.

A broker in Ventura, California, wanted to buy a particular house. He spoke with the sellers, who owned their house free and clear. They wanted to buy a house in Santa Paula. The buyer agreed to find them a bargain house, in return for his buying their house with no downpayment. First, he obtained title to their house, and quickly took out a mortgage. Then he checked out houses in Santa Paula, found one that appealed to the Ventura family and arranged to purchase it, using the money from the mortgage he had on the Ventura house to make the downpayment. Finally, he turned over the Santa Paula house to the Ventura family. What he did, in effect, was trade his real estate services for the downpayment on the Ventura house.

While these approaches create tax problems that you should review with your accountant, they do address your pressing need to find an alternative to a downpayment.

Ask yourself: What services can I provide to a seller in return for a downpayment? If you run a travel agency, for example, you might offer the sellers a trip somewhere, at a discount—because you'll refund to them the commission you've earned. If you're handy, you can offer to repair whatever is wrong with their house—fix the plumbing, replace the kitchen cabinets, paint, whatever. They can then raise the price of the house and lower your downpayment by an amount equal to the labor you performed, plus the cost of any materials.

This strategy, as mentioned, will work when the seller doesn't need cash immediately and is willing to give the buyer a mortgage. Traditional lenders would be skeptical of granting you a mortgage for a sweat-equity downpayment.

But there's nothing kinky about this arrangement. The lawyer, the secretary, and the broker could have performed their services for other people, and used the money they received for the downpayment. But by dealing directly with the seller, they saved time. Consult with your accountant about the tax problems created by barter or service exchange situations. The value of the services rendered in exchange for a break on the price of a house may be taxable.

TRADE SOMETHING ELSE

If the sellers don't need cash, what they want, above all, is to know that their house has been sold. For the most part, you can forget about the possibility that the sellers will accept something else you own—a car, truck, a motorcycle, a recreational vehicle, a coin collection, a parcel of land out in the boondocks—as part of a downpayment. Sell whatever you were thinking of trading—you should get a better price that way—and put the proceeds toward the downpayment. Yet sometimes you can successfully trade something for a downpayment.

CASE STUDIES: Don Developer wanted to purchase a house that needed sprucing up. At the time, he owned a small commercial store that sold carpeting and paint. The tenants were six months behind in their rent. He negotiated with the house sellers to trade them a new paint job and new carpeting throughout their house in return for no downpayment, and a selling price boosted to the value of the redecorating. Meanwhile, he obtained the carpeting and the paint free from the store owner, in return for forgiving them the back rent.

Another time, he offered to buy a woman's home if she would accept as a downpayment a room in a duplex he owned, rent free for a year. She was delighted.

Still another time, he offered to buy a house if the sellers would accept, in place of a downpayment, a note backed by a piece of property he owned in northern California. They accepted. They didn't want the land; they just wanted to sell their house, and the piece of paper, secured by the land, gave them the assurance they needed. It was naive of them to accept, perhaps, but Developer had a good reputation—and the land was certainly worth a few thousand dollars.

As always, consult your accountant. This type of transaction creates a host of tax problems. You may have to report the gain of the property you transferred as if you sold it.

BORROW FROM YOUR WHOLE-LIFE INSURANCE

You may have access to money you're not even aware of. Perhaps you own whole-life insurance policies. These are life insurance contracts that have a savings account—a "cash value." (They are also called "permanent" insurance.) If you have owned any of them for several years, you may have a few thousand dollars built up. If your parents bought whole-life insurance for you long ago, you might have even more.

You can borrow the cash value automatically. It's supposedly your money, and most insurance companies have no option: they must lend you the money. The interest rate you will be charged may be low, depending on how long the policy has been in effect. You might pay 8 percent interest—or even 5 percent, if you have an old policy.

You can deduct part of the interest you pay—20 percent in 1989, 10 percent in 1990. But beginning in 1991, none of the interest will be deductible.

Actually, in some cases, you might be best off just canceling any whole-life policies you have, especially if you're young, healthy, and have other insurance (perhaps through your employer). With the premium you're paying, you could buy four or five times the same coverage with "term" insurance—plain vanilla insurance, without any cash value. What you might do is cancel your whole-life policies, use some of the cash value for your downpayment, and use the rest to buy term life insurance.

If you keep the whole-life policies, don't hesitate to borrow the cash value. The interest you're getting on that money may be low. And if you die, the insurance company will keep the cash value; all that your beneficiaries will receive is the face amount of your policy. True, the amount you borrow will reduce the insurance coverage you have. But your beneficiaries may gain a commensurate amount by your ownership of a house.

You can also borrow on the cash value if you have whole-life insurance on your children, but you may want to consider dropping the policies altogether—not borrowing the cash value. Insuring the lives of children is astonishingly common, especially in the Midwest. Yet children don't need life insurance, let alone whole-life insurance.

CAUTION: Never drop any life insurance coverage you have without being sure that you have qualified for new coverage. If your health has deteriorated, perhaps without your even knowing about it, you might have trouble obtaining new coverage. Wait until you're guaranteed new coverage, after passing a physical, before dropping any coverage you have. Review any such steps carefully with your insurance advisers before taking action.

Some life insurance agents will discourage you from cashing in any whole-life policies you have. If they sold you those policies originally, it will look bad on their records. But at least one insurance salesman, in California, strongly advises all his young clients to borrow on their whole-life policies—specifically to buy houses. The salesman is a real estate agent on the side.

Check any other insurance policies you might own—annuities, single-premium life insurance contracts, endowment policies. See if you can borrow or withdraw any money without stiff tax penalties and without stiff penalties from the insurance companies. Of course, if you're young and cash poor, you're not likely to have these coverages. On the other hand, your parents may have them—and may have forgotten about them, even while trying hard to lend you money for a house.

BORROW FROM YOUR PENSION PLANS

Do you contribute to a 401(k) or "salary reduction plan"? Or to a profit-sharing plan? These are other excellent sources of borrowed money. Generally, you cannot permanently withdraw money from any retirement plan funds without penalty until you reach age 59½ or quit your job. But you can borrow if you suffer a financial hardship. What's a financial hardship? You have an immediate and heavy financial need.

TIP: Consider borrowing from your 401(k), recommends Johnathan Kenter, a pension attorney with New York City law firm Shea & Gold. There will be no tax penalty. And almost all employers allow you to borrow from your 401(k) if you're buying a house for yourself (not a child or other relative).

EXAMPLE: You need to make a downpayment on a house that will be your main residence. You must also prove that you have no other option except borrowing money from your 401(k). You have to state to your employer that you can't borrow what you need anywhere else, cash in any other pension-plan accounts, or liquidate any investments. An alternative to proving to your employer that you can't raise money elsewhere is to be barred from putting new money into the 401(k) for a year, and to have your first year's deposit after that be limited.

Either way, don't withdraw money from your 401(k) plan to buy a house. The 10-percent tax penalty is a killer. If you withdraw $20,000 and you're in the 28-percent tax bracket, you'll pay $7,400 (38 percent). You'll avoid a tax penalty only if you're disabled, or you're borrowing to pay medical bills that exceed 7.5 percent of your adjusted gross income.

An exception: The only time you might consider withdrawing money from your 401(k) to buy a house is to buy a "creampuff "—a house in tip-top condition in a fine area selling for a bargain-basement price, and you have to act immediately.

If you're borrowing from a pension plan to buy a house, you have at least five years to repay the money—maybe longer. You must repay the loan in level installments, four times a year. In some plans, moreover, the interest you will pay will go directly to your own 401(k). In other plans, the interest goes to all plan participants. Employers have a lot of options on 401(k) plans. The old rule was that you could borrow half your pension assets, up to $50,000 in some cases, but you could always borrow up to $10,000. Now the amount you can borrow depends on what you've borrowed in the previous 12 months.

EXAMPLE: If you have $100,000 in your plan, you might be able to borrow half, $50,000. But let's say you've already borrowed $40,000 within the year, but repaid it. Then you borrowed another $10,000. Now you want to borrow more.

Subtract the $10,000 you still owe from the $40,000 you've borrowed and repaid. That's $30,000. Subtract that $30,000 from your $50,000 limit: $20,000 is what you can borrow.

With IRAs, the story is grim. There's no real borrowing, and you'll face a 10-percent tax penalty for cashing in an IRA. There are a few exceptions: if you're 59½ or disabled, or you withdraw the money in accordance with your life expectancy (that is, as an annuity). Otherwise, if your tax bracket is 15 percent, you'll pay 25 percent on the money withdrawn. If your tax bracket is 28 percent, you'll pay 38 percent on the money; that means that if you have a $10,000 IRA, you'll pay $3,800 in taxes and penalties to cash it in—an enormous loss.

The only time you might consider cashing an IRA, as suggested with 401(k) plans, is when you have a once-in-a-lifetime opportunity to buy a wonderful house at a bargain price.

TIP: If you need cash for just 60 days and no more, you can withdraw your IRA money, use if for 60 days, then restore it (to the same institution, or another one) without tax penalty. That might be a useful ploy to pay closing costs, say, providing you expect another source of money within two months. But check with your tax adviser and don't miss the deadline.

THE CAR IS THE ENEMY OF THE HOUSE

The biggest mistake many young would-be homeowners make is spending too much on transportation—buying expensive, luxurious cars and paying for them on time.

Right out of high school or college, many young people seem to want, above everything else, a car that knocks their friends and neighbors for a loop. They don't understand that automobiles depreciate; houses appreciate. In 10 years, they'll be lucky to get rid of their car without paying someone to haul the scrap heap away. In 10 years, any house they buy may be worth double what they paid for it.

Yet recall how much of their incomes renters paid for transportation, according to a 1985 survey conducted for the National Association of Realtors. Transportation amounted to 18.5 percent of their annual expenditures compared to 29.9 percent for housing. (See Chapter 1.) And look again at what percentage of Americans think a car contributes to the "good life": 84 percent, according to the National Association of Realtors—only slightly lower than the 87 percent figure for owning your own home. (See Chapter 1.)

In the first case, transportation ranks second to housing, and in the second case, a car ranks second to a home. Clearly, many Americans do not just have a love affair with their cars; they are obsessed with them.

You must remember that your car can be the enemy of your goal to purchase a house. If you need a car for work, buy a good, cheap car. Or, better yet, a used car. Forget about the snazzy sports cars. Don't pay for a car on the installment plan, either—unless you're getting a break on the interest rate. You're buying a house—your first house. You can't live in a car, and don't even want an apartment with a grumpy, bossy landlord and loud, angry neighbors. You want your own house, with a lawn and a yard, a room for your office, and a place for your workshop. And, yes, a garage for your cheap little car.

Cut back on transportation costs however you can. Trade in your new or not-so-old car for a smaller, older model. Or give up cars altogether—so you won't be paying for auto insurance, gas, oil, tuneups, new tires. Use public transportation, or join a car pool. Do it even for just a year—and bank the savings for your downpayment.

ASK YOUR EMPLOYER FOR HELP

Around 50 major companies now provide housing help to their employees, reports David Schwartz, a Rutgers University professor. Among the companies are Colgate-Palmolive, Clorox, Chevron, Mutual Benefit Life Insurance, Connecticut National Bank, Hawaii Bell, and Hartz Mountain. These companies may guarantee their employees' mortgage loans, the way the Veterans Administration does. Or they may "buy down" the lenders' interest rates by giving them a sum of money. Or they give their employees money directly, and share in the appreciation of their houses. Your employer might be willing to help you out, following the example of the companies mentioned above.

If you're a valuable employee, your boss might realize that it's in his or her own interest to help provide you with roots in the vicinity—so you'll be less likely to skip off across the country for a job that pays a little more.

SAVE FOR THE DOWNPAYMENT

Here are other ways—some obvious and some perhaps not so obvious—to cut back on your spending or raise more cash:

- If you're getting married, ask wedding guests for cash. Or ask the father of the bride for a modest wedding—and the downpayment on a house.

- Drop insurance you don't need. Experts say that you don't need accidental death and dismemberment insurance as part of life insurance. You don't need travel insurance—if you have sufficient life insurance, travel insurance is redundant. And consider increasing your deductibles—on your auto insurance, your tenant policies.

- Dine out less. Brown-bag it more.

- Get rid of all of your credit cards, especially if you ever owe money because of late payments, and if there's a yearly charge. If a card is a necessity, obtain one that has no yearly charge and pay your debts before you are assessed interest.

- Get a second job. A second job as a real estate agent would be perfect. A part-time job selling houses would be an open sesame to your finding the perfect house on the perfect terms. But be willing to settle for being a waiter or waitress, taxi driver or bus driver. Even when jobs are scarce, it seems that housecleaners are in demand. Yes, even college graduates—young people with advanced degrees—work as housecleaners these days.

- Turn your hobby into a business. If you're a photographer, offer to take photos for weddings and for passports. Or perform your magical tricks at children's parties. Or start a new sideline business—raising purebred pets, running a housecleaning service, recaning chairs. Investigate carefully first. Talk to others who do the same thing to learn the perils.

- Dispense with or economize on vacations.

- To make sure you do save, arrange with your employer, or with your bank or credit union, to regularly put a portion of your salary check or your checking account into savings.

- Have less withholding taken out of your salary; being a homeowner should reduce your tax obligations. (See Chapter 15.)

- Sell securities that you own and are keeping (1) only because you've lost money on them and want to break even, (2) because you have a sentimental attachment to them—like the AT&T stock your aunt left you. In general, to raise cash, sell volatile securities—stocks that bounce up and down—if they're up now.

- Take a course in home repair at a local school, and buy a good book on the subject. If you recognize your limitations and confine yourself to installing new light fixtures and fixing leaky faucets, you'll do fine. Avoiding repairpeople whenever possible will save you money during your first year in your new home—and every year thereafter.

CASE STUDY: One young couple sold almost everything they owned to make a downpayment on a house. They sold their old car, their furniture, their appliances, all their stocks and bonds. They depleted every last nickel of their savings. Thus, they managed to make a 20-percent downpayment and get a good mortgage at a low interest rate. They didn't have to pay for mortgage insurance; they had no trouble qualifying for the loan.

But with no cash whatsoever, they were now in a very precarious financial situation. Then, as agreed, one of their fathers gave them a second mortgage on their house for $20,000. Now they had enough cash to deal with emergencies and to buy furniture and other necessities—new.

MORE WAYS TO GET A DOWNPAYMENT

Here are still other ways of dealing with the downpayment problem:

- Ask your real estate broker to lend you (to defer collecting) the commission he or she receives from the seller, to help you make the downpayment. Agents can do this if they are the listing brokers—they accepted the contract to sell the house, and don't have to split the commission with anyone. They might be interested if they trust you and feel they might not easily and quickly sell the house otherwise. Don't expect brokers to jump at this alternative, however. In addition, if this is done the broker will need a note, and don't be surprised if the broker wants a second mortgage on the house to protect his or her commission.

- In a very unusual situation, it may make sense for a very short period of time to use a credit card advance to obtain a downpayment—for example, if you have a great deal, must close quickly, have a large sum of cash coming soon to pay off the advance, and so forth. Be careful; the rates are very high and most of the interest expense won't be deductible. This should be viewed as a short term and very rare option.

- Accommodate the seller in certain ways and, at the same time, try hard to strike a deal with a lower downpayment. The seller may desire to close quickly, or perhaps stay in the house after closing. By offering to accommodate the seller in ways that other buyers won't, you may be able to get the seller to reciprocate by accepting a lower downpayment.

- For qualifying first-time home buyers tax-exempt mortgage bonds may offer some assistance. The law providing for these was due to expire at the end of 1988, but Congress recently extended it for one year. Borrowers using these bonds may have to repay some of the subsidy if they sell their homes within 10 years. Borrowers must meet certain income levels to qualify. Check with your accountant and local housing agencies.

- If you're moving to a new house in a more expensive part of the country because of a job assignment, check with your employer. Many employers have formal programs to assist relocating employees.

- Innovative real estate brokerage firms may have programs that can help the first-time or cash-tight buyer get a house.

CASE STUDY: Schlott Realtors has instituted its Power House Program to help home buyers. Qualifying sellers, with homes priced at market value, agree to pay the points on the buyer's mortgage which the buyer would normally be responsible for, up to 2¾ points.

Buyers purchasing homes from sellers participating in Schlott's program can conserve substantial amounts of cash that would otherwise be necessary to close on the house. If the seller actually pays the buyer's points, rather than just giving the buyer a payment equal to the points at the closing, the buyer's tax deduction for the mortgage points will be lost. While Schlott acknowledges this drawback, the benefits to a cash-tight homeowner still can be important—this may be the only way for cash-tight buyers to get the house they want.

- Use the house you buy to make the downpayment. This can happen if the owners don't see certain possibilities—for example, that you can sell off something valuable related to the house or land.

CASE STUDY: George Rosenberg, a California real estate broker, wanted to buy a house that the owners used as a chicken farm. The owners agreed to defer a downpayment for six months, and took back a mortgage. Rosenberg then subdivided the land, separating the house from about a half acre of remaining property. He checked with neighbors and, yes, one wanted the land to start a worm farm. Besides the land, Rosenberg also sold the chickens and the chicken wire for a few thousand dollars. He ended up with more than enough for the downpayment. (Rosenberg publishes a listing of agents called *Who's Who in Creative Real Estate*. It can be obtained by writing P.O. Box 23275, Ventura, CA 93002.)

CHAPTER SUMMARY

Other ways to lower the downpayment, or come up with enough money to make a downpayment, include: doing some work for the sellers in place of a downpayment; trading something for the downpayment, like household items that will increase the value and price of the house; borrowing the cash value of your whole-life insurance, or canceling the policies; borrowing from your 401(k) plan; reducing your expenditures for transportation, particularly on new cars; asking your employer for help; and amassing more savings, either by spending less or saving more. Be certain to check with your lawyer and accountant about the legal and tax implications of any of these methods.

15 MORE WAYS UNCLE SAM CAN HELP—TAX SAVINGS

INTRODUCTION

When looking for every angle to help get yourself into that first house, don't overlook some of the tax benefits that may be available. If you can find some substantial tax benefits relating to your purchase of your home in the year you buy it, those tax savings may be put to use almost immediately by reducing the tax withheld from your paycheck, or the amount of estimated taxes you must pay. This extra cash can be used to help offset closing costs, or to add to the savings you plan to use for your downpayment. This chapter will review a few of the common tax deductions you may be able to take advantage of and then give you some pointers on how to get the most benefit the fastest.

EXAMPLE: Bob and Betty Buyer are tight on cash for the downpayment for the home they are trying to buy. They have managed to save about $6,000 from working at the restaurant they own, Buyers' Buffet. They figure they need an additional $3,500 to cover closing and moving costs and the minimum downpayment the seller and the bank will accept. After making some calculations, the Buyers determine that the $2,200 in moving costs they will have to incur will be tax deductible. The $3,000 in points they will have to pay at the closing to get their mortgage will also be deductible. Finally, $750 of the closing costs will be for property taxes, which will also be deductible. The Buyers are in a 28-percent tax bracket. These tax deductions will provide them with about a $1,666 tax savings [($2,200 + $3,000 + $750) × 28%]. This tax savings is almost half of what they need to make up the shortfall. The Buyers will reduce their remaining estimated tax payments to obtain some of this benefit before the closing.

MOVING EXPENSES

Moving expenses are one of the major costs of going to a new home. Fortunately, for many taxpayers some or even all of their moving expenses are tax deductible. You must, however, meet all the requirements discussed below. If you do, you can deduct the following costs:

Direct Costs (Deductible without Limit)

- Moving household goods (furniture, clothing, dishes, and so forth) from your former home to your new home. This can include costs to pack, crate, insure, move, and store (up to 30 days) your household possessions. Other preparation costs, such as disconnecting appliances in preparation of the move, can be deducted.

- Traveling from your old home to your new home (including meals and hotels). This includes costs for yourself and your family. Food and lodging for the day before you leave on the trip and for one day after you arrive can be included.

NOTE: The cost of meals and food must be kept track of separately since only 80 percent of these expenses can be deducted. If your employer reimburses you for meal expenses and treats the reimbursements to you as wages, your employer will be subject to the limitation instead of you.

Indirect Costs (Deductible up to Specified Limits Only)

- Premove house-hunting trips. This item includes traveling from your old home to the area where your new job is located (after you've been hired), to look for a new home. While it is not necessary to find a house to deduct the cost of a house-hunting trip, your principal purpose for the trip must be to find a place to live. The maximum amount of house-hunting and temporary living expenses combined (see below) that you can deduct is $1,500.

TIP: The best way to prove the purpose of the trip is to keep a log, diary, or appointment book, recording all of your meetings and the house leads you followed up on. If you started with a newspaper and circled all the house listings you called or visited, save the paper and your notes in a "Moving Expense Deduction" file.

• Temporary living expenses. These include meals and hotel costs (lodging) in the area where your new job is located for the 30-day period after you're hired and while you're living in temporary quarters. These expenses don't have to be incurred within the first 30 days after starting work to be deductible. They are deductible whether you are living in temporary quarters because you haven't yet found a new residence, or because you are waiting for your new residence to be available so you can move into it. The maximum amount of temporary living expenses and house-hunting-trip expenses you can deduct is $1,500.

TIP: The 30-day period during which you can deduct temporary living expenses must be one consecutive 30-day period. However, you have the option of deciding when the 30-day period begins, so long as it's after the day you obtain employment at the new job location. Begin counting the 30-day period so that you include the days when you incur the greatest expenses.

• Certain expenses of terminating your old apartment lease and buying a new home. Your lease expenses could include legal fees, commissions, payments to your landlord to break a lease early, and so forth. These don't include rent prepayments or security deposits. This deduction includes qualifying expenses incidental to purchasing your new home, such as legal fees, title insurance costs, survey, appraisal, and other expenses that would be included in the adjusted basis of your new home. (See Chapter 3.) The maximum amount of expenses in the indirect category (house-hunting, temporary living, and expenses of buying and breaking a lease) is $3,000. As noted above, the maximum in the first two categories combined is $1,500.

To qualify to deduct moving expenses, a number of requirements must be met, including the following:

(1) *Distance Test:* The distance (measured by the most commonly traveled route, not as the crow flies) between the location of your new job and your old home must be at least 35 miles more than the distance from the location of your old job and your old home. The

idea is that you should be moving to get a better commute than you would have if you stayed in the same house and commuted to your new job. In addition, if the distance between your new place of work and your new residence is greater than the distance between your old residence and your new place of work, the IRS will probably disallow the deduction under the work connection test described below.

(2) *Work Time Test:* During the 12-month period immediately after the move, you must work full time for at least 39 weeks. The 39 weeks of work don't have to be consecutive, and you don't have to have the job lined up before you move. However, if you don't actually work, no deduction is allowed. If you become self-employed before meeting this test, you must meet the self-employed test described below.

If you're self-employed, you must also work full time for a minimum of 78 weeks in the 24-month period immediately after the move. A self-employed person is considered to have begun work when substantial arrangements to begin work have been made. If either you or your spouse meet the appropriate test, and you file a joint return, you qualify to deduct moving expenses.

You may claim moving expense deductions even if enough time hasn't passed before the end of the year for you to have worked 39 weeks at your new job location. You must claim the deductions in the year you pay or incur them. Claim the deductions for the year you moved, and if you later find that you don't meet the test, report the improperly deducted amount as income in the year you fail to meet the test.

(3) *Work Connection Test:* The move must be connected with your starting at a new principal place of work. The move must be reasonably proximate in both time and place to the commencement of your new job. A new principal place of work is defined as the plant, office, shop, store, or other property where services are performed. For a self-employed person, it is defined as the center of his or her business activities. The principal place of work of someone employed by a number of employers on a short-term basis through an employment agency is the employment agency. The moving expenses must be incurred within one year from the date you first start your new job, unless you can demonstrate extenuating circumstances.

EXAMPLE: Mary Mover is transferred by her employer from Boston to Washington, DC. Mary moves to a new home in Washington, DC and commences work on February 1, 1995. Mary's husband Tom and their two children stay in Boston until June, 1996 so that the children can complete their grade-school education in the old school. In June, 1996 Mary and Tom sell their Boston home, and Tom and the children then move to Washington, DC. Considerable expenses are incurred in June, 1996 in connection with the move. These expenses are allowable as a deduction even though they were incurred 16 months after the date Mary commenced work at her new job location, since Mary moved to the new location and incurred some of the expenses before the expiration of the one-year period.

---

(4) *Reasonableness Test*: Only reasonable expenses may be deducted. For example, travel expenses should be reasonable if they are incurred along the shortest and most direct route from your old home to your new home. Costs to travel a longer but more scenic route, or to permit a stopover, are not allowed. Expenses for travel arrangements that are lavish or extravagant can't be deducted. You can deduct expenses of your move and the move of your family and household if their principal residence both before and after the move is your residence.

To claim moving expense deductions, fill out Form 3903, "Moving Expenses." Moving expenses can be deducted only when you itemize deductions. Note: The 2 percent of adjusted-gross-income floor (the hurdle rate you must exceed to claim miscellaneous itemized deductions) doesn't apply to moving expenses.

MORTGAGE COSTS AND POINTS

Points paid on getting a mortgage to pay for your new home can be very expensive. Points are a cost that most lenders charge for making a loan, and they are usually based on a percentage of the loan made. Points are really interest expense paid up front when the loan is made. Fortunately, a special tax rule lets homeowners deduct points in the year they are paid. This can be an important tax savings.

To qualify for this favorable treatment, (1) the loan must be used to buy or improve your principal residence; (2) it must be secured by your principal residence; (3) the number of points can't exceed the number of points generally charged in the area where the loan is made; and (4) paying points is an established business practice in the area where the loan is made.

CAUTION: Loan processing and other service fees are not considered interest and can't be deducted. To deduct points, you must actually pay them. If the bank lent Mary $100,000 as in our example, but paid her only $97,000 at the mortgage closing, Mary would not be able to deduct the points. Instead, Mary should insist that the bank pay her the full $100,000 loan, and she should write a check to the bank for the $3,000 points.

NOTE: If you take out a federally insured mortgage loan and the lending institution charges you discount points to increase its yield to a competitive position, you can deduct these points, too.

PROPERTY TAXES

When you buy a house, property taxes usually enter into the adjustments that are made at the closing (the transaction where the final documents are signed, checks are handed over, and the deed and ownership of the property are given to you). For example, if the seller paid property taxes for a period for which you will end up owning the house, you will have to reimburse the seller for these taxes. Sometimes a large property tax payment may be due at the closing or shortly thereafter. All such property tax payments should be deductible by you, and these deductions can be a substantial benefit.

Deciding what property taxes can be deducted and by whom can be a bit complicated. Fortunately, the lawyers will have to figure all of this out for you at the closing, so that the proper payments can be made. If you really want to dig through the rules, the discussions below will help you. The easiest way to explain the general rule for dividing up property taxes is with an example.

EXAMPLE: Sam Seller sold his house to Bonnie Buyer on June 30. Property taxes are $3,650 per year. Assume the county assesses taxes on a January 1 through December 31 basis. To figure the division of the property taxes, first determine how many days Sam and Bonnie each owned the house during the property tax assessment period:

Sam: January 1–June 29* = 180 days
Bonnie: June 30–December 31 = 185 days

* The seller's tax is allocated to the day before the sale.

Next, determine the portion of the assessment period in which each owned the house and multiply it by the entire tax to determine the tax the buyer and seller are each responsible for:

Sam: $180/365 \times \$3,650 = \$1,800$
Bonnie: $185/365 \times \$3,650 = \$1,850$

Unfortunately, dividing up the property taxes is never so easy. The county (or other taxing authority) usually has a property tax assessment period other than a calendar year. Assume instead that the county property tax assessment period runs from April 1 to March 31 of the following year. Now the question is, how many days during the property tax assessment period do the buyer and seller own the house?

Sam: April 1–June 29 = 90 days
Bonnie: June 30–March 31 = 275 days

The property taxes are then allocated as follows:

Sam: $90/365 \times \$3,650 = \$900$
Bonnie: $275/365 \times \$3,650 = \$2,750$

What happened to the property taxes prior to April 1? Sam already paid them during the prior assessment period. What will happen to the property taxes after March 31 of the following year? Bonnie owns the house and will pay them entirely on her own.

The above example, showing how property taxes are divided up on the sale of a home, with and without the complication caused by the taxing authority's (the county in our example) use of a tax year different from a regular calendar year, should make property tax division easier to understand.

The rule is that real estate taxes must be prorated (divided) between the buyer and seller as of the date of the closing (transfer of ownership of the house from the seller to the buyer). Only taxes properly allocable to the buyer (or seller) can be deducted by the buyer (or seller). This follows the general rule discussed in an earlier question—only the person liable for and paying the property taxes can deduct them. Simply stated, the buyer and seller are each responsible for the property taxes for the portion of the year each owns the house. Unfortunately, the calculation gets complicated from here.

The seller and buyer pay tax on a calendar year basis (the period from January 1 through December 31). Most property taxes, however, are assessed on the basis of some fiscal year period—for example, July 1 through June 30 of the following year. This is the period under local (state) law to which the tax relates. The allocation is based on the number of days in the taxing authority's fiscal year in which the buyer and seller each owned the property. The seller is responsible for paying (and can deduct when he or she pays) taxes owed through the date one day before the sale. The buyer is responsible for paying (and can deduct when he or she pays) taxes from the date of sale onward.

To make matters more confusing, the laws in some places call property taxes a lien on the property, or a liability of the owner before or after the real property tax assessment year to which the taxes relate. The rule is that the taxes are deductible by the person who owns the house during the real property assessment period. If the real property taxes become a lien on the property or a liability for the seller before the property tax assessment period to which the taxes relate, and the house is sold before that assessment period begins, the seller can't deduct these taxes. Similarly, if the real property taxes become a personal liability of the buyer or a lien on the property after the end of the real property assessment period to which the taxes relate, the buyer can't deduct them.

EXAMPLE: Real property taxes for 1989 became a lien on the property on October 1, 1988. You bought the house on November 12, 1988. Even though the real property taxes for 1989 were a lien on the house while the seller owned the house in 1988, the seller can't deduct any of the 1989 property taxes.

HOW YOU CAN REDUCE THE TAXES WITHHELD FROM YOUR PAYCHECK

The amount of federal income tax to be withheld from your wages depends on the amount of income you earn during each pay period and the information you report to your employer on IRS Form W-4, "Employee's Withholding Allowance Certificate." Form W-4 is usually filled out when you first start a new job. But you can also fill it out if there is a substantial change in your tax picture that affects the amount of withholding that should be taken out of your paycheck. Buying your first home may be just such a situation. The greater the number of allowances you claim on Form W-4, the lower the amount of tax withheld. One factor to consider is what deductions to your income you expect to have for the year.

Be certain to check with your employer as to the date that the new withholding allowances you claim will be reflected in your paycheck. Employers can (but don't have to) delay the use of the new information until the first status determination date that occurs at least 30 days after you submit the new Form W-4. Status determination dates occur on January 1, May 1, July 1, and October 1.

CAUTION: If you make any statements or claims on your Form W-4 that are false in order to decrease the amount of tax withheld, and there is no reasonable basis for these statements, a number of penalties, including one for $500, can be assessed.

Don't overclaim allowances and find yourself having paid in less than the required tax at year end. Be sure to read the instructions for Form W-4 and have your accountant review your calculations.

HOW YOU CAN REDUCE THE AMOUNT OF ESTIMATED TAXES YOU MUST PAY

Taxpayers who work as independent contractors (rather than as employees) or who have their own businesses, or even taxpayers with a substantial amount of income other than wages subject to income tax withholding, usually must make estimated tax payments. Generally, you must make estimated tax payments if your estimated tax for the year will be $500 or more, and the total of your tax withheld and tax credits will be less than the lower of: (1) 90 percent of the tax that will be due on your tax return (Form 1040); or (2) 100 percent of the total tax you owed in the prior year. To determine how much 90 percent of your estimated tax will be, use the worksheets and instructions the IRS provides with its tax Form 1040-ES. Estimated tax payments are generally due on the following dates:

April 15
June 15
September 15
January 15 (of the following year)

If your moving expenses, home mortgage interest and property tax deductions will substantially increase your overall tax deductions, it may pay to recalculate the amount of estimated tax you must pay. If a lesser amount is due, you can reduce the amount paid in the remaining installments. This is likely to be true for first-time home buyers who had few itemized deductions before the purchase (particularly when a lot of points were paid).

Have your accountant review your calculations and assumptions. If you underpay the amount of estimated tax, you could be subject to a stiff penalty. See IRS Form 2210 and IRS Publication No. 505, *Tax Withholding and Estimated Tax*.

CHAPTER SUMMARY

When looking for the downpayment to purchase a house, don't overlook the tax benefits that buying and moving into a home can bring. Although these benefits alone are unlikely to supply the funds you need, they can be an important component of your overall strategy for coming up with the downpayment. Because the tax laws are very complicated and are constantly changing, make sure to consult with your accountant before changing your withholding or estimated tax payments. You wouldn't want to find yourself facing interest charges and a stiff penalty for making a mistake.

FOR YOUR NOTEBOOK

Form W-4 and Form 1040-ES, including worksheets to make the necessary calculations and instructions, are reproduced here.* The illustrations were prepared by the international accounting firm, Ernst & Whinney. They will help you implement the planning ideas suggested in the chapter. However, it's always best to check with your accountant before filing a tax return. Forms can be obtained from your nearest IRS office. Your employer should have Form W-4 available.

EXAMPLE: Sam and Jenny Starr are a married couple renting an apartment. The following summarizes their current projected 1989 tax information:

(1) *Income:* Wages $40,000 and Interest $500.

(2) *Deductions:* State Taxes $3,000 and Contributions $1,800.

Since their total itemized deductions do not exceed the federal standard deduction of $5,000, there is no tax benefit for them in itemizing their deductions. Their federal tax liability is $5,000.

The Starrs are contemplating buying a home for $150,000. Their down-payment of $50,000 would be supplemented by a mortgage of $100,000. If they make the purchase on July 1, 1989, the following items would affect their above tax calculations:

(1) Points on the mortgage of $3,500 would be fully deductible.

(2) Real estate taxes of $2,000 for the six months of ownership would be fully deductible.

(3) Mortgage interest for the six months of $5,000 would also be fully deductible.

Since their itemized deductions now total $15,300, they can benefit from itemizing on Form 1040 Schedule A. The couple's resulting tax liability has decreased to $3,200.

---

* Tax forms and examples were prepared by Ernst & Whinney, New York, NY.

Simply by making this home purchase, they will have saved $1,800 in 1989 taxes. The savings can be realized immediately either by adjusting their employee Form W-4s for the remainder of 1989, or reducing their quarterly estimated tax voucher (Form 1040-ES) payments for the last six months of the year.

	Apt. Rental Jan–June	Home Purchase July–Dec
W-4 Federal Withholding Exemptions	2	15
Quarterly Estimated Federal Payments	$1,250	$350

Income Statement for 1989

Sam & Jenny Starr

	Apt. Rental	Buy House
Earned Income		
Wages & Salaries	$ 40,000	$ 40,000
	$ 40,000	$ 40,000
Interest Dividends		
Interest	$ 500	$ 500
	$ 500	$ 500
Adjusted Gross Income	$ 40,500	$ 40,500
Deductions		
State Taxes Paid	$ 3,000	$ 3,000
Real Estate Taxes Paid	40,000	2,000
Mortgage Interest	0	8,500
Charitable Contributions	1,800	1,800
Gross Deductions	$ (4,800)	$(15,300)
Standard Deduction	5,000	5,000
Allowed Deductions	$ (5,000)	$(15,300)
Personal Exemptions	(3,900)	(3,900)
Taxable Income	$ 31,600	$ 21,300
Total Federal Tax	$ 4,988	$ 3,199
Federal Tax Bracket	28%	15%

19**89**   Form W-4

Department of the Treasury
Internal Revenue Service

Purpose. Complete Form W-4 so that your employer can withhold the correct amount of Federal income tax from your pay.

Exemption From Withholding. Read line 6 of the certificate below to see if you can claim exempt status. If exempt, only complete the certificate; but do not complete lines 4 and 5. No Federal income tax will be withheld from your pay.

Basic Instructions. Employees who are not exempt should complete the Personal Allowances Worksheet. Additional worksheets are provided on page 2 for employees to adjust their withholding allowances based on itemized deductions, adjustments to income, or two-earner/two-job situations. Complete all worksheets that apply to your situation. The worksheets will help you figure the number of withholding allowances you are

entitled to claim. However, you may claim fewer allowances than this.

Head of Household. Generally, you may claim head of household filing status on your tax return only if you are unmarried and pay more than 50% of the costs of keeping up a home for yourself and your dependent(s) or other qualifying individuals.

Nonwage Income. If you have a large amount of nonwage income, such as interest or dividends, you should consider making estimated tax payments using Form 1040-ES. Otherwise, you may find that you owe additional tax at the end of the year.

Two-Earner/Two-Jobs. If you have a working spouse or more than one job, figure the total number of allowances you are entitled to claim on all jobs using worksheets from only one Form

W-4. This total should be divided among all jobs. Your withholding will usually be most accurate when all allowances are claimed on the W-4 filed for the highest paying job and zero allowances are claimed for the others.

Advance Earned Income Credit. If you are eligible for this credit, you can receive it added to your paycheck throughout the year. For details, obtain Form W-5 from your employer.

Check Your Withholding. After your W-4 takes effect, you can use **Publication 919**, Is My Withholding Correct for 1989?, to see how the dollar amount you are having withheld compares to your estimated total annual tax. Call 1-800-424-3676 (in Hawaii and Alaska, check your local telephone directory) to obtain this publication.

Personal Allowances Worksheet

A   Enter "1" for **yourself** if no one else can claim you as a dependent . . . . **A** ___1___

B   Enter "1" if:
  1. You are single and have only one job; or
  2. You are married, have only one job, and your spouse does not work; or
  3. Your wages from a second job or your spouse's wages (or the total of both) are $2,500 or less.
  . . . . **B** _____

C   Enter "1" for your **spouse**. But, you may choose to enter "0" if you are married and have either a working spouse or more than one job (this may help you avoid having too little tax withheld) . . . . **C** ___1___

D   Enter number of **dependents** (other than your spouse or yourself) whom you will claim on your tax return . . . . **D** _____

E   Enter "1" if you will file as a **head of household** on your tax return (see conditions under "Head of Household," above) . **E** _____

F   Enter "1" if you have at least $1,500 of **child or dependent care expenses** for which you plan to claim a credit . . . . **F** _____

G   Add lines A through F and enter total here . . . . ▶ **G** ___2___

For accuracy, do all worksheets that apply.

- If you plan to **itemize or claim adjustments to income** and want to reduce your withholding, turn to the Deductions and Adjustments Worksheet on page 2.
- If you are **single** and have **more than one job** and your combined earnings from all jobs exceed $25,000 OR if you are **married** and have a **working spouse or more than one job,** and the combined earnings from all jobs exceed $40,000, then turn to the Two-Earner/Two-Job Worksheet on page 2 if you want to avoid having too little tax withheld.
- If **neither** of the above situations applies to you, **stop here** and enter the number from line G on line 4 of Form W-4 below.

- - - - - - - - - - - - - - - - **Cut here and give the certificate to your employer. Keep the top portion for your records.** - - - - - - - - - - - - - - - - -

Form **W-4**
Department of the Treasury
Internal Revenue Service

Employee's Withholding Allowance Certificate
▶ **For Privacy Act and Paperwork Reduction Act Notice, see reverse.**

OMB No. 1545-0010

19**89**

OLD

1 Type or print your first name and middle initial Sam	Last name Starr	**2** Your social security number 111-11-1111

Home address (number and street or rural route)
567 Yourtown Drive

City or town, state, and ZIP code
Gotham City, Metropolis 12345

3 Marital Status
☐ Single   ☒ Married
☐ Married, but withhold at higher Single rate.
Note: If married, but legally separated, or spouse is a nonresident alien, check the Single box.

4 Total number of allowances you are claiming (from line G above or from the Worksheets on back if they apply) . . . **4** | 2

5 Additional amount, if any, you want deducted from each pay . . . . **5** $

6 I claim exemption from withholding and I certify that I meet **ALL** of the following conditions for exemption:
- Last year I had a right to a refund of **ALL** Federal income tax withheld because I had **NO** tax liability; **AND**
- This year I expect a refund of **ALL** Federal income tax withheld because I expect to have **NO** tax liability; **AND**
- This year if my income exceeds $500 and includes nonwage income, another person cannot claim me as a dependent.

If you meet all of the above conditions, enter the year effective and "EXEMPT" here . . . . . . ▶ **6** | 19

7 Are you a full-time student? **(Note:** Full-time students are not automatically exempt.) . . . . **7** ☐Yes   ☐No

Under penalties of perjury, I certify that I am entitled to the number of withholding allowances claimed on this certificate or entitled to claim exempt status.

Employee's signature ▶ _Sam Starr_   Date ▶ _July 1_ , 19_88_

8 Employer's name and address (**Employer:** Complete 8 and 10 **only if sending to IRS)**
Courtesy of Ernst & Whinney
787 7th Avenue, New York, NY 10019

9 Office code (optional)

10 Employer identification number

254

Deductions and Adjustments Worksheet

Note: *Use this worksheet only if you plan to itemize deductions or claim adjustments to income on your 1989 tax return.*

1 Enter an estimate of your 1989 itemized deductions. These include: qualifying home mortgage interest, 20% of personal interest, charitable contributions, state and local taxes (but not sales taxes), medical expenses in excess of 7.5% of your income, and miscellaneous deductions (most miscellaneous deductions are now deductible only in excess of 2% of your income) . . . . 1 $ _____

2 Enter: { $5,200 if married filing jointly or qualifying widow(er)
$4,550 if head of household
$3,100 if single
$2,600 if married filing separately } . . . . 2 $ _____

3 Subtract line 2 from line 1. If line 2 is greater than line 1, enter zero . . . . 3 $ _____

4 Enter an estimate of your 1989 adjustments to income. These include alimony paid and deductible IRA contributions . 4 $ _____

5 **Add** lines 3 and 4 and enter the total . . . . 5 $ _____

6 Enter an estimate of your 1989 nonwage income (such as dividends or interest income) . . . . . 6 $ _____

7 Subtract line 6 from line 5. Enter the result, but not less than zero . . . . 7 $ _____

8 **Divide** the amount on line 7 by $2,000 and enter the result here. Drop any fraction . . . . 8 _____

9 Enter the number from Personal Allowances Worksheet, line G, on page 1 . . . . 9 _____

10 **Add** lines 8 and 9 and enter the total here. If you plan to use the Two-Earner/Two-Job Worksheet, also enter the total on line 1, below. Otherwise, **stop here** and enter this total on Form W-4, line 4 on page 1 . . . . 10 _____

Two-Earner/Two-Job Worksheet

Note: *Use this worksheet only if the instructions at line G on page 1 direct you here.*

1 Enter the number from line G on page 1 (or from line 10 above if you used the Deductions and Adjustments Worksheet) . 1 _____

2 Find the number in **Table 1** below that applies to the **LOWEST** paying job and enter it here . . . . . . 2 _____

3 If line 1 is **GREATER THAN OR EQUAL TO** line 2, subtract line 2 from line 1. Enter the result here (if zero, enter "0") and on Form W-4, line 4, on page 1. **DO NOT** use the rest of this worksheet. . . . . 3 _____

Note: *If line 1 is **LESS THAN** line 2, enter "0" on Form W-4, line 4, on page 1. Complete lines 4–9 to calculate the additional dollar withholding necessary to avoid a year-end tax bill.*

4 Enter the number from line 2 of this worksheet . . . . 4 _____

5 Enter the number from line 1 of this worksheet . . . . 5 _____

6 **Subtract** line 5 from line 4 . . . . 6 _____

7 Find the amount in **Table 2** below that applies to the **HIGHEST** paying job and enter it here . . . . . . 7 $ _____

8 **Multiply** line 7 by line 6 and enter the result here. This is the additional annual withholding amount needed 8 $ _____

9 Divide line 8 by the number of pay periods each year. (For example, divide by 26 if you are paid every other week.) Enter the result here and on Form W-4, line 5, page 1. This is the additional amount to be withheld from each paycheck . . . 9 $ _____

Table 1: Two-Earner/Two-Job Worksheet

Married Filing Jointly		All Others	
If wages from **LOWEST** paying job are—	Enter on line 2 above	If wages from **LOWEST** paying job are—	Enter on line 2 above
0 - $4,000	0	0 - $4,000	0
4,001 - 8,000	1	4,001 - 8,000	1
8,001 - 18,000	2	8,001 - 13,000	2
18,001 - 21,000	3	13,001 - 15,000	3
21,001 - 23,000	4	15,001 - 19,000	4
23,001 - 25,000	5	19,001 and over	5
25,001 - 27,000	6		
27,001 - 32,000	7		
32,001 - 38,000	8		
38,001 - 42,000	9		
42,001 and over	10		

Table 2: Two-Earner/Two-Job Worksheet

Married Filing Jointly		All Others	
If wages from **HIGHEST** paying job are—	Enter on line 7 above	If wages from **HIGHEST** paying job are—	Enter on line 7 above
0 - $40,000	$300	0 - $23,000	$300
40,001 - 84,000	560	23,001 - 50,000	560
84,001 and over	660	50,000 and over	660

Privacy Act and Paperwork Reduction Act Notice.—We ask for this information to carry out the Internal Revenue laws of the United States. We may give the information to the Department of Justice for civil or criminal litigation and to cities, states, and the District of Columbia for use in administering their tax laws. You are required to give this information to your employer.

The time needed to complete this form will vary depending on individual circumstances. The estimated average time is: **Recordkeeping** 46 mins., **Learning about the law or the form** 10 mins., **Preparing the form** 70 mins. If you have comments concerning the accuracy of these time estimates or suggestions for making this form more simple, we would be happy to hear from you. You can write to the **Internal Revenue Service,** Washington, DC 20224, Attention: IRS Reports Clearance Officer, TR:FP; or the **Office of Management and Budget,** Paperwork Reduction Project, Washington, DC 20503.

Form **1040-ES** | **1988**
Payment-
Voucher

Department of the Treasury
Internal Revenue Service

REVISED

Return this voucher with check or money order payable to the Internal Revenue Service.
Please write your social security number and "1988 Form 1040-ES" on your check or
money order. Please do not send cash. Enclose, but do not staple or attach, your payment
with this voucher.
File only if you are making a payment of estimated tax.

OMB No. 1545-0087
Expires 9-30-90

(Calendar year—Due Sept. 15, 1988)

1 Amount of payment
$ 350

2 Fiscal year filers
enter year ending

----------- (month and year)

Please type or print

Your first name and initial	Your last name	Your social security number
Sam	Starr	111-11-1111
(If joint payment, complete for spouse) Spouse's first name and initial	Spouse's last name if different from yours	If joint payment, spouse's social security number
Jenny		

Address (number and street)
567 YourTown Drive

City, state, and ZIP code
Gotham City, Metropolis   12345

For Paperwork Reduction Act Notice, see instructions on page 1.

Tear off here

Form **1040-ES** | **1988**
Payment-
Voucher

Department of the Treasury
Internal Revenue Service

OLD

Return this voucher with check or money order payable to the Internal Revenue Service.
Please write your social security number and "1988 Form 1040-ES" on your check or
money order. Please do not send cash. Enclose, but do not staple or attach, your payment
with this voucher.
File only if you are making a payment of estimated tax.

OMB No. 1545-0087
Expires 9-30-90

(Calendar year—Due June 15, 1988)

1 Amount of payment
$ 1250

2 Fiscal year filers
enter year ending

----------- (month and year)

Please type or print

Your first name and initial	Your last name	Your social security number
Sam	Starr	111-11-1111
(If joint payment, complete for spouse) Spouse's first name and initial	Spouse's last name if different from yours	If joint payment, spouse's social security number
Jenny		222-22-2222

Address (number and street)
567 YourTown Drive

City, state, and ZIP code
Gotham City, Metropolitan   12345

For Paperwork Reduction Act Notice, see instructions on page 1.

Tear off here

Form **1040-ES**	**Estimated Tax for Individuals**	OMB No. 1545-0087 Expires 9-30-90
Department of the Treasury Internal Revenue Service	▶ **This form is primarily for first-time filers of estimated tax .**	**1988**

Instructions

Paperwork Reduction Act Notice.— We ask for this information to carry out the Internal Revenue laws of the United States. We need it to ensure that taxpayers are complying with these laws and to allow us to figure and collect the right amount of tax. You are required to give us this information.

Changes You Should Note.—The Tax Reform Act of 1986 made changes in the tax law for 1988 that may affect your 1988 estimated tax. For summaries of some of the major changes see **Tax Law Changes Effective for 1988**, on page 4. **Caution:** At the time this form went to print, Congress was considering legislation that would impose a supplemental premium on individuals who for 1988 are covered by the Medicare Part B insurance program. This premium would be payable as an addition to tax. If this legislation is passed, IRS will use various means to furnish you details about the subject. If you are required to pay the premium, you may want to increase the amount of your estimated tax payments.

See **Publication 505,** Tax Withholding and Estimated Tax, for some of the other items that may be changed by legislation.

Purpose of Form.—Use this form to figure and pay your estimated tax.

Estimated tax is the amount of tax you expect to owe for the year after subtracting the amount of tax you expect to have withheld and the amount of any credits you plan to take.

This form is primarily for first-time filers. After your first payment-voucher is received in the Internal Revenue Service, IRS will mail you a 1040-ES package. Your name, address, and social security number will be preprinted on the vouchers. You should use these vouchers in making the **remaining** payments of estimated tax for the year. Using the preprinted vouchers will speed processing, reduce the chance of error, and help save processing costs.

This form can also be used if you did not receive a 1040-ES package, or if you lost it. Complete the appropriate payment-voucher and mail it with your payment.

A. Who Must Make Estimated Tax Payments

The rules below are for U.S. citizens or residents of Puerto Rico, Virgin Islands, Guam, Northern Mariana Islands, and American Samoa. (If you are a nonresident alien, use **Form 1040-ES (NR).**)

Generally, you must pay estimated tax if you expect to owe, after subtracting your withholding and credits, at least $500 in tax for 1988; and you expect your withholding and credits to be less than:

1. 90% of the tax shown on your 1988 tax return, **OR**

2. **100% of the tax shown on your 1987 tax return** (assuming the return covered all 12 months).

Exceptions.—Generally, you do not have to pay estimated tax if your 1988 income tax return will show (1) a tax refund, or (2) a tax balance due of less than $500. Also, you do not have to pay estimated tax if you were a U.S. citizen or resident and you had no tax liability for the full 12-month preceding tax year.

Note: If you must make estimated tax payments and receive salaries and wages, you may not be having enough tax withheld during the year. To avoid making estimated tax payments, consider asking your employer to take more tax out of your earnings. To do this, file a new **Form W-4,** Employee's Withholding Allowance Certificate, with your employer and make sure you will not owe $500 or more in tax.

B. How To Figure Your Estimated Tax

Use the Estimated Tax Worksheet on page 3, the 1988 Tax Rate Schedules on page 4, the instructions on pages 4 and 5, and your 1987 tax return as a guide for figuring your estimated tax. See the 1987 Instructions for Form 1040 for information on figuring your income, deductions, and credits, including the taxable amount of **social security income.**

Note: You may not make joint estimated tax payments if: (1) either you or your spouse is a nonresident alien, (2) you are separated under a decree of divorce or separate maintenance, or (3) you and your spouse have different tax years.

Most of the items on the worksheet are self-explanatory. However, the instructions below provide additional information for filling out certain lines.

Line 7—Additional taxes.—Enter on line 7 any additional taxes from:

● **Form 4970,** Tax on Accumulation Distribution of Trusts, **OR**

● **Form 4972,** Tax on Lump-Sum Distributions.

Line 9—Credits.—For details on credits you may take, see Form 1040, lines 40 through 46, and the related instructions.

Line 11—Self-employment tax.—If you and your spouse make joint estimated tax payments and both have self-employment income, figure the estimated self-employment tax separately. Enter the total amount on line 11.

Line 12—Other taxes.—Enter on line 12 any other taxes from:

● Recapture of investment credit;

● Tax on premature distributions (Form 5329, Part II only);

● Section 72 penalty taxes;

● Advance earned income credit payments;

● Alternative minimum tax; **AND**

● Excise tax on golden parachute payments.

C. How To Use the Payment-Voucher

Each payment-voucher has the date when the voucher is due for calendar year taxpayers. Please use the correct voucher.

(1) Enter your name, address, and social security number in the space provided on the payment-voucher. If you are filing a joint payment-voucher, your spouse's name and social security number should be included on the voucher.

(2) Enter the net amount of your payment on line 1 of the payment-voucher. If you paid too much tax on your 1987 Form 1040, you may have chosen to apply the overpayment to your estimated tax for 1988. If so, you may apply all or part of the overpayment to any voucher. **Send the payment-voucher to IRS ONLY when you are making a payment.**

(3) Enclose, but do not staple or attach, your check or money order with the payment-voucher. Make the check or money order payable to Internal Revenue Service. Please write your social security number and "1988 Form 1040-ES" on your check or money order. **Do not** include any balance due on your Form 1040 with your check for estimated tax. Please fill in the Record of Estimated Tax Payments on page 2 so you will have a record of your payments.

(4) Mail your payment-voucher to the address for the place where you live shown on page 2.

D. When To Pay Your Estimated Tax

In general, you must make your first estimated tax payment by April 15, 1988. The April 15th date applies whether or not you are outside the United States and Puerto Rico on April 15. You may either pay all of your estimated tax at that time or pay in four equal amounts that are due by April 15, 1988; June 15, 1988; September 15, 1988; and January 17, 1989. Exceptions to these rules are listed below.

(1) Other payment dates.—In some cases, such as a change in income, you may have to make your first estimated tax payment after April 15, 1988. The payment dates are as follows:

If the requirement is met after:	Payment date is:
● March 31 and before June 1	June 15, 1988
● May 31 and before Sept. 1	Sept. 15, 1988
● August 31	Jan. 17, 1989

(Continued on page 2)

Note: *You may use the "Amended Estimated Tax Schedule" on page 3 to figure your amended estimated tax.*

If the first payment you are required to make is due:

- June 15, 1988, enter ½;
- September 15, 1988, enter ¾;
- January 17, 1989, enter all

of line 16 (less any 1987 overpayment applied to this installment) on line 17 of the worksheet and on line 1 of the payment-voucher.

If you file your 1988 Form 1040 by January 31, 1989, and pay the entire balance due, then you do not have to make the payment which would otherwise be due January 17, 1989.

(2) Farmers and fishermen.—If at least two-thirds of your gross income for 1987 or 1988 is from farming or fishing, you may do one of the following:

- Pay all of your estimated tax by January 17, 1989; OR
- File Form 1040 for 1988 by March 1, 1989, and pay the total tax due. In this case, you do not need to make estimated tax payments for 1988.

(3) Fiscal year.—If your return is on a fiscal year basis, your due dates are the 15th day of the 4th, 6th, and 9th months of your fiscal year and the 1st month of the following fiscal year. If any date falls on a Saturday, Sunday, or legal holiday, use the next regular workday.

E. Penalty for Not Paying Enough Estimated Tax

You may be charged a penalty for not paying enough estimated tax, or for not making the payments on time in the required amount (even if you have an overpayment on your tax return). The penalty does not apply if each required payment is timely and the total tax paid:

- Is at least 90% (66⅔% for farmers and fishermen) of the amount of income tax (including alternative minimum tax) and self-employment tax due as shown on your return for 1988, or 90% of the tax due if no return was filed;
- **Is 100% of the tax shown on your return for 1987** (you must have filed a return for 1987 and it must have been for a full 12-month year); OR

- Is 90% of the tax figured by annualizing the taxable income, alternative minimum taxable income, and adjusted self-employment income received for the months ending before the due date of the installment.

Note: *The penalty may be waived under certain conditions. Get **Publication 505**, Tax Withholding and Estimated Tax, for details.*

Caution: *You may be required to make payments of past due amounts to avoid further penalty. You may have to make these payments if you do not make your estimated tax payments on time, or if you did not pay the correct amount for a previous payment date.*

Example: On June 1, 1988, you find out that you should have made an estimated tax payment for April 15. You should immediately fill out the payment-voucher due April 15, 1988, and send in the required amount (¼ × 1988 estimated tax).

For more details about the penalty, get Publication 505.

If you changed your name because of marriage, divorce, etc., and you made estimated tax payments using your old name, you should attach a brief statement to the front of your 1988 Form 1040. In it explain all the estimated tax payments you and your spouse made during 1988, the address where you made the payments, and the name(s) and social security number(s) under which you made payments.

F. Where To File Your Payment-Voucher

Mail your payment-voucher to the Internal Revenue Service at the following address.

If you are located in:	Use this address:
New Jersey, New York (New York City and counties of Nassau, Rockland, Suffolk, and Westchester)	P.O. Box 162 Newark, NJ 07101-0162
New York (all other counties), Connecticut, Maine, Massachusetts, Minnesota, New Hampshire, Rhode Island, Vermont	P.O. Box 371999 Pittsburgh, PA 15250-7999
Delaware, District of Columbia, Maryland, Pennsylvania	Philadelphia, PA 19255
Alabama, Florida, Georgia, Mississippi, South Carolina	P.O. Box 62001 Philadelphia, PA 19162-0300
Kentucky, Michigan, Ohio, West Virginia	Cincinnati, OH 45999
Arkansas, Indiana, North Carolina, Tennessee, Virginia	Memphis, TN 37501
Illinois, Iowa, Missouri, Wisconsin	P.O. Box 6413 Chicago, IL 60680-6413
Kansas, Louisiana, New Mexico, Oklahoma, Texas	Austin, TX 73301
Alaska, Arizona, California (counties of Alpine, Amador, Butte, Calaveras, Colusa, Contra Costa, Del Norte, El Dorado, Glenn, Humboldt, Lake, Lassen, Marin, Mendocino, Modoc, Napa, Nevada, Placer, Plumas, Sacramento, San Joaquin, Shasta, Sierra, Siskiyou, Solano, Sonoma, Sutter, Tehama, Trinity, Yolo, and Yuba), Colorado, Idaho, Montana, Nebraska, Nevada, North Dakota, Oregon, South Dakota, Utah, Washington, Wyoming	Ogden, UT 84201
California (all other counties), Hawaii	Fresno, CA 93888
American Samoa	Philadelphia, PA 19255
Guam	Commissioner of Revenue and Taxation Agana, GU 96910
Northern Mariana Islands	Philadelphia, PA 19255
Puerto Rico (or if excluding income under section 933) Virgin Islands: Nonpermanent residents	Philadelphia, PA 19255
Virgin Islands: Permanent residents	V.I. Bureau of Internal Revenue P.O. Box 3186 St. Thomas, VI 00801
A.P.O. or F.P.O. address of:	Miami—Atlanta, GA 39901 New York—Holtsville, NY 00501 San Francisco—Fresno, CA 93888 Seattle—Ogden, UT 84201
Foreign country: U.S. citizens and those filing Form 2555 or Form 4563, even if you have an A.P.O. or F.P.O. address	Philadelphia, PA 19255

Record of Estimated Tax Payments

Payment number	(a) Date	(b) Amount	(c) 1987 overpayment credit applied	(d) Total amount paid and credited (add (b) and (c))
1				
2				
3				
4				
Total . . . . ▶				

Note: If you are not required to make the estimated tax payment due April 15, 1988, at this time, you may have to make a payment by a later date. See Instruction D(1).

Page 2

Amended Estimated Tax Schedule (Use if your estimated tax changes during the year.)

1 Amended estimated tax		**1**
2a Amount of 1987 overpayment chosen for credit to 1988 estimated tax and applied to date	**2a**	
b Estimated tax payments to date	**2b**	
c Total of lines 2a and 2b		**2c**
3 Unpaid balance (subtract line 2c from line 1)		**3**
4 Amount to be paid (see Instructions D(1) and E)		**4**

1988 Estimated Tax Worksheet (Keep for Your Records—Do Not Send to Internal Revenue Service)

1 Enter amount of Adjusted Gross Income you expect in 1988	**1**
2 If you plan to itemize deductions, enter the estimated total of your deductions. If you do not plan to itemize deductions, see **Standard Deduction** on page 4. Enter the amount here	**2**
3 Subtract line 2 from line 1. Enter the difference here	**3**
4 Exemptions (multiply $1,950 times number of personal exemptions). If you are eligible to be claimed as a dependent on another person's return, see **Personal Exemption** on page 4	**4**
5 Subtract line 4 from line 3	**5**
6 Tax. (Figure your tax on line 5 by using Tax Rate Schedule X, Y, or Z on page 4. DO NOT use the Tax Table or Tax Rate Schedule X, Y, or Z in the 1987 Form 1040 Instructions.)	**6**
7 Enter any additional taxes (see line 7 Instructions)	**7**
8 Add lines 6 and 7	**8**
9 Credits (see line 9 Instructions)	**9**
10 Subtract line 9 from line 8	**10**
11 Self-employment tax. Estimate of 1988 self-employment income $ - - - - - - - - - - - - - - - - - ; if $45,000 or more, enter $5,859; **if less, multiply the amount by .1302** (see line 11 Instructions for additional information)	**11**
12 Other taxes (see line 12 Instructions).	**12**
13a Total. Add lines 10 through 12	**13a**
b Earned income credit and credit from **Form 4136**	**13b**
c Total. Subtract line 13b from line 13a	**13c**
14a Enter 90% (66 ⅔% for farmers and fishermen) of line 13c.	**14a**
b Enter 100% of the tax shown on your 1987 tax return	**14b**
c Enter the smaller of lines 14a or 14b. This is your required annual payment	**14c**

Caution: Generally, if you do not prepay at least the amount on line 14c, you may be subject to a penalty for not paying enough estimated tax. To avoid a penalty, make sure your estimate on line 13c is as accurate as possible. If you are unsure of your estimate and line 14a is smaller than line 14b, you may want to pay up to the amount shown on line 14b. For more information, get Publication 505.

15 Income tax withheld and estimated to be withheld (including income tax withholding on pensions, annuities, certain deferred income, etc.) during 1988	**15**
16 Balance (subtract line 15 from line 14c). (**Note:** If line 13c less line 15 is less than $500, you are not required to make estimated tax payments.) If you are applying an overpayment from 1987 to 1988 estimated tax, see Instruction C(2), page 1	**16**
17 If the first payment you are required to make is due April 15, 1988, enter ¼ of line 16 (less any 1987 overpayment that you are applying to this installment) here and on line 1 of your payment-voucher(s). You may round off cents to the nearest whole dollar	**17**

Page 3

259

GLOSSARY

A

Abstract of title. A document listing the transactions affecting a property's ownership, including sales, mortgages, liens, and so forth.

Acceleration clause. A provision in a mortgage that the lender may demand immediate payment of the entire balance of the debt under certain circumstances, such as a late payment.

Adjustable-rate mortgage (ARM). A mortgage whose interest rate will fluctuate in line with an index, such as the rate on one-year Treasury bills.

Adjusted sales price. For tax purposes, the selling price of a property, minus certain expenses, like commissions paid to brokers.

Adjusted tax basis. The original cost of a property, reduced by depreciation deductions and increased by improvements and other capital expenditures.

Adjustments. Expenses a buyer or seller must pay at a closing, for prepaid taxes, for remaining fuel, and so forth.

Affidavit of title. A written declaration that the seller owns a property free and clear. The document is typically affirmed by an authorized official.

Agent. A person who acts on another person's behalf, as in buying or selling property. A real estate agent can be either a broker or a salesperson.

Amortization. The gradual repayment of a loan, including interest, and increasing reduction of the principal.

"As is." Without any guarantees as to condition of a property.

Asking price. The amount that a seller would like to receive for property. It is the same as the listing price, but may differ from the selling price.

Assessed valuation. An estimate for property tax purposes of a property's financial value.

Assumption of a mortgage. The takeover by a buyer of the existing mortgage on a property.

B

Balloon mortgage. A mortgage in which the principal must be paid off at a certain date, even if regular payments have been based on a date further in the future.

Basis. For tax purposes, the cost of a property, including not just the purchase price and purchase expenses, but the value of improvements.

Binder. A preliminary contract for the purchase of property.

Biweekly mortgage. A mortgage for which you make payments twice a month, not just once a month.

Blanket mortgage. A mortgage for the purchase of more than one piece of real estate.

Blended mortgage. A new mortgage whose interest rate is higher than that of an existing mortgage, but not as high as market rates.

Break clause. A provision in a sales contract that allows the seller to keep a house on the market when the buyer has inserted a contingency clause in the sales contract. If another buyer comes along, the first buyer has a limited time to go ahead with the purchase.

Bridge loan. A short-term loan to enable a buyer to purchase another house, before obtaining the proceeds from the sale of his or her present house.

Broker. A person who, for a fee or commission, negotiates sales, as of real estate. A real estate broker has an office, unlike a real estate salesperson.

Building and loan association. A type of savings and loan association.

Building code. A community's rules governing new construction and existing buildings.

Buy down. A seller lowers a buyer's mortgage payments by giving the lender a sum of money.

Buyer's broker. An agent who represents the buyer in purchases of real estate. Traditionally, agents have represented sellers.

C

Cap. A limit on how much the rate of interest, or the monthly payment, on an adjustable-rate mortgage can fluctuate.

Capital gain. Profit on the sale of an asset (like a house), which may be taxable.

Carrying charges. Expenses associated with owning property, such as taxes and interest.

Caveat emptor. The notion that buyers purchase any articles with no guarantee as to their condition, unless any defects were not easily noticeable. Latin for "Let the buyer beware."

Certificate of eligibility. A statement issued by the Veterans Administration indicating that a person qualifies for a VA-guaranteed mortgage.

Certificate of title. A document affirming the true ownership of a property.

Chain of title. A chronological record of all changes of ownership in a piece of property.

Chattel. An item of personal property not permanently installed in a house, like a piece of furniture or jewelry.

Chattel mortgage. A mortgage secured by personal property, such as an automobile.

Clear title. Title to a property that is free of encumbrances, such as liens.

Closing. The meeting between buyer and seller and their representatives during which the title to property is transferred.

Closing statement. A document listing all the expenses and monetary transfers related to a real estate transaction.

Cloud on the title. Any claim against a property.

Collateral. Property pledged as security for a debt, such as a house for a mortgage.

Commercial bank. A financial institution that can offer a variety of services, including granting mortgages.

Commission. A payment earned by someone for services rendered.

Comparables. Properties similar to one being sold that can provide a benchmark for the market price of that property.

Condominium. A residence in which an individual owns a unit within a multi-unit building and has a shared interest in the common areas, like stairways and grounds.

Contingency clause. A statement inserted into a contract that permits the cancelation of the contract unless a certain condition is met, such as the buyer obtaining a mortgage at a specific rate of interest.

Contract rent. The amount of rent a tenant is obligated to pay, not including any other expenses, like the cost of utilities.

Conventional mortgage. A mortgage that is not insured or guaranteed by an agency of the U.S. government; also, a fixed-rate mortgage with a set maturity date.

Conveyance. The transfer of title to property.

Cooperative. A multi-unit dwelling owned by all its residents, who are shareholders.

Creative financing. Unusual ways for buyers to purchase property, typically by means of sellers giving the buyers mortgages.

D

Deed. A written document conveying title to real property.

Deed of trust. A document used in certain states instead of a mortgage. Title to a property is held by a trustee until the buyer completes payment of the debt.

Default. The failure to perform an obligation, such as making mortgage payments.

Defect in the title. See Cloud on the title.

Deficiency judgment. A court ruling, after a foreclosure sale, calling for the payment of the balance of a mortgage.

Detached house. A residence that has no walls shared with another residence, in contrast to a townhouse.

Discount broker. A real estate agent who charges less than the traditional 6-percent to 7-percent commission on the sales price.

Distressed property. Property that is in foreclosure.

Downpayment. The cash that a buyer must pay before a lender will provide a mortgage for the balance.

Due-on-sale clause. A statement in a mortgage contract that if the house is sold, the balance of the mortgage principal must be paid immediately, and the buyer cannot take over the mortgage.

Duplex. Two units sharing one roof; also, an apartment with rooms on two floors.

E

Earnest money. A deposit a buyer makes while offering to purchase a property. Usually nonrefundable.

Easement. A right given to an individual or a company to use property, such as to use it to cross over to another property.

Encroachment. The extension of a building beyond the owner's property line.

Encumbrance. A restriction on the value or use of a property, such as a claim that people have not been paid for having worked there.

Equity. The value of property you own free and clear.

Escrow. The custody of money or contracts by a third party until certain conditions are met. Such items are said to be "held in escrow."

Escrow agent. A neutral party who has custody of items placed in escrow.

Estate. An individual's total assets.

Estate tax. Federal and state taxes on the assets left by someone who has died.

Extended coverage. Insurance that provides coverage missing in standard contracts.

Extension. An agreement between two parties to delay a specific time mentioned in a contract.

F

Fair market value. The price at which an item can be sold at the present time between two unrelated people, neither under compulsion to buy or sell.

Federal Home Loan Mortgage Corporation (Freddie Mac). An organization that purchases mortgage loans.

Federal National Mortgage Association (Fannie Mae). A private organization regulated by the Department of Housing and Urban Development that buys and sells mortgages and other securities.

Financial statement. A document listing an individual's assets and liabilities.

Financing. Borrowing money to purchase property.

First mortgage. The first loan secured by a property. Payment of the first mortgage takes precedence over other, junior mortgages.

Fixed-rate mortgage. A loan with an interest rate that does not change during the life of the loan.

Fixture. An article attached to land or dwelling that is considered part of the land or dwelling, as opposed to personal property.

Fix-up costs. Expenses incurred by a seller to spruce up property not more than 90 days before a sale, and paid within 30 days after the sale. Such expenses are deductible from the adjusted sales price when the seller calculates capital gains.

Floater. Insurance that covers movable property, like jewelry, wherever it goes.

Floating-rate mortgage. See Adjustable-rate mortgage.

Foreclosure. The legal procedure by which a mortgagor in default is deprived of his or her ownership of the property.

Foundation. The construction that supports a building. It may be partly or entirely underground.

G

Gentrification. The replacement of low-income residents in a neighborhood by middle- to high-income residents, with an upgrading of the dwellings.

Governmental National Mortgage Association (Ginnie Mae). An organization that guarantees payments to investors who buy mortgage-backed securities.

Graduated-payment mortgage. A mortgage allowing for initially low but increasingly higher regular payments of interest and principal.

Grantee. The legal term for a buyer in a real estate transaction.

Grantor. The legal term for a seller in a real estate transaction.

Ground lease. A lease conveying the use of land.

Growing-equity mortgage. A mortgage whose interest rate is fixed, but whose monthly payments can increase to reduce the principal owed.

Guarantee. To pay the issuer of a mortgage a part of any difference between the money owed and the selling price of the property in case a borrower defaults.

H

Handyman's special. A house up for sale in poor condition.

Holdback. Money set aside to be paid when certain conditions are met.

Homeowners policy. Insurance that protects homeowners against financial losses due to fire and other disasters, thefts, liability, and other hazards.

House inspector. A professional who can evaluate the structural soundness and operating systems of a residence, recommend repairs, and estimate their costs.

I

Impound account. Money set aside for future needs. A bank may impound a homeowner's money to pay property taxes.

Improvement. A change to your house. A "capital" improvement is one that materially adds to the value of a house, appreciably prolongs its useful life, or adapts it to new uses. The cost can be added to the tax basis of a house to calculate the seller's capital gains. Contrast with Repair.

Imputed interest. The interest rate that the U.S. Government will assume is reasonable for tax purposes when, for example, a seller gives a buyer a mortgage for an unusually low rate, perhaps raising the selling price as compensation.

Index. A number that indicates a current financial situation, such as the level of interest rates.

Installment contract. Where the buyer obtains a loan from the seller, but does not receive title to the property until the loan is mostly repaid.

Interest-only mortgage. A mortgage that calls on the borrower to pay only interest until the date of maturity, when the entire principal must be paid.

J

Joint tenancy. Ownership of real estate by two or more people, each of whom can inherit the property if the other dies.

Junior mortgage. Any mortgage but a first mortgage. After a foreclosure sale, holders of junior mortgages cannot be paid until the holder of the first mortgage has been paid.

L

Land contract. A written agreement that enables the buyer to use property, but title does not pass until specified conditions have been met.

Lease. A contract that allows someone to use property in return for paying rent for a specified time.

Lease option. An arrangement in which a possible buyer lives in the seller's house and pays rent, but has the right to buy the house in the future. In some cases, part of the rent is applied toward the purchase price of the house.

Liability insurance. Protection against lawsuits arising from injuries to individuals or damage to other people's property.

Lien. A legal claim on a property for a debt.

Life-of-loan cap. The maximum amount that the interest rate on an adjustable-rate mortgage can rise during its term.

Liquidity. The ease with which assets can be sold for cash.

Listing. A written agreement giving a broker the right to sell another person's property.

Listing broker. The broker who first contracts with a homeowner to sell his or her property. The listing broker is always entitled to part of any sales commission even if another broker makes the sale.

Loan application fee. A charge made by a lender when you apply for a mortgage.

Loan origination fee. A charge made by a lender for processing your mortgage application.

Loan-to-value ratio. The amount of a mortgage compared with the value of the property being purchased. A house valued at $100,000 with an $80,000 mortgage has an 80 percent loan-to-value ratio.

M

Manufactured home. A house constructed at a factory, then brought to the building site.

Marketable title. Title to property that a buyer would ordinarily accept.

Market value. A property's value in the current marketplace.

Maturity. When the principal of a loan must be repaid.

Mechanic's lien. A legal claim on property from workers who have provided materials or labor for repairs or improvements, but who have not been paid.

MGIC. Mortgage Guarantee Insurance Corporation, one of the largest companies that issues private mortgage insurance.

Mobile home. A factory-built dwelling, towed on wheels to a lot and erected on a foundation.

Modular home. A factory-built dwelling, constructed in large units, and transported to a building site.

Mortgage. A loan backed by real property.

Mortgage banker. Someone who originates and services mortgage loans.

Mortgage broker. Someone who finds a lender for a buyer, for a fee.

Mortgage commitment. A written document from a lender agreeing to grant a mortgage for a specified amount for a specified property.

Mortgage insurance. An organization's pledge to reimburse the lender for part or all of the outstanding mortgage if the buyer defaults.

Mortgagee. The holder of a mortgage—the lender.

Mortgagor. The borrower.

Multiple listing. An arrangement where brokers share their listings.

Mutual savings bank. A state-chartered bank, typically in the Northeast, that makes mortgage loans. Such banks are owned by their depositors.

N

National Association of Realtors. The trade association of real estate brokers.

Negative amortization. A situation in which the buyer of a house owes more on his or her mortgage after a period of time than originally. Negative amortization can result from an adjustable-rate mortgage that limits the total monthly payment a buyer makes, even if the interest rate has risen.

Note. A written statement acknowledging a debt and promising payment.

O

Open-end mortgage. A mortgage allowing the borrower to repay the loan before maturity without penalty, or to refinance it.

Option. The right to buy a property at a specific price within a specific time. The fee paid for an option is usually forfeited if it isn't exercised.

P

Personal property. Items not permanently fixed to a house, such as furniture and jewelry.

PITI. Abbreviation for principal, interest, taxes, and insurance, all of which may be included in the monthly mortgage payment a homeowner must make.

Points. Charges assessed by a lender for granting a mortgage. Usually, points allow the lender to lower the interest rate. A point is 1 percent of the amount of the loan.

Precut home. A house whose components are cut in a factory, then shipped to a site for assembly.

Prepayment penalty. A charge assessed the borrower if he or she pays the balance due on a mortgage within the first few years. Typically it's six months' interest. Such penalties are illegal in some states.

Prime rate. The lowest interest rate that lenders charge their best customers.

Principal. The amount of money a mortgage or other loan provides before including interest.

Principal residence. The dwelling where one lives most of the time, and which one intends as his or her permanent home, as opposed to a second or vacation home.

Private mortgage insurance. See Mortgage insurance.

Prorate. To allocate bills proportionately—for example, to charge the buyer and the seller certain amounts for property taxes in the year when the property is sold.

Purchase-money mortgage. A mortgage that the seller grants to the buyer.

Q

Qualify a buyer. To investigate whether a buyer has enough income to purchase a residence and pay the mortgage.

R

Real estated owned (REO). Property acquired by a lender after a foreclosure.

Real Estate Settlement Procedures Act (RESPA). A law requiring, among other things, that lenders inform buyers in advance about closing costs on one- to four-dwelling units.

Real property. Land and anything permanently attached to it, such as a building. Also called real estate.

Realtor. A real estate broker who belongs to the National Association of Realtors. A salesperson who works for a broker may be a Realtor Associate.

Record. To file documents such as deeds in a county courthouse or similar place for public inspection.

Refinance. To substitute a new mortgage for an old one.

Repair. An alteration that merely maintains your home in an ordinary, efficient operating condition, and that doesn't add value to your home, or appreciably prolong its life, according to the IRS. Repair costs are not deductible from capital gains taxes when you sell a private residence.

Replacement cost rider. A guarantee from an insurance company that you will be paid the replacement cost of damaged articles, even if they were old.

Restriction. A legal limitation on the use of a property.

Right of first refusal. A potential buyer's privilege to match a third party's bid for a property.

Rollover mortgage. A mortgage whose interest rate will be renegotiated after a few years. Also called a "renegotiable mortgage."

S

Sale-leaseback. The purchase of property and its immediate rental back to the seller.

Salesperson. A real estate agent who works for a broker.

Savings and loan association. A financial institution that usually specializes in mortgages.

Secondary financing. Money obtained through junior mortgages.

Secondary market. The market where mortgages are bought and sold.

Second mortgage. A mortgage supplementing, and junior to, a first mortgage.

Secure. To provide collateral for a loan. Real estate serves as collateral for a mortgage loan.

Self-amortizing mortgage. A mortgage that will be entirely paid off through regular payments of principal and interest.

Settlement costs. See Closing costs.

Shared-appreciation mortgage. A mortgage in which an investor provides financial help to the buyer in return for a percentage of the house's growing value.

Siding. The covering on the exterior walls of a house.

Stick-built house. One constructed on the site, as opposed to a manufactured house.

Stipulations. The terms in a contract.

Survey. A map of a tract of land showing the boundaries, size, elevation, and so forth.

Sweat equity. The value added to your property by your own work.

T

Teaser. An unusually low interest rate, offered for perhaps six months, on an adjustable-rate mortgage.

Tenancy by the entirety. A form of property ownership in which, when one owner dies, the other automatically takes title. See Joint tenancy.

Tenancy in common. A form of property ownership in which each owner has an undivided interest in the property. If one dies, that person's interest goes to the deceased's heirs, not to the other tenants in common.

Time is of the essence. A phrase in a contract stipulating that the contract's terms must be fulfilled by a certain date.

Title. Legal ownership.

Title defects. Claims and similar clouds on property ownership.

Title insurance. Insurance againt loss occurring through defects in the title (ownership) to property.

Title search. An examination of title records to determine a property's rightful owner.

Torrens system. A system in some states where land is registered, and title searches are not needed.

Townhouse. A building that shares at least one outside wall with another house.

Transfer tax. A tax assessed by a local government when a house is sold.

Trust deed. A deed given by the seller to a third party to hold in trust, pending the fulfillment of an obligation, such as the amortization of a mortgage.

Trustee. A person or institution holding property in trust for another.

U

Unit. Rooms making up living quarters for one tenant or family in a multi-family project.

Utilities. Gas, electricity, water, telephone, and other services a building typically requires.

V

VA-guaranteed. A mortgage guaranteed by the Veterans Administration and available to qualified veterans.

Valuation. The estimated value of real property.

Variance. An exception to a zoning ordinance.

W

Warranty deed. A deed affirming that the seller will protect a title transferred to a buyer against possible claimants.

Wraparound mortgage. A mortgage that covers both the seller's old mortgage and the buyer's new mortgage.

Index